gp

Selected and Current Works

# goettschpartners

**THE MASTER ARCHITECT SERIES**

Selected and Current Works

# goettschpartners

goettsch
kaufman
nilles
prendergast
weldon
zheng

Publishing

Published in Australia in 2007 by
The Images Publishing Group Pty Ltd
ABN 89 059 734 431
6 Bastow Place, Mulgrave, Victoria 3170, Australia
Tel: +61 3 9561 5544  Fax: +61 3 9561 4860
books@images.com.au
www.imagespublishing.com

Copyright © The Images Publishing Group Pty Ltd 2007
The Images Publishing Group Reference Number: 700

All rights reserved. Apart from any fair dealing for the purposes of private study, research, criticism or review as permitted under the Copyright Act, no part of this publication may be reproduced, stored in a retrieval system or transmitted in any form by any means, electronic, mechanical, photocopying, recording or otherwise, without the written permission of the publisher.

National Library of Australia Cataloguing-in-Publication entry:

Goettsch Partners: selected and current works.

Bibliography.
Includes index.

ISBN 978 186470 168 5.
ISBN 1 86470 168 4.

1. Goettsch Partners.  2. Architectural firms – Chicago.
I. Pridmore, Jay.  (Series: Master architect series. VIII).

720.977311

Coordinating editor: Robyn Beaver

Designed by Goettsch Partners

Production by The Graphic Image Studio Pty Ltd, Mulgrave, Australia
www.tgis.com.au

Digital production by Splitting Image Colour Studio Pty Ltd, Australia

Printed by Everbest Printing Co. Ltd., in Hong Kong/China

IMAGES has included on its website a page for special notices in relation to this and our other publications.
Please visit www.imagespublishing.com

# Contents

6 Introduction

## Selected Works
14 111 South Wacker
24 Charles Square Center
34 UBS Tower
44 Suzhou Genway Tower
54 Blue Cross Blue Shield of Illinois Headquarters
68 Grand Hyatt São Paulo
76 Mary and Leigh Block Museum of Art Expansion
84 North Burnham Park and Soldier Field Redevelopment

## Office
94 Suzhou International Tower
98 SIP Administration Center
102 CBS 2 Broadcast Center
104 Lujiazui Diamond Tower
110 Jenner & Block
112 Sunbelt Tower
114 Freeborn & Peters
116 155 North Wacker and 222 West Randolph

## Hospitality/Residential
122 Hyatt Lodge at McDonald's Campus
126 Enhance Anting Golf Club Complex
128 Grand Hyatt Mumbai
132 Ningbo Marriott
134 Hyatt Regency Suzhou
138 Four Seasons Mumbai
140 J.W. Marriott Grand Rapids

## Mixed-Use
144 Nanjing International Center
150 Greenland Mixed-Use Development
152 Product Research and Data Service Center
154 Hyatt Regency at Chicony Plaza
156 Grand Hyatt Guangzhou
158 Ovation Plaza
162 Shanghai Caohejing Development
164 Bahagia Mixed-Use Development
166 Beijing Silvertie Center

## Institutional
168 U-505 Submarine Exhibit
172 CCS Bard Hessel Museum
178 Regenstein Center for African Apes
182 Sky Pavilion
186 Chicago Tower
190 Suzhou Jinji Lake Yacht Club

## Repositioning
194 360 North Michigan Avenue
198 1 North LaSalle Street
200 231 South LaSalle Street
204 120 South LaSalle Street
208 35 East Wacker Drive

## Firm Profile
214 Office
220 Partners
226 Staff
230 Project Chronology
250 Selected Works Project Credits
251 Selected Works Collaborators
252 Acknowledgments
253 Photography Credits
255 Index

# Introduction
by Jay Pridmore

The encouraging news in commercial architecture is that skylines over many American cities are coming back to earth, moving away from the architectural glitter and pyrotechnics of the recent past. On skylines layered with signposts of changing tastes and discarded styles, the best new buildings of the 21st century are showing the simple lines and sure touch of classic design. They're proving that form, after some aimless fluttering in recent decades, still follows function, and they indicate that commercial architecture is returning to the timeless rules of architecture—including the Vitruvian concept of "commodity, firmness, and delight"—that are guiding major commercial projects which also require efficiency, sustainability, and "smart" infrastructure.

Gone is the ubiquitous use of overblown ornament and ponderous curtain walls of exotic stone. A new taste for restraint and simple elegance is evident, especially compared to other buildings of the not-too-distant past, which are aging, as a reformed ex-postmodernist once put it, like "women with too much jewelry."

To declare a new era of "classic modernism" may be premature, since the inventiveness that heralds the modern and the purity of form that marks a classic are confirmed only by time. Yet a succession of new buildings of the 21st century appears uncomplicated and composed compared to those of a decade or two ago. They show a balance between what's comfortable and familiar in architecture along with notes that look forthrightly to the future. It's an optimistic trend and one that is richly represented in the recent work of Goettsch Partners.

Though Goettsch Partners is a new name, this is an old firm, a direct descendant of the practice founded by Mies van der Rohe, who immigrated to the U.S. and began the second phase of his career in Chicago in 1938. Since Mies' death, the firm has undergone several transformations, with changing personnel and the dominant style evolving and shifting in kind. Yet the strength of Goettsch Partners' current work reflects a longtime philosophy that has not changed: the modernist tenet that architecture should reveal, not conceal, its underlying structure.

The rationalist spirit at work here is refreshing, but it's important to remember that it's hardly new; rather it has recurred continuously throughout history and particularly in Chicago. Now as in the past, resurgent architecture begins with changes in practical conditions, calling for a creative response and, eventually, artistic discovery. In the late 19th century, for example, the first Chicago School of Architecture absorbed new economic and technical realities so deeply that it adopted the proportions of the basic metal frame as the basis of a new classic American style. Later with Mies' great success, the second Chicago School embraced the mass-produced building materials of his time, "expressing the essence" of glass and steel stripped of extraneous ornament.

Today, economics and construction methods are changing high-rise architecture anew. Conditions are certainly different from earlier periods, even recent ones. But as in the past, the powerful new construction, combined with urgent financial imperatives, are ushering in an important new phase in commercial architecture. Now as before, impatience with the recent past is forcing change. As has occurred at many points in architectural history, an interest in practical innovation—a new rationalism—is leading to a renewed sense of what's classic in architecture. Or as a French critic said many years ago, when neoclassicism was fresh (and French democracy was new): "Nothing is beautiful but what is true."

## Embedded in tradition

In this portfolio of Goettsch Partners' work of the last 10 years, the striking impression is of the size of many projects and their wide diversity, which together signal the firm's confident new direction. This work includes sleek office towers in Chicago, multi-use centers in China, dazzling hotels in South America and Asia, and even a new ape house at Chicago's Lincoln Park Zoo. On the surface, such an impressive list is not surprising from a firm of this stature and with its legacy. What is remarkable, however, and a foreshadowing of things to come in architecture, is the firm's consistent signature. Profiles are strong. Details are striking—and integral to structure. Efficiency and technology are distilled into images of sculptural clarity. If all this sounds complex, it is quietly so. The Goettsch Partners recipe often results in buildings of tranquil repose, not jarring shouts for attention.

How did the firm place itself on commercial architecture's leading edge? Clearly, it is attuned to change, staying current with the latest construction technologies and how they can be translated into distinctive form. Yet the firm's architects also recognize deep historical roots and often find themselves referring to the lessons of Chicago's architectural history.

President and design leader James Goettsch says he feels the heritage of the first Chicago School, when Louis Sullivan and John Wellborn Root defined what became known as "organic architecture," in which all elements of a building, from structural walls to ornamental detail, from financial costs to a building's transcendent spirit, were inextricably linked. The concept applied as much to soaring towers as to houses filled with natural light.

For Sullivan, organic architecture could transform useful office buildings into works of art that he described as "poems in stone …" Though architects at Goettsch Partners may bridle at such seeming sentimentalism, weaving artistic form with practical construction remains their simple, inspired objective. More prosaically, the idea is to "unite architecture and construction in an identical expression," as put by the visionary Swiss critic Sigfried Giedion who in the mid-20th century identified Chicago as the font of a modern movement.

This basic premise of modern architecture hasn't changed. And its practical problems are, if anything, more urgent than ever. The cost of commercial construction is high and getting higher; financing packages are increasingly fragile. The strains of high-density urban centers—strains that are relieved or aggravated by architecture—are obvious to anyone who lives in a large city. And sustainable or "green" design is now regarded as indispensable not only by activists but by tenants and realtors as well. It stands to reason, therefore, that the best new buildings of our era will meet these requirements with imaginative new forms.

Some elements of new architecture are obvious. The demand for economy and physical freedom is leading to spare structures filled with light, unencumbered by weighty signs of luxury. These are among the consistent marks of Goettsch Partners' work and are evident in the projects illustrated in this book. But reaching beyond the merely practical and rendering spare structures with strong, expressive form is a harder architectural objective, and this is where Goettsch Partners appears to have broken new ground.

## Rational buildings, unique in spirit

Genuine change in architecture does not usually arrive with the drama of a Brunelleschi dome, and rarely with the flourish of a Frank Gehry scherzo. Change occurs "truly at the appointed time," wrote John Wellborn Root, "solely by those who, with intelligence and soberness, are working out their ends with the best means at hand." Root rightly believed that architecture evolves by accretion and not in dazzling crescendos—evolution not revolution. Thus we can watch the work of Goettsch Partners move forward in discernible steps. With clear intention, the firm has evolved while keeping its hard focus on architecture's moving targets, specifically the means of financing commercial structures and the methods of constructing them.

Goettsch Partners' aversion to subjective formalism is bred in the bone. Clarity was the hallmark of Mies' work, as it was for some time after his death in 1969, when the office was renamed. Carried on by the early partners who had been among Mies' closest protégés, the firm was noted for its doctrinaire modernism, dedicated to basic materials, rectilinear forms, and repetitive modules. Today, there is little on the surface that connects that older firm with Goettsch Partners' present make-up. Yet deep down, the foundations of the approach have not changed—that architectural form develops from the building's function and technologies of construction; only rarely does it happen the other way around.

In the 1980s, when the office was reconstituted and led by Mies' grandson Dirk Lohan, it shifted away from a Miesian approach. Lohan's tenure was noted for an effort to soften the cold precision of modernism with the inclusion of elements that were seen as warmer and more humanistic. In this period, the firm turned out a number of sprawling suburban corporate headquarters projects, including McDonald's corporate campus in Oak Brook, Illinois; Frito-Lay in Plano, Texas; and TRW in Lyndhurst, Ohio.

By the early 1990s the firm enjoyed a modest reputation but not a unique style. It went on to design highly visible work such as major additions to historical buildings including the Adler Planetarium and Shedd Aquarium, both in Chicago. To the latter, a 1929 neo-classical gem, the firm added a prominent modern wing: the "Oceanarium," as it's called, remains a harmonious (not to mention highly popular) addition to the lakefront.

## A quiet revolution

James Goettsch joined the firm as a design partner in 1992, contemporaneously with a general impatience for superficial and decorative postmodernism. The economy was stumbling, and moreover, soaring vacancy rates in many cities shouted for a more value-conscious approach to commercial architecture. Goettsch had come from his former position as executive vice president of Murphy/Jahn, where structural rationalism was touched by postmodernism but never overcome by it.

What clearly interested Goettsch as he entered the new firm was the timeless principle that architectural form could, and must, emerge from the means and methods of conventional construction. Corollary to this idea is that efficient construction techniques are changing almost every year. And if construction and design are indeed aspects of the same innovative expression, then the potential for an ever-evolving and endlessly creative architecture is inherently possible.

In its quiet way, Goettsch Partners has introduced important ideas that have influenced the trajectory of commercial architecture. An important milestone came in 1997 with the completion of a new Chicago headquarters for Blue Cross Blue Shield of Illinois. The client, a health insurer, had a complex and, frankly, difficult program and invited proposals from several design-build groups. Economy was paramount, followed closely by the desire for a prominent but restrained exterior to reflect the company's public-service image. Another need was expandability, and this requirement was potentially the toughest to meet, given the limited site on the edge of Grant Park.

Goettsch Partners' winning design for Blue Cross features a profile that is imposing—the broad façade fills the property line—but also spartan. Its interior, with open office areas for the majority of the company's employees, provides splendid views of the lakefront. All of this was important to the client, but what clinched the job for Goettsch Partners were elements to enable a future addition, not on vacant land to the side but into vertical airspace above.

The foundations and mechanical systems were designed with the full expansion in mind. Many other details were also taken into consideration to enable the expansion and allow the 4,000 Blue Cross Blue Shield employees to continue working without interruption. Some of these elements remained

invisible, but others did not. Among the latter is the tower's dramatic glass atrium, rising to the building's full height of the first phase, 32 stories, and plans for a second phase to add another 25 stories (construction to begin January 2007). This soaring vertical space itself makes the building unforgettable to visitors and a pleasure for employees. Yet the feature was motivated less by the desire to dazzle and more by another strictly functional need: to leave a portion of the core vacant for future elevators. It is a brilliant blend of form and function, and a demonstration of how contemporary buildings can recall the deeply organic concepts of Root's Rookery and Adler and Sullivan's Auditorium.

## New notes of modernism

Blue Cross Blue Shield struck an almost instantaneous chord with the business community. That Goettsch Partners was on the right track with Blue Cross was proved a short time later with another commission in downtown Chicago, UBS Tower, which was completed in 2001. Significantly, the client for the UBS high-rise was the John Buck Co., developer of two previous buildings with historic overtones—Chicago towers by Philip Johnson and Kevin Roche, each with heavy stone cladding and elaborate profiles. For Buck in particular, hiring Goettsch a decade after the other two was a sign that commercial architecture was moving, anticipating the future as opposed to recalling the past.

UBS, like Blue Cross, emphasizes practical engineering related to construction and long-term efficient use. At the same time, the functional elements are assembled in an architectural design of distinction. UBS remains eloquent in stating that economy is valued more than majesty, efficiency more than grandiosity. The project also demonstrated that function—long interior spans and "transparent" infrastructure to facilitate mechanical and telecommunications upgrades—could be wrought in a form that appears sleek, spare, and smart.

"To us, architecture is an expression of engineering driven by economics," said Steve Nilles, a partner whose understanding of developer clients is largely responsible for the firm's success in this area. "But these buildings need to be eye-catching as well as economical to be successful." The UBS lobby, a space of remarkable transparency, is enclosed with a mullionless cable-net wall and low-iron, non-reflective glass, and is one of the eye-catching elements. The application of the net wall was the first use of this technology in the United States.

Knowing that repetition is a sure sign of evolving classic form, Goettsch Partners followed its success at UBS with a related design on a nearby site and for the same client. The 53-story high-rise known by its address, 111 South Wacker, was completed in 2005 using a one-way, cable-supported glass lobby enclosure and taking it a step further with a reduced number of ground-floor columns to create a greater sense of openness. The building has positively changed an important intersection, once crowded and canyon-like and now open and filled with daylight. The rational design of 111 South Wacker is accompanied, moreover, by the world's first LEED-CS Gold certification, a high honor in efforts to create sustainable architecture.

## The multicultural modern

While Goettsch Partners is a firm of modernists, no one will mistake its work for the rectilinear style of its forebears. This stylistic shift reflects normal evolution; even Mies foresaw a diversity of forms, at least in theory, as modernism would progress. For this firm, diversity is particularly apparent in its work in China. Here, basic objectives are not too different from those in the West: they include economy, comfort, and delight. The difference is that the Chinese environment is more explosive, and tastes are more exuberant. "Chinese cities are growing so fast, and many areas are completely vacant when we start to work on a site," said James Zheng, partner and director of the firm's Chinese work. "There is no existing context, so it's natural that developers insist on bold architectural statements."

The firm's first major commission in China, Suzhou International Tower, was completed in 1999. Primary requirements for this 18-story office building addressed basic economics, but the client also repeated the common mantra: "It must be unique." The answer was a blend of contrasting modern forms: an oval-shaped tower of transparent glass with a woven pedestal-like base clad with sections of glass and stone. The circle-and-square plan can be seen by the symbol-conscious Chinese as representative of heaven and earth. In architectural terms, the building straddles the turn of the new century with a masonry building, redolent of the 1990s, wrapped around a 21st-century glass façade that appears to defy gravity.

Goettsch Partners' work in China and elsewhere in Asia is evolving, but it already represents an instructive contrast to the firm's American designs. In Shanghai, Beijing, Suzhou, Nanjing, and other Chinese cities, as well as in two major hotel projects in Mumbai, India, the need for distinctive form drives each design along with the practical elements of pure function. Yet, the difference between Asia and America is only a matter of degree. "In classic modernism, the objective is relatively constant: to discover the balance between innovation and a design that's going to remain fresh over time," said Michael Kaufman, the partner who leads design efforts for large hotels and institutional buildings, as well as the firm's successful practice in restoration and renovation.

## The complex ingredients of simplicity

Goettsch Partners' best work, like successful design anywhere, resists strict analysis. Far from formulaic, its architecture embraces complexity and draws on the firm's skills in many different areas. "With a clear understanding of materials and construction, one can push the limits of modern design without jeopardizing long-term performance and sustainability," said Larry Weldon, the partner who oversees the firm's Enclosures Group. As the firm's longest-serving partner, Weldon has helped to set the office apart from competitors. With his deep understanding of new structural and curtain wall systems, creative design solutions come naturally to the firm at large.

In a similar way, Goettsch Partners' interior architecture practice applies knowledge of organizational behavior to overall designs through its belief that a symbiotic relationship exists between a client's business objectives and the physical arrangement of space; that the potential of both is determined by the degree to which they are connected to one another. "In all our work, we believe the answer is imbedded in a deep understanding of the problem," said Jim Prendergast, the partner who leads the firm's interior architecture practice.

Another of the firm's special areas of interest is a long-established practice in city planning, which was a key element in the 2003 renovation of Soldier Field, one of Chicago's most controversial projects in recent history. This planning process, combined with the adaptive reuse of a stadium that was built in 1924, took environmental design in the city to new levels of complexity.

The Soldier Field project required the transformation of an old and nearly obsolete structure into a modern football venue. The commission called for parking, green space, event engineering, and historical preservation on a lakefront site that became a political lightning rod. Its success owes largely to the technical prowess of Goettsch Partners, along with their distinguished design partner on the project, Wood + Zapata, who rendered a complex architectural idea with strength and substantial simplicity. A daring structure is now the centerpiece of a reconstituted stretch of lakefront and referred to as a "stadium in a park."

## The test of time

Whether Goettsch Partners' recent work represents true architectural milestones, and whether its version of 21st-century modernism will influence architects of the future, remains to be seen. Ultimate success can be affirmed only by the test of time. Yet the rich dialogue carried on by this firm between the certainties of the past and the kaleidoscope of the future remains valuable and instructive.

Poetically, the architects of Goettsch Partners have grasped the process of forging images of force and clarity in an environment of swirling complexity. The case studies included in this book demonstrate that its work incorporates the most recent technical developments in unitized curtain walls, low-iron glass, and long-span construction, not to mention the intricacies of city planning. Mastery of the technical is very much what leads to creative successes, entrenched in economic realities and committed to harmony with the world around.

The architectural values expressed in this book are clearly those of classic modernism—they have been articulated in one way or another for more than 100 years. The strength of these values in the 21st century resides in their fundamental utility and truth, certainly, but also in their having adapted to the times, to new economics and evolving construction.

The dialogue between value-laden absolutes and moving architectural targets is as important in venerable old cities like Chicago as it is in mercurial new ones in China. The key is the architect's ability to address the many demands placed on a new building—from the functional to the social—and arrive at designs that are simple and eloquent. In any era, and especially this one, it is the architect's deepest challenge—and in this case Goettsch Partners' truest goal—to practice architecture as a widely collaborative process and create buildings that appear as the work of a single, confident hand.

# Selected Works

14 **111 South Wacker**
Chicago, Illinois

24 **Charles Square Center**
Prague, Czech Republic

34 **UBS Tower**
Chicago, Illinois

44 **Suzhou Genway Tower**
Suzhou, China

54 **Blue Cross Blue Shield of Illinois Headquarters**
Chicago, Illinois

68 **Grand Hyatt São Paulo**
São Paulo, Brazil

76 **Mary and Leigh Block Museum of Art Expansion**
Evanston, Illinois

84 **North Burnham Park and Soldier Field Redevelopment**
Chicago, Illinois

Chicago, Illinois
Design/Completion 2000/2005
Client: The John Buck Co.
1,457,000 square feet (135,360 square meters)

# 111 South Wacker

### Site
The building is located along the prime office corridor at the western edge of the central business district with easy access to rail lines, mass transit, and expressways.

### Program
This 53-story, multi-tenant building provides 1,149,000 square feet of office space. The street level features a 44-foot-high lobby, a restaurant and sundry shop. Above the lobby, there are seven levels of parking for 389 cars. At the midpoint of the building, a double-height floor includes a conference center and mechanical equipment rooms; a fitness center is included on the 10th floor. Loading docks are accessed from lower Wacker Drive, as well as two levels of parking for another 100 cars.

### Concept
The building is designed to attract tenants who require large, open floor plans, state-of-the-art data and communication services, and tenant-dedicated emergency power and supplemental cooling systems. Maximum planning efficiency and flexibility is optimized on the typical office floors with column-free, 50- and 60-foot spans from the core to the exterior wall and 40-foot column spacing along the curtain wall.

The building's lobby design is one of its most unique aspects. To compensate for a building footprint that covers almost the entire quarter-block site, the 40-foot perimeter columns transfer to 80-foot spans as they pass through the garage levels. The underside of the parking ramp serves as a dynamic orientation device that encircles the building core. The radial pattern of the ramp is reflected in the lobby's stepped ceiling and lighting. This pattern is further reflected in the granite and marble floor that extends beyond the lobby enclosure, across the plaza to the edge of the curb, unifying the pedestrian experience with the lobby interior. The openness of the lobby is enhanced by the cable-supported, water-white, non-reflective glass enclosure. This ultra-transparent glass wall allows the indoor and outdoor areas to be perceived as a single, continuous space.

111 South Wacker was the first building ever to receive Gold-level certification in the USGBC's LEED Green Building Rating System® for core and shell development. The sustainable design initiatives include a green roof, a high-performance building envelope, and high-efficiency heating, cooling, and lighting systems. Additionally, the structure incorporates existing caissons and foundation walls that helped minimize material usage and energy consumption during construction.

### Elements
Reinforced concrete core with perimeter structural steel frame, unitized aluminum-and-glass curtain wall with linen-finish stainless steel fins, cable-supported glass lobby enclosure, Carrara and Rossa Verona marble cladding on the lobby walls, Shivakashi granite and Carrara marble on the floor

111 South Wacker

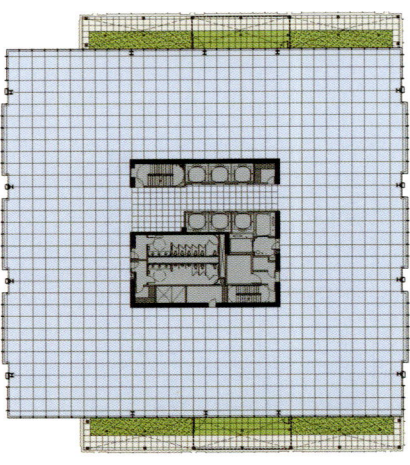
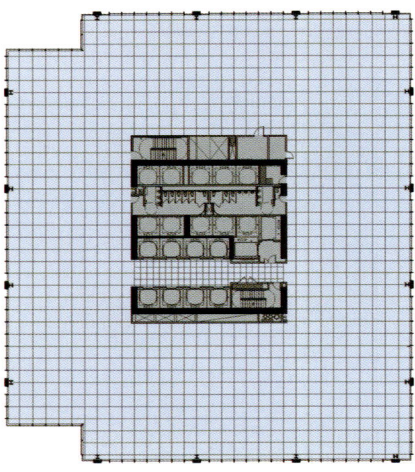
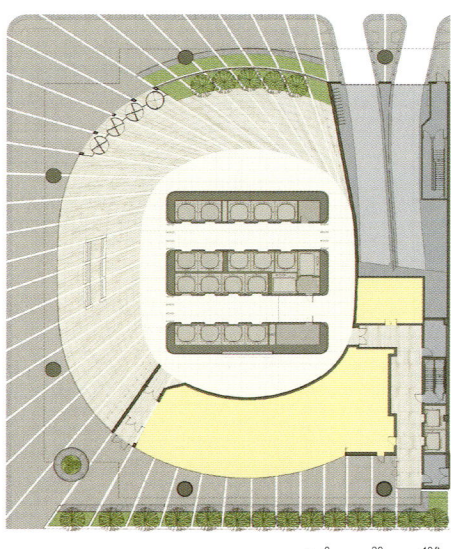

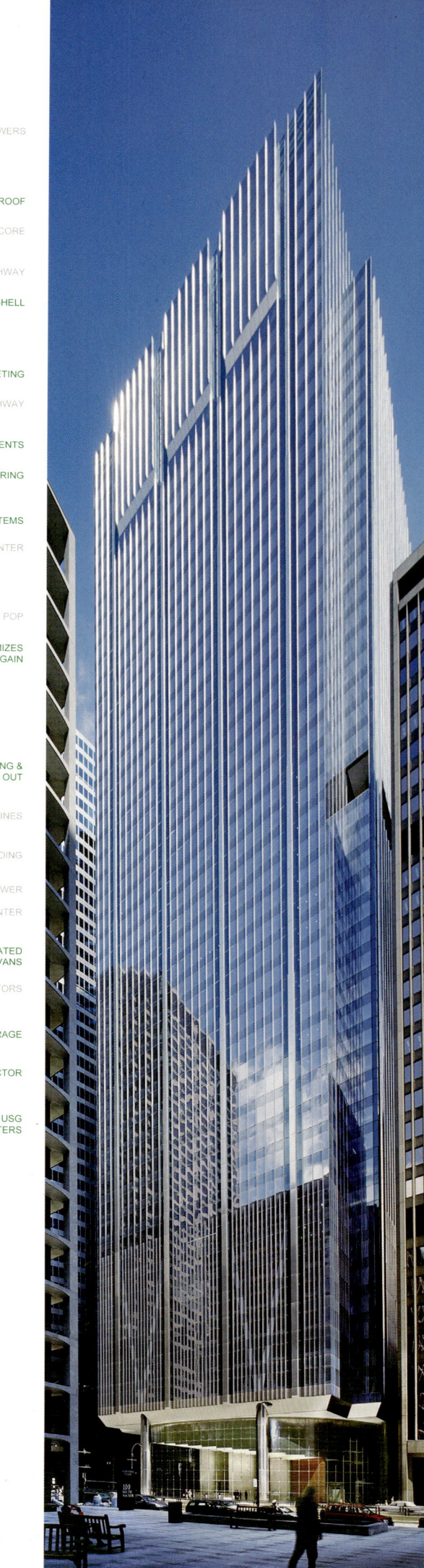

- FUTURE TENANT COOLING TOWERS
- GREEN ROOF
- DEDICATED TENANT EXHAUST SYSTEM WITHIN CORE
- ROOFTOP TECHNOLOGY PATHWAY
- LOW VOC PAINT THROUGHOUT CORE & SHELL
- GREEN LABEL CERTIFIED CARPETING
- FUTURE TENANT COOLING AND BACKUP POWER PATHWAY
- RECYCLED AND RECYCLABLE BUILDING COMPONENTS
- CARBON DIOXIDE MONITORING
- COMMISSIONING OF MEP SYSTEMS
- TENANT AMENITY: CONFERENCE CENTER
- NET POP
- HIGH PERFORMANCE UNITIZED CURTAINWALL MAXIMIZES DAYLIGHTING/MINIMIZES SOLAR HEAT GAIN
- COLUMN FREE INTERIOR PROVIDES MAXIMUM DAYLIGHTING & VIEWS AND GREATEST FLEXIBILITY FOR TENANT BUILD OUT
- REDUNDANT TELECOMMUNICATION LINES
- EXISTING 311 MONROE OFFICE BUILDING
- BASE BUILDING HVAC & POWER
- TENANT AMENITY: FITNESS CENTER
- ZONING MINIMUM FULLY ENCLOSED PARKING WITH DEDICATED PARKING FOR ALTERNATIVE FUEL VEHICLES & CARPOOL VANS
- FUTURE TENANT GENERATORS
- BICYCLE STORAGE
- RECYCLING PROGRAM & COMPACTOR
- REUSED CAISSONS AND FOUNDATION WALLS FROM OLD USG HEADQUARTERS

*Selected Works*

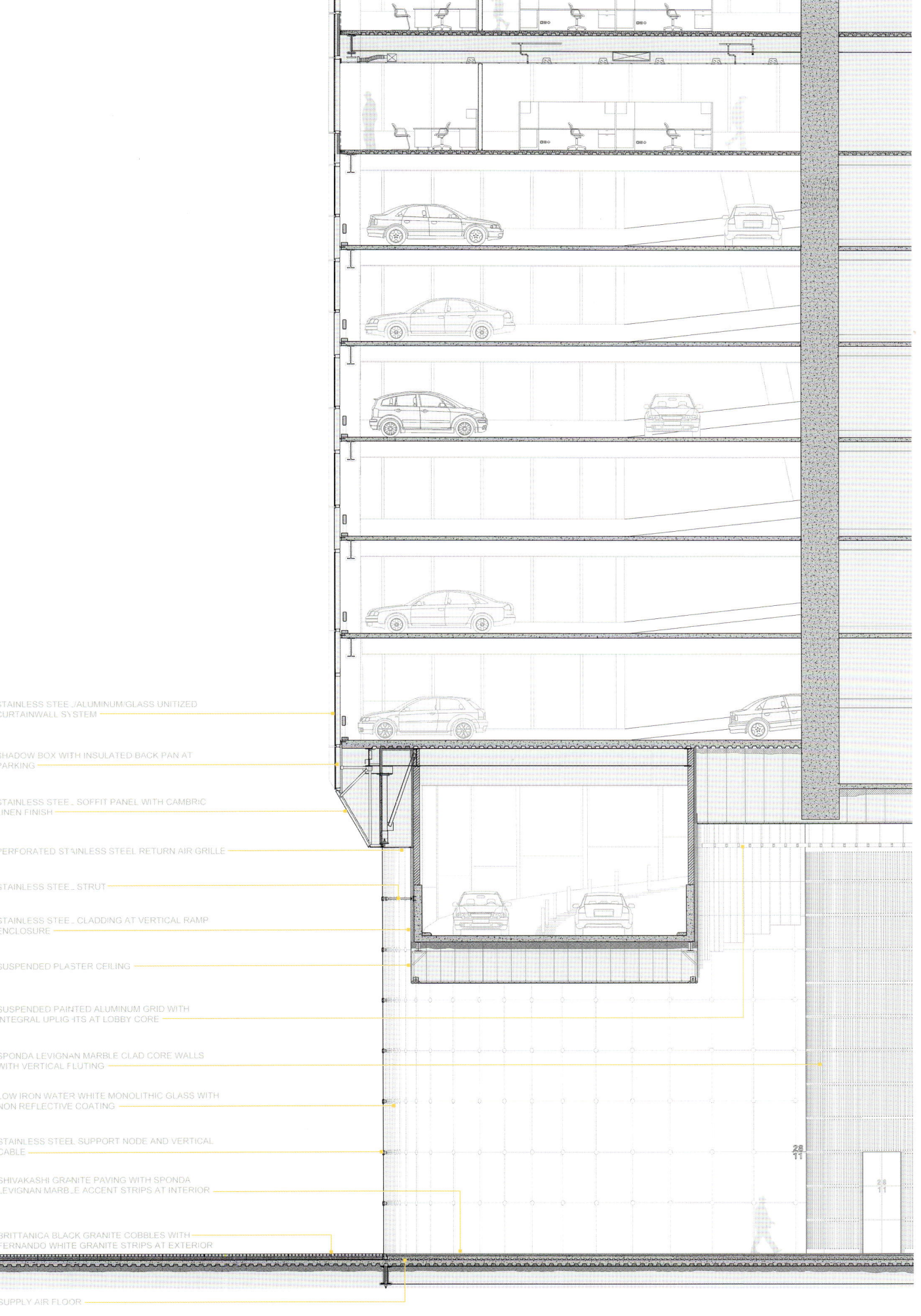

111 South Wacker

Prague, Czech Republic
Design/Completion 1997/2002
Client: GE Capital Golub Europe, LLC
290,500 square feet (26,990 square meters)

# Charles Square Center

### Site
The building is located on historic Charles Square, one of the oldest and largest public spaces in Prague.

### Program
The developer's goal was to provide a state-of-the-art, American-style office building in the historic city center. The eight-story building was constructed above an existing metro station and includes 165,000 square feet of Class A office space, 61,000 square feet of retail, and below-grade parking for 150 cars.

### Concept
Prague is a city that is uniquely conscious of its history. The opportunity to construct a new building is rare, as the demolition of existing buildings is seldom permitted. The site for this building was bombed during WWII and had not been built upon since. The primary challenge was to design a contemporary office building that fulfilled today's business requirements for flexibility and technology, while respecting Prague's historic architectural context. The massing of the building recognizes the street wall and cornice lines of adjacent buildings. Fritted glass and embossed aluminum curtain wall panels provide the façade with a sense of scale and detail that complements the architectural traditions of Prague.

The first two floors are occupied by retail tenants that benefit from a skylit atrium and foot traffic from the metro station below. The atrium is reminiscent of the traditional Prague courtyard building, as the hard-edged street wall gives way to an interior moment of light and air. The typical office floor plates provide planning efficiencies and advanced building systems that are rare within the historic city core.

### Elements
Reinforced concrete structure; unitized curtain wall system with fritted glass and embossed metal spandrel panels; vaulted, glass-enclosed atrium; wood-paneled office lobby; granite flooring at grade; backlit glass floors with wood paneling on the typical-floor elevator lobbies

*Charles Square Center*

Selected Works

*Charles Square Center*

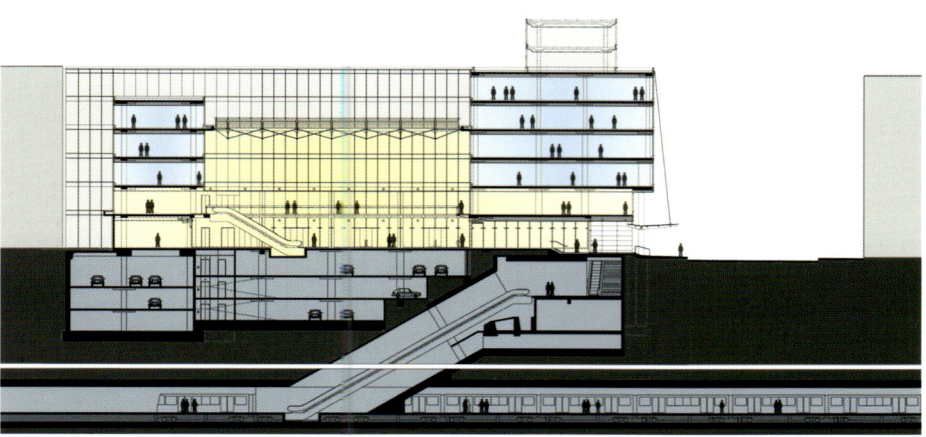

Selected Works

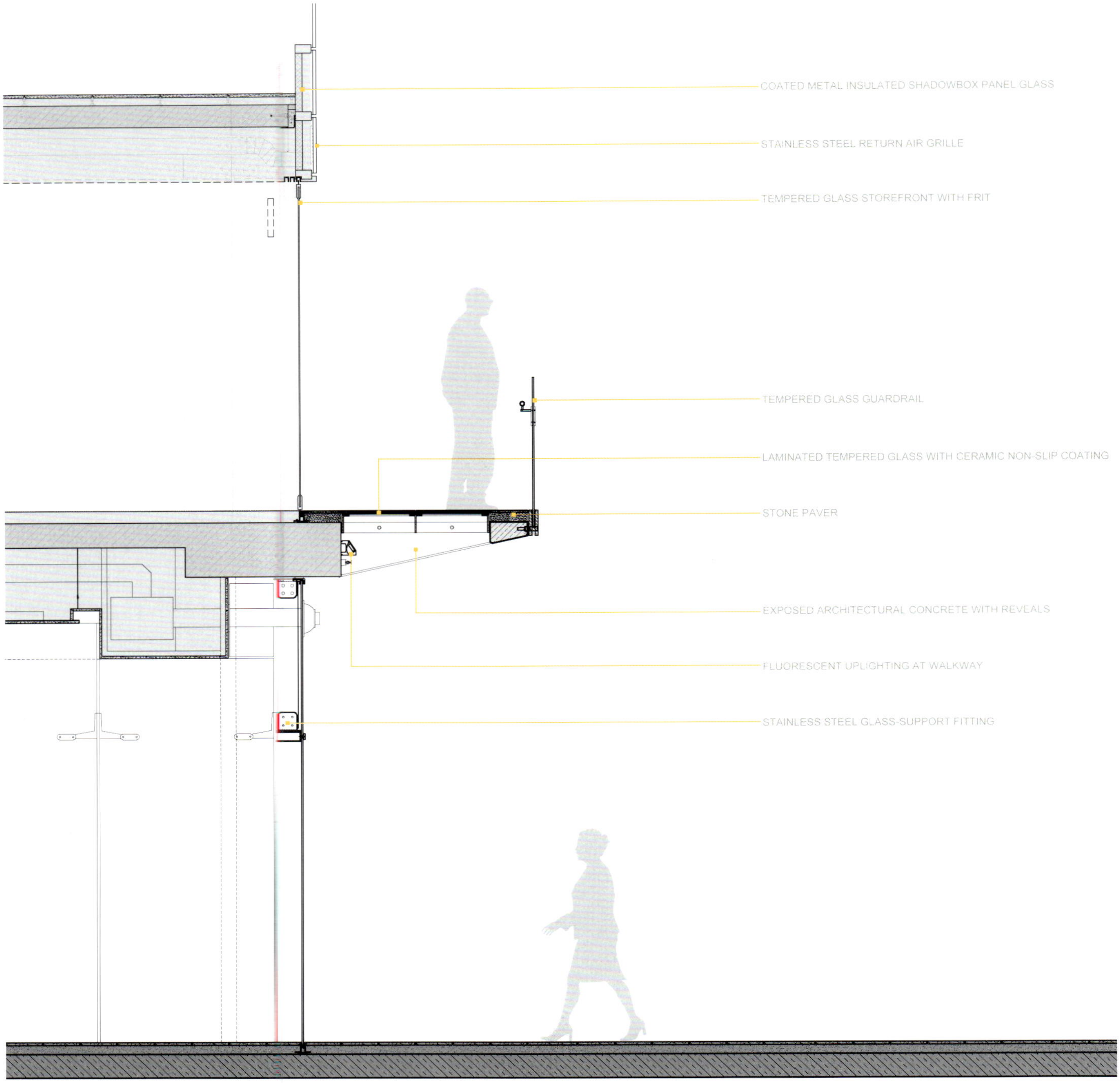

- COATED METAL INSULATED SHADOWBOX PANEL GLASS
- STAINLESS STEEL RETURN AIR GRILLE
- TEMPERED GLASS STOREFRONT WITH FRIT
- TEMPERED GLASS GUARDRAIL
- LAMINATED TEMPERED GLASS WITH CERAMIC NON-SLIP COATING
- STONE PAVER
- EXPOSED ARCHITECTURAL CONCRETE WITH REVEALS
- FLUORESCENT UPLIGHTING AT WALKWAY
- STAINLESS STEEL GLASS-SUPPORT FITTING

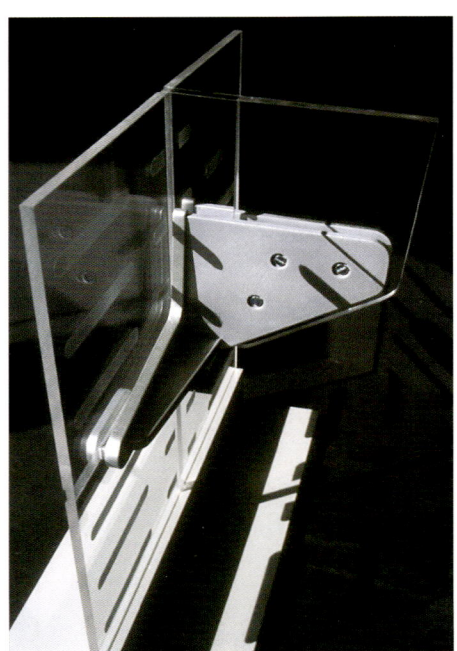

*Selected Works*

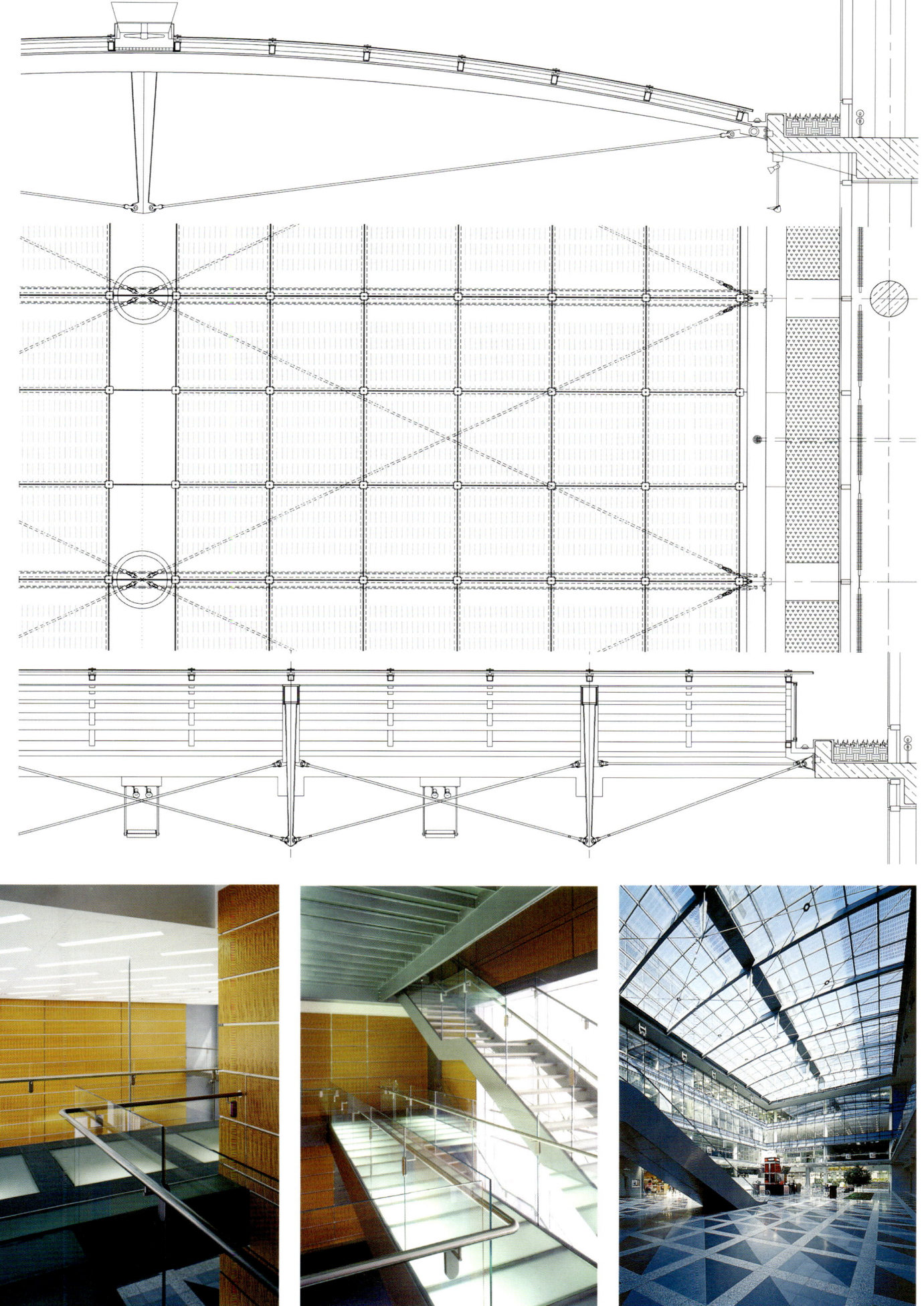

*Charles Square Center*

Chicago, Illinois
Design/Completion 1998/2001
Client: The John Buck Co.
1,754,000 square feet (162,950 square meters)

# UBS Tower

### Site
The building is located a block north of 111 South Wacker, also designed by the firm, along the western edge of Chicago's Loop, with easy access to major transportation routes.

### Program
The 51-story office tower provides three distinct floor plates of 29,300, 33,300, and 37,900 square feet in order to appeal to a range of tenants. Building amenities include a mezzanine-level conference center with a 250-seat auditorium, meeting rooms and teleconferencing equipment; a fitness center; and a white-tablecloth restaurant on the ground floor. Loading docks and two levels of parking are located on lower Wacker Drive.

### Concept
As Chicago's first multi-tenant office building in more than a decade, the project was driven by the developer's objective to build and market a contemporary, visually compelling tower—one that would be a clear departure from competing properties. The developer wanted to attract premier tenants with flexible, 45-foot column-free lease spans, the latest data and communication services, and exclusive emergency power and auxiliary cooling systems.

The building is enclosed with a unitized curtain wall clad with linen-finish stainless steel and utilizing an energy-efficient vision glass. Circular steel columns extend the building's full height and rise above the roofline, providing a distinctive image on the skyline and setting a clear organizational rhythm for the building's architecture. The east and west façades are slightly curved.

The lobby is enclosed with a dramatic, 40-foot-high cable-supported net wall—the first of its kind in the U.S.— that uses water-white glass with a non-reflective coating to create a highly transparent lobby enclosure. This ultra-clear enclosure exposes a rich stone interior to passersby as well as views from within of the historic Lyric Opera Building and other neighboring structures.

Locating the tower in the northwest corner of the site allows the building to define the Wacker Drive street wall. This location also opens up the east side to a large plaza with fountains and creates a major pedestrian connection along Madison Street. This east–west connection is enlivened with large granite benches encircling mounded landscape elements and cypress trees. Together, these elements reinforce the building's design and provide seating and shade for thousands of pedestrians who pass through the site daily.

### Elements
Reinforced concrete core with perimeter steel structural frame, pre-glazed unitized curtain wall system, linen-finish stainless steel and aluminum cladding, cable-supported glass lobby enclosure, Blue Orissa granite and Carrara marble cladding on the elevator core walls

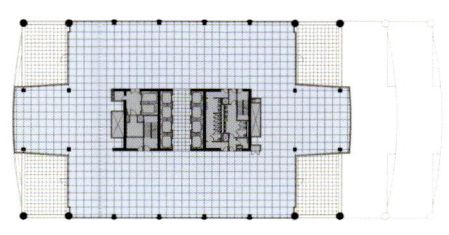
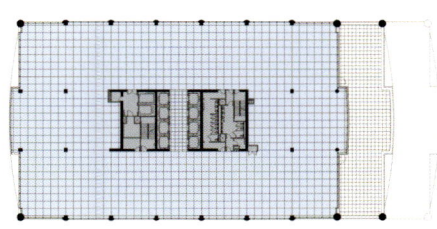
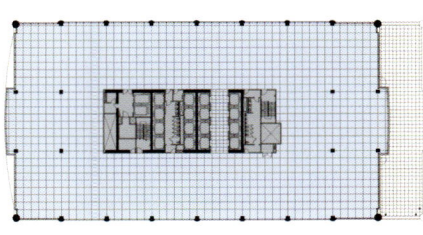
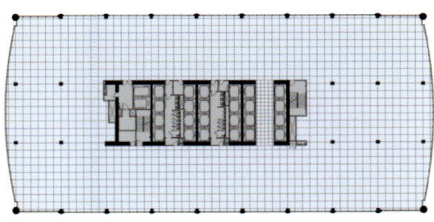
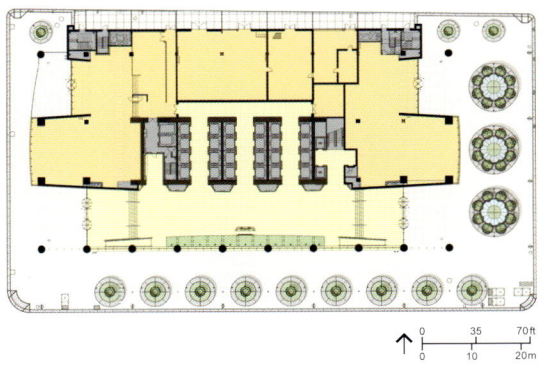

*UBS Tower*

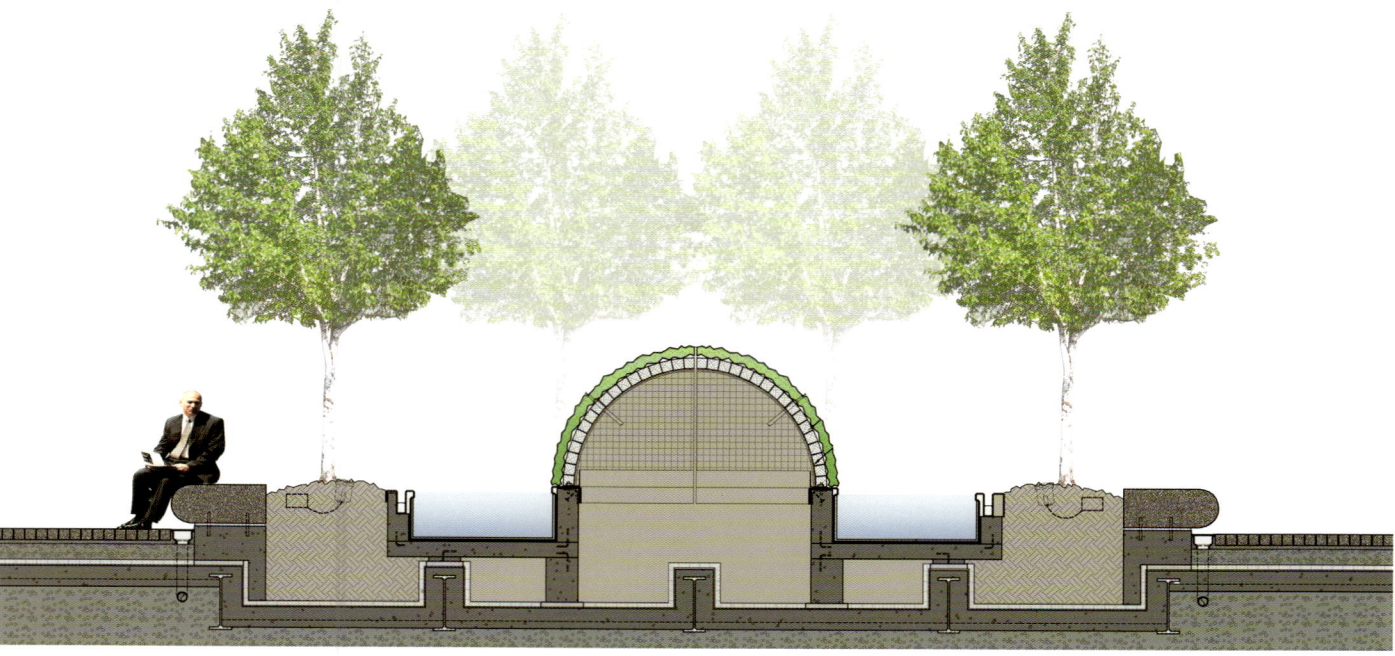

Selected Works

*UBS Tower*

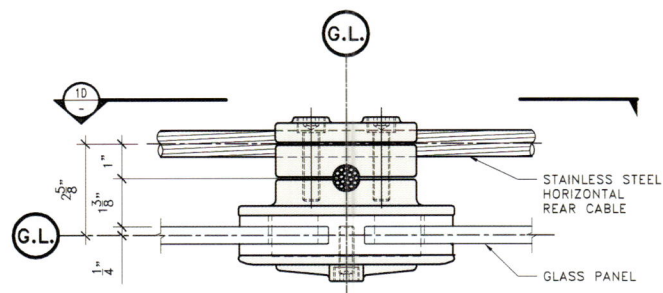
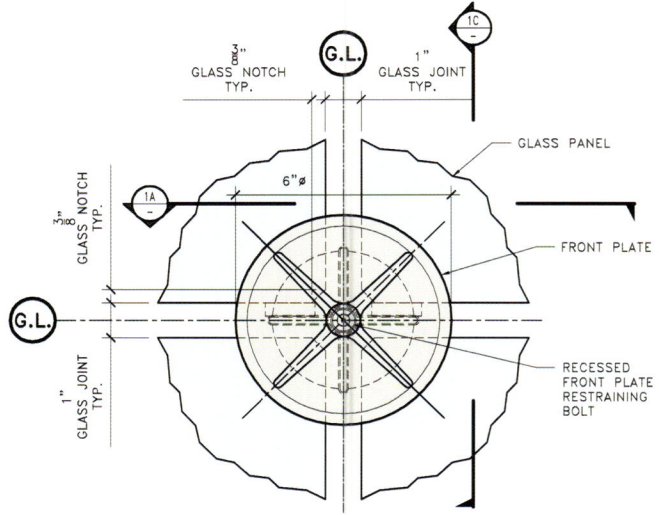
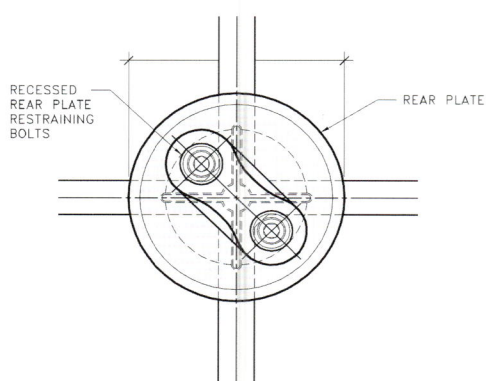

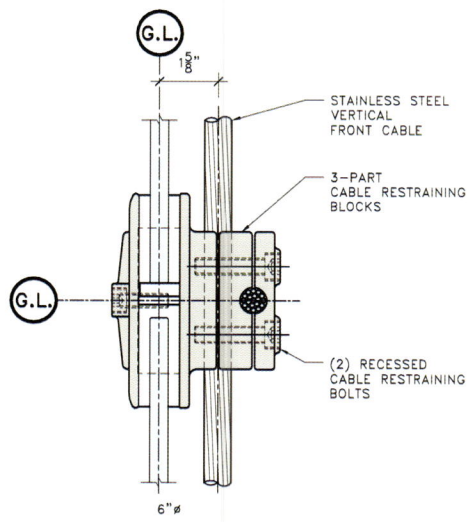

*UBS Tower*

Suzhou, China
Design/Completion 2003/2005
Client: Suzhou Industrial Park Genway Development Company
646,000 square feet (60,000 square meters)

# Suzhou Genway Tower

### Site
On the edge of the historic city of Suzhou, the Suzhou Industrial Park (SIP) is a fully planned, 24-hour community designed to attract leading electronics and pharmaceutical manufacturing companies. This complete and newly constructed town offers international-quality housing, educational, civic, cultural, and recreational facilities for residents and visitors. The building is located in the second phase of the SIP, in the development's Government Center, for which the firm also created the master plan.

### Program
The building houses the tax collection bureau. The three podium floors provide public contact areas for tax collection, which can be accessed from the street or the lobby, as well as a cafeteria and retail. The 20-story tower provides office space with a conference center on the top floor.

### Concept
The building is designed to serve as a boundary marker for the SIP Government Center, sited on the southwest corner; its L-shaped plan is a mirror image of an adjacent building. The tower's massing is distinguished by the articulation of two interlocking forms: one emphasizing horizontal mullions, the other a two-story grid pattern. The west façades of the tower and podium taper slightly to provide a distinctive profile. The main entrance is defined by a dramatic, glass-enclosed three-story lobby. A prominent feature of the lobby is an elevator core that is clad with yellow back-painted glass panels. An extension of the SIP canal system runs between the podium and the tower, which are connected by a bridge featuring a floor, ceiling, and side walls built entirely of glass.

### Elements
Reinforced concrete core; unitized aluminum-and-glass curtain wall; podium clad with flamed and polished granite; glass-enclosed lobby

Suzhou Genway Tower

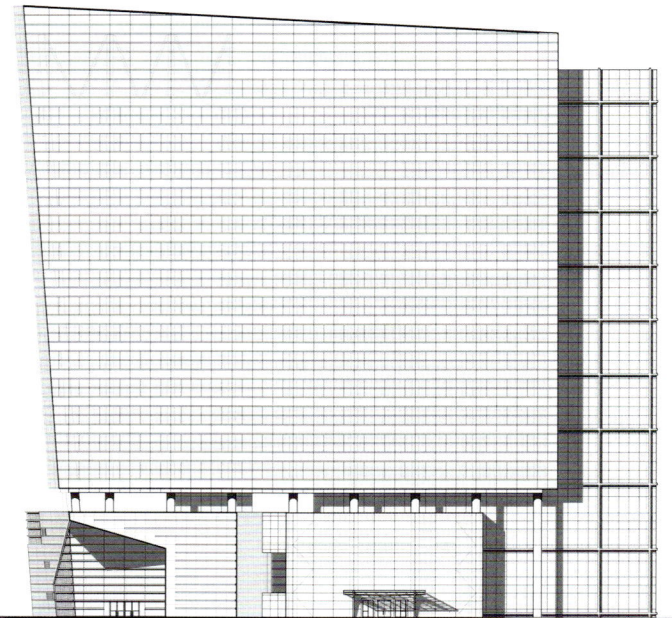

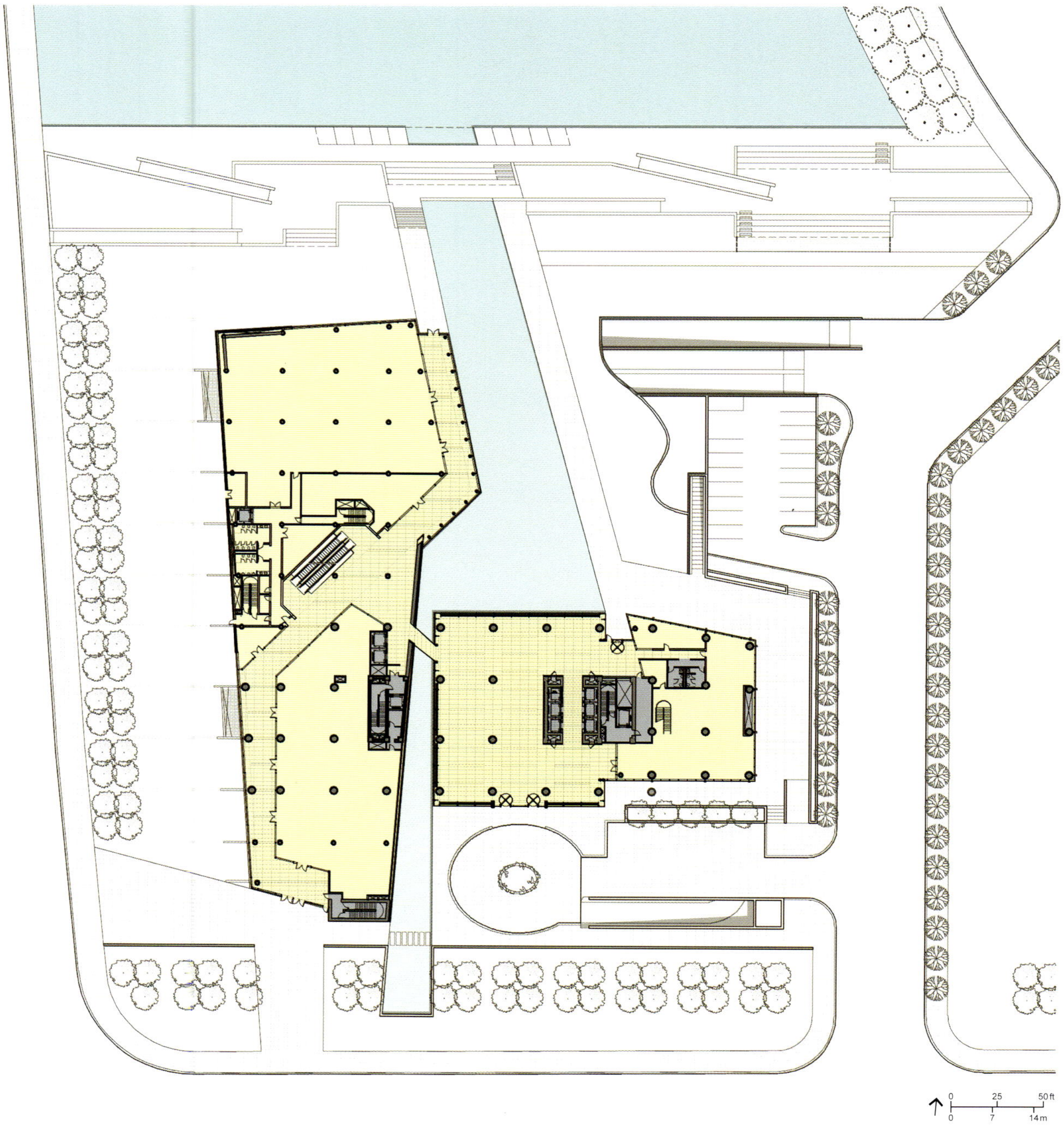

46

*Selected Works*

*Suzhou Genway Tower*

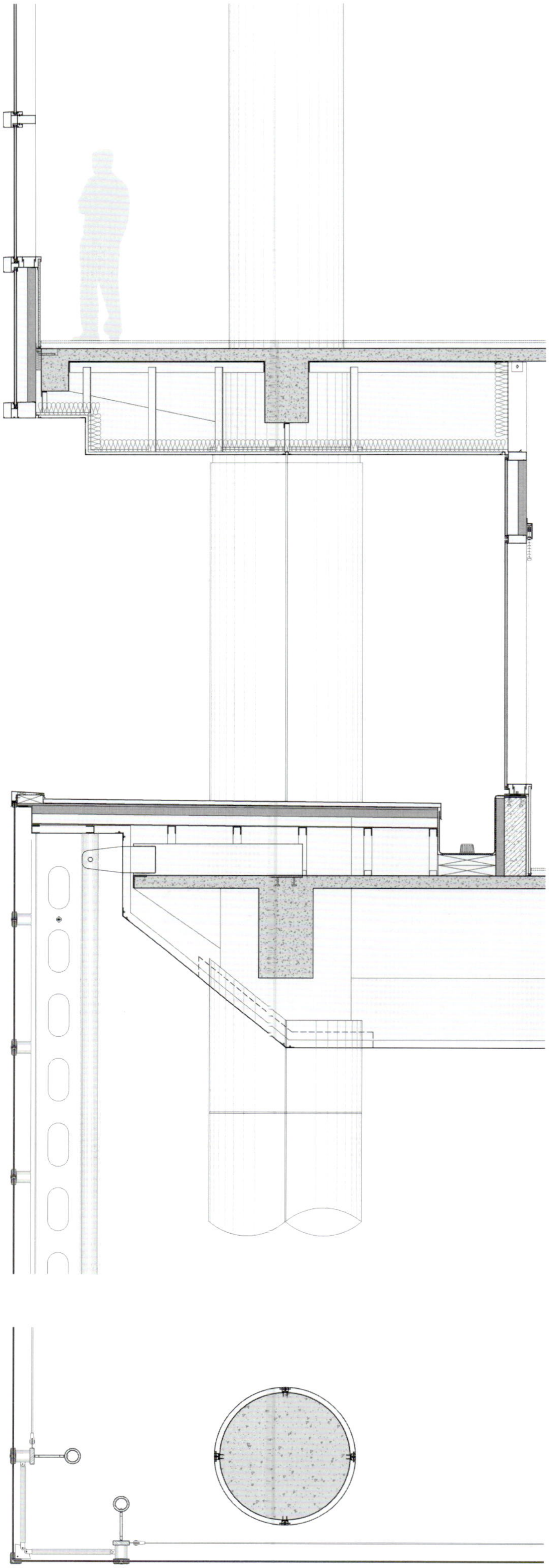

*Selected Works*

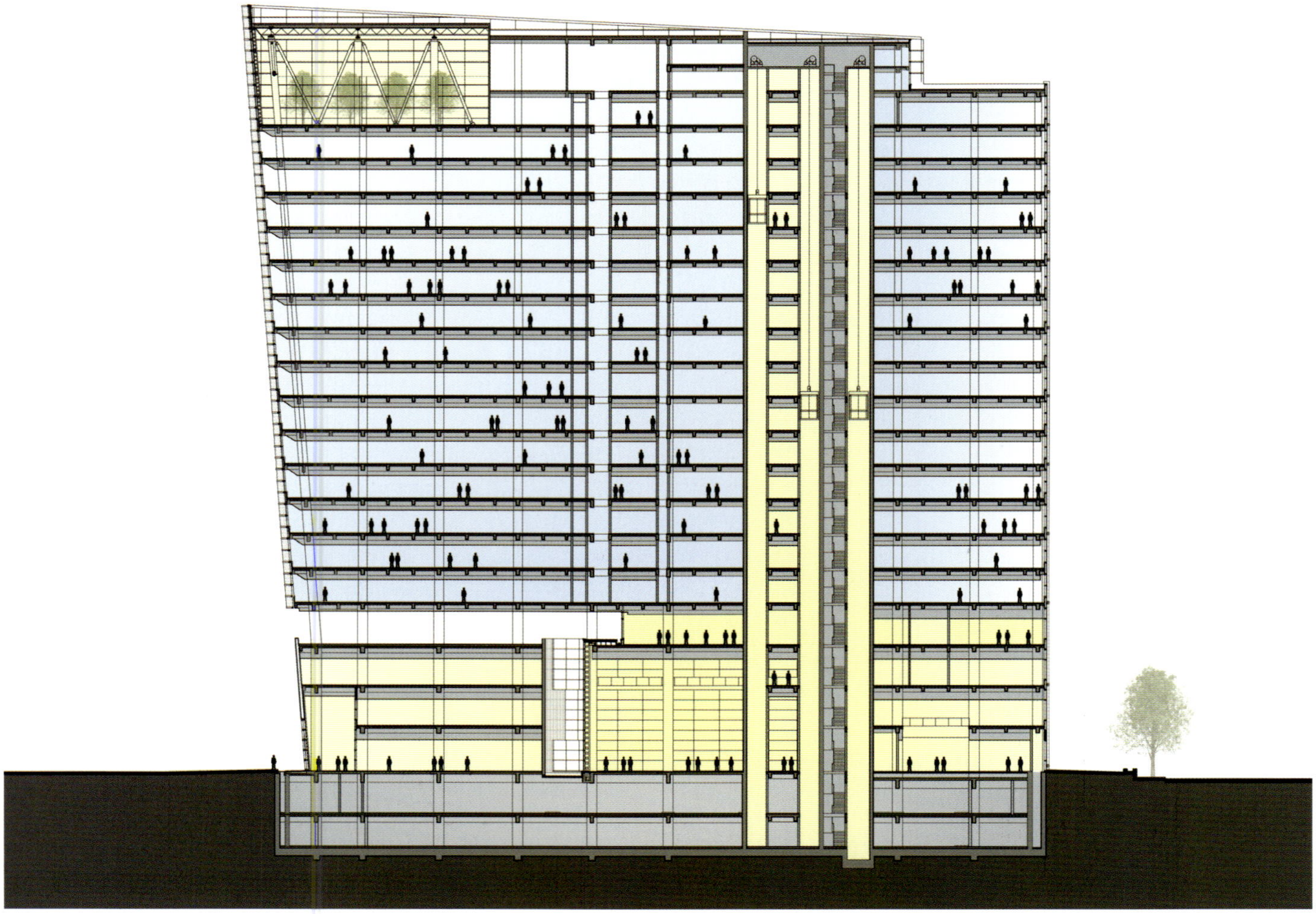

*Selected Works*

Chicago, Illinois
Design/Completion 1994/1997 (Phase 1), 2010 (Phase 2)
Client: Blue Cross Blue Shield of Illinois
Phase 1: 1,430,000 square feet (132,850 square meters)
Phase 2: 860,000 square feet (79,900 square meters)

# Blue Cross Blue Shield of Illinois Headquarters

### Site
Located in downtown Chicago at the north end of Grant Park, the building overlooks Michigan Avenue, Millennium Park, and Lake Michigan.

### Program
The building serves as the headquarters for a health care insurance company that required flexibility in its expansion plans to accommodate its growth. Phase one provides 1,430,000 square feet on 32 office floors, designed to accommodate staff in an open-office environment. A third-floor employee cafeteria serves 900 people, and a three-level podium space sits below a street-level landscaped plaza. The podium houses a conference and training facility, executive parking, and the physical plant.

### Concept
With the client's challenge of future growth in mind, the unique solution for this high-rise is its expansion. The building is designed to be vertically expanded from the original 32 floors to 57 floors without disrupting the existing structure or building services. The major challenge was to accommodate vertical shafts for future elevators without constructing large, unutilized voids that would compromise the efficiency of the initial building.

The soaring atrium comprises five 40- by 30-foot open structural bays. Two of the bays are used for two eight-car banks of passenger elevators; two will be used for the phase two expansion with two additional eight-car banks. The center bay is reserved for an open stair to facilitate inter-floor circulation, and every three floors, the center bay is fully built out and utilized for meetings and lounge space.

On the north elevation, the building's massing and exterior expression reflect the interior organization. By utilizing two split service and structural cores, the typical floors provide a very open plan. Visitor access to the building is controlled through the ground-floor lobby, where a large, stainless steel concierge desk is defined by an illuminated oval-shaped disc overhead. Employees enter through optically controlled turnstiles adjacent to the concierge desk.

### Elements
Split concrete cores with a steel frame, unitized aluminum-frame curtain wall with stainless steel and granite panels, Rossa Verona marble cladding on lobby core walls with stainless steel column cladding

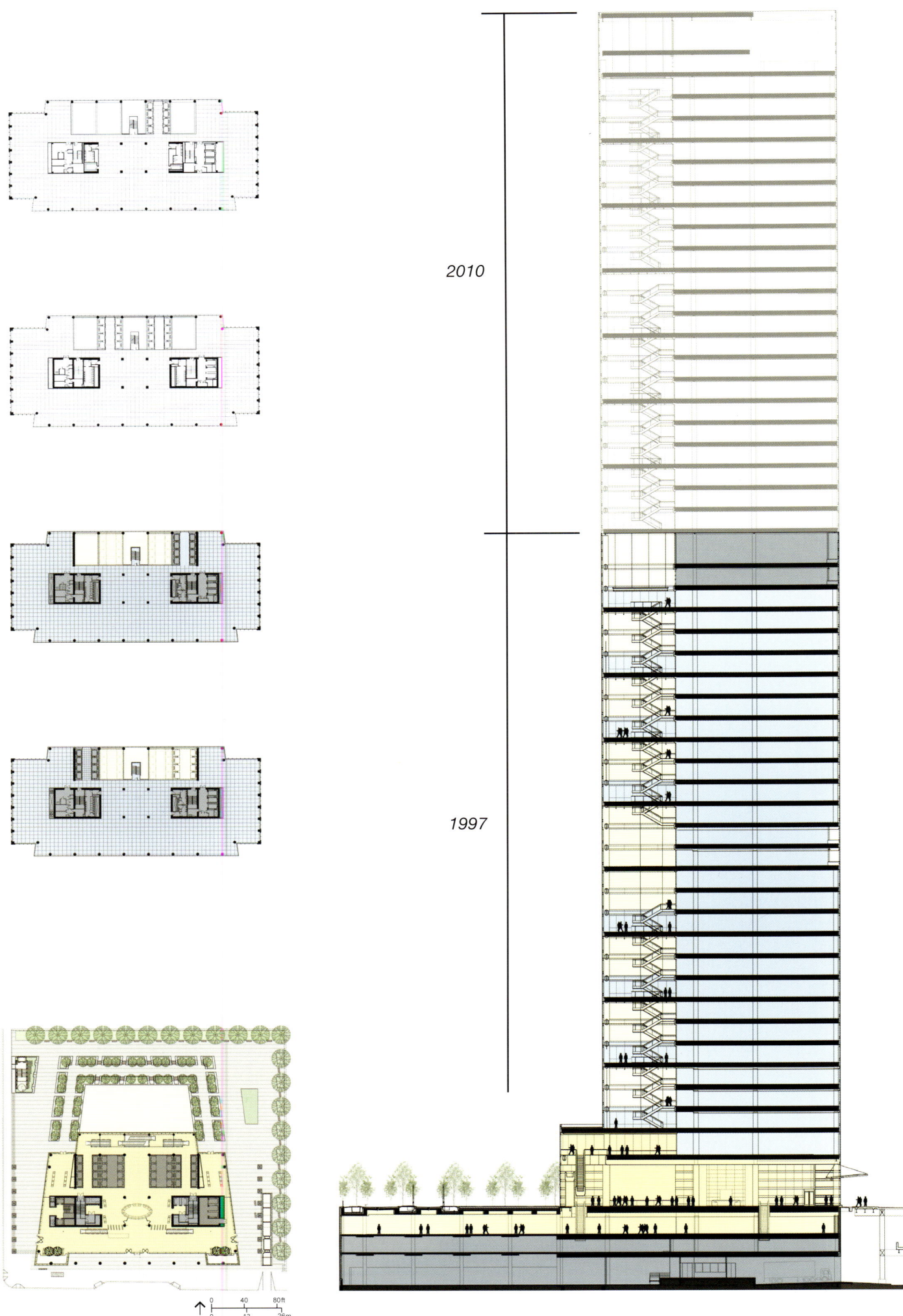

*Selected Works*

*Blue Cross Blue Shield of Illinois Headquarters*

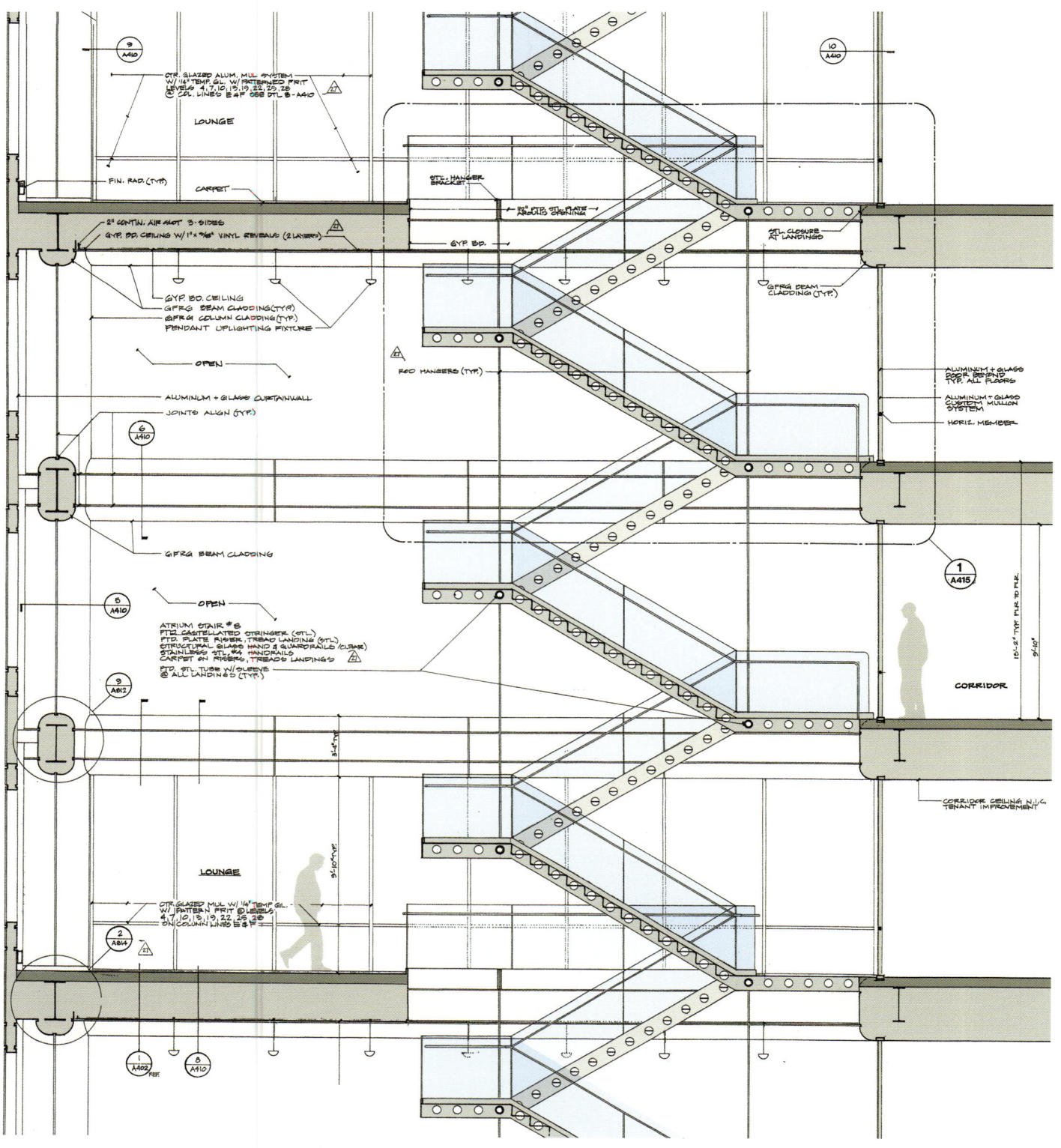

62

*Selected Works*

*Blue Cross Blue Shield of Illinois Headquarters*

# Expansion, Blue Cross Blue Shield of Illinois Headquarters

Having relocated four times in its 25-year history of extensive growth, Blue Cross Blue Shield developed its headquarters building with plans to limit such frequent moves in the future. The company's goal for its new building was to satisfy immediate physical requirements and yet be able to expand in order to accommodate expectations for continued strong growth.

Phase one was designed with the structural and mechanical infrastructure to support the additional 25 floors and 860,000 square feet. Additional riser space was also provided to accommodate independent mechanical, electrical, and plumbing systems for the expansion floors. The exterior of the building is clad with glass, stainless steel, and aluminum—all materials that age well and can be matched easily as the building is expanded.

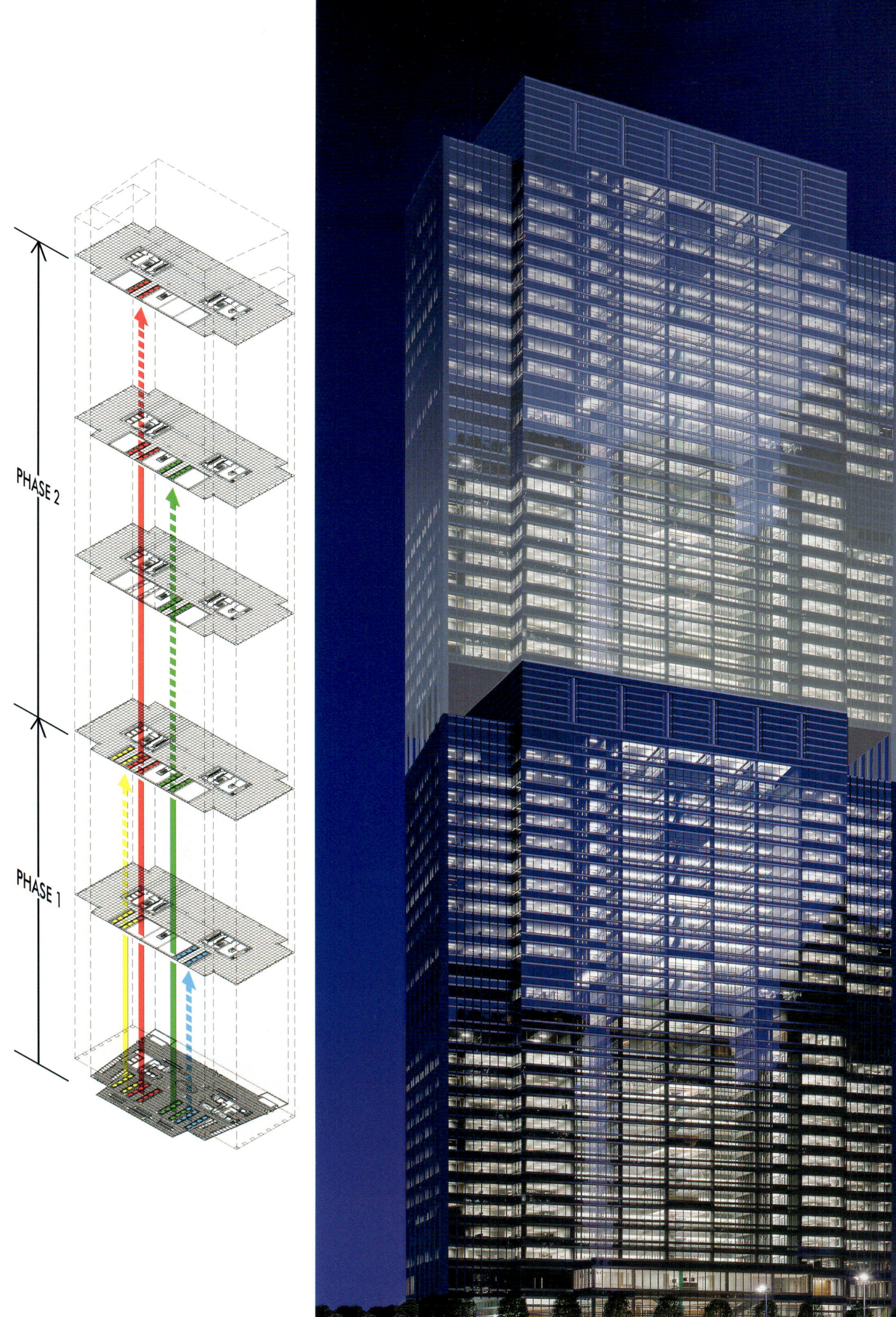

# Pedway, Blue Cross Blue Shield of Illinois Headquarters

A 275-foot-long pedway was constructed to connect the Blue Cross Blue Shield headquarters facility with public parking across the street. The Blue Cross pedway is a part of the city's underground pedway system that links many of the city's major buildings, parking structures, and subways. The steel-and-glass structure is suspended between the upper and intermediate levels of a three-level roadway system that surrounds the Blue Cross building and connects Lake Shore Drive and Michigan Avenue.

The challenge was to design and construct the bridge on a limited budget without disrupting traffic on the street below. The materials of steel, glass, and precast concrete are composed to provide a structural expression that appears to "fly" across the roadway below. Its light-filled interior is inviting, memorable, and exciting, as well as economical and practical in terms of construction and utility.

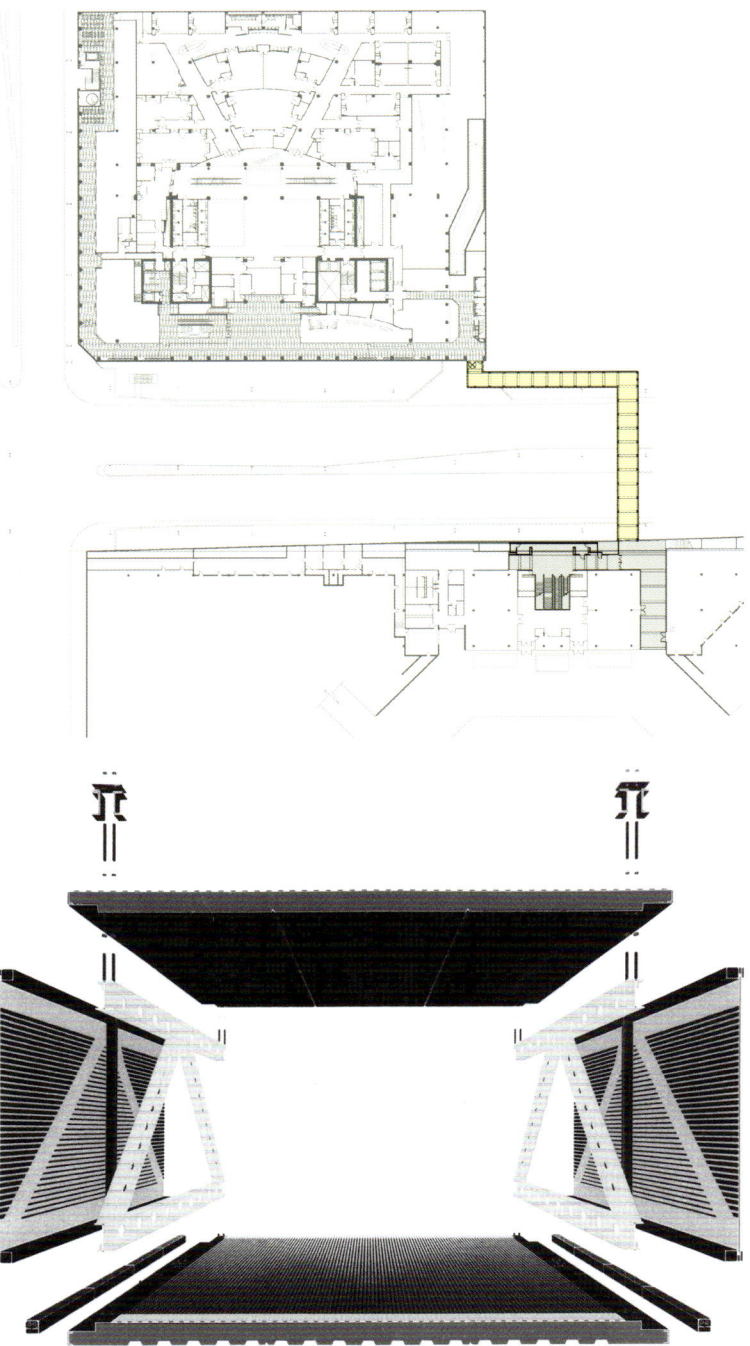

São Paulo, Brazil
Design/Completion 1998/2002
Client: Sociedad Latinoamericana de Inversiones S.A.
592,000 square feet (55,000 square meters)

# Grand Hyatt São Paulo

### Site
The hotel is sited between two skyscrapers in the Marginal Pinheiros business and financial district, with spectacular views of the city and the Tietê River.

### Program
The five-star hotel maximizes its relatively dense urban site, providing 470 guest rooms, a two-story dining and entertainment complex, a convention facility with 33,000 square feet of meeting space, and a fitness center and spa. The facility also includes a business center and on-site parking for 600 cars.

### Concept
In its downtown location, the complex caters to international business travelers with three distinct elements: a hotel tower, a conference center, and a separate dining facility that also serves residents of São Paulo. The hotel is a crisply sculpted tower of stone, glass, and steel that addresses its corporate neighbors and provides a distinct presence on the skyline. Two efficient, double-loaded corridors linked to a central elevator core provide visual access to landscaped gardens and pools that lend a resort-like quality to the otherwise all-business hotel.

The glass-enclosed lobby is 33 feet high and features granite and native orange-hued Louro Faia wood. A glass bridge and exposed elevator connect the fitness center and spa to a large outdoor pool. The conference center is housed in a connected, yet clearly distinct, structure and has two ballrooms and seven meeting rooms with natural daylight and private terraces. The exterior details of the restaurant complex mirror those of the other structures while its gray-colored stone differentiates it from the yellow hue of the hotel and conference center.

### Elements
Concrete frame, aluminum-and-glass window system, painted aluminum louvers, limestone cladding with granite highlights

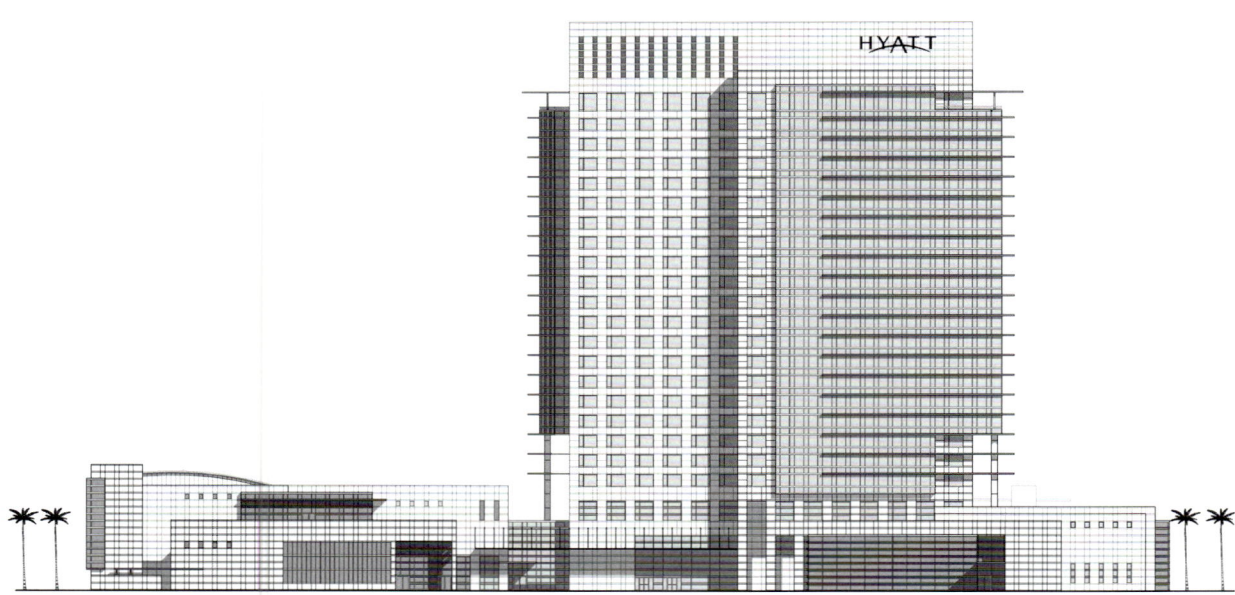

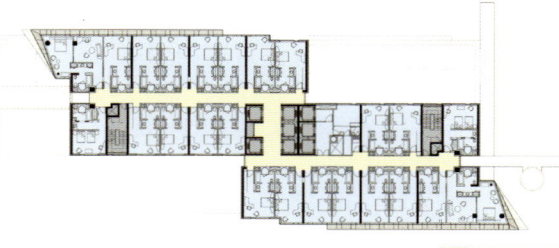

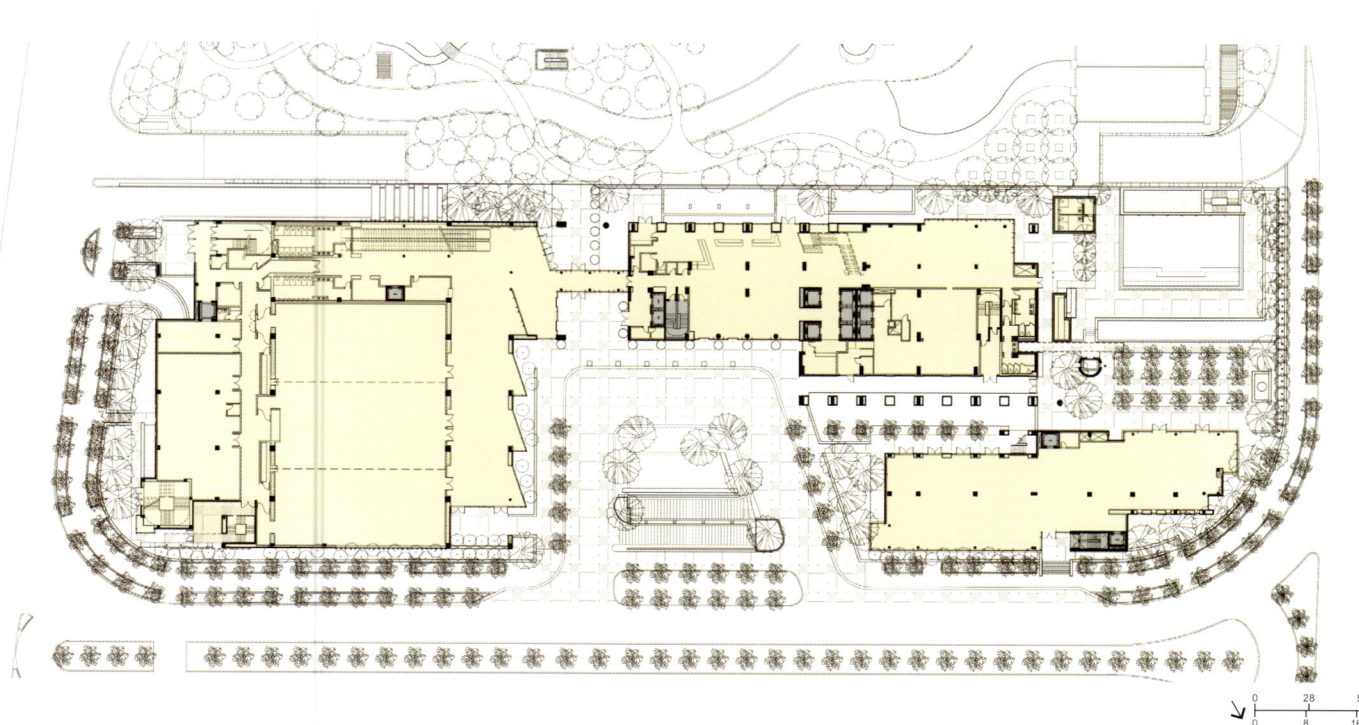

*Selected Works*

*Grand Hyatt São Paulo*

Selected Works

*Grand Hyatt São Paulo*

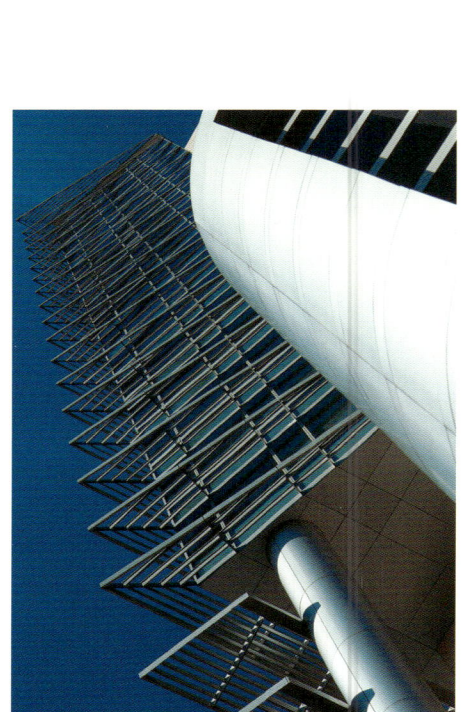
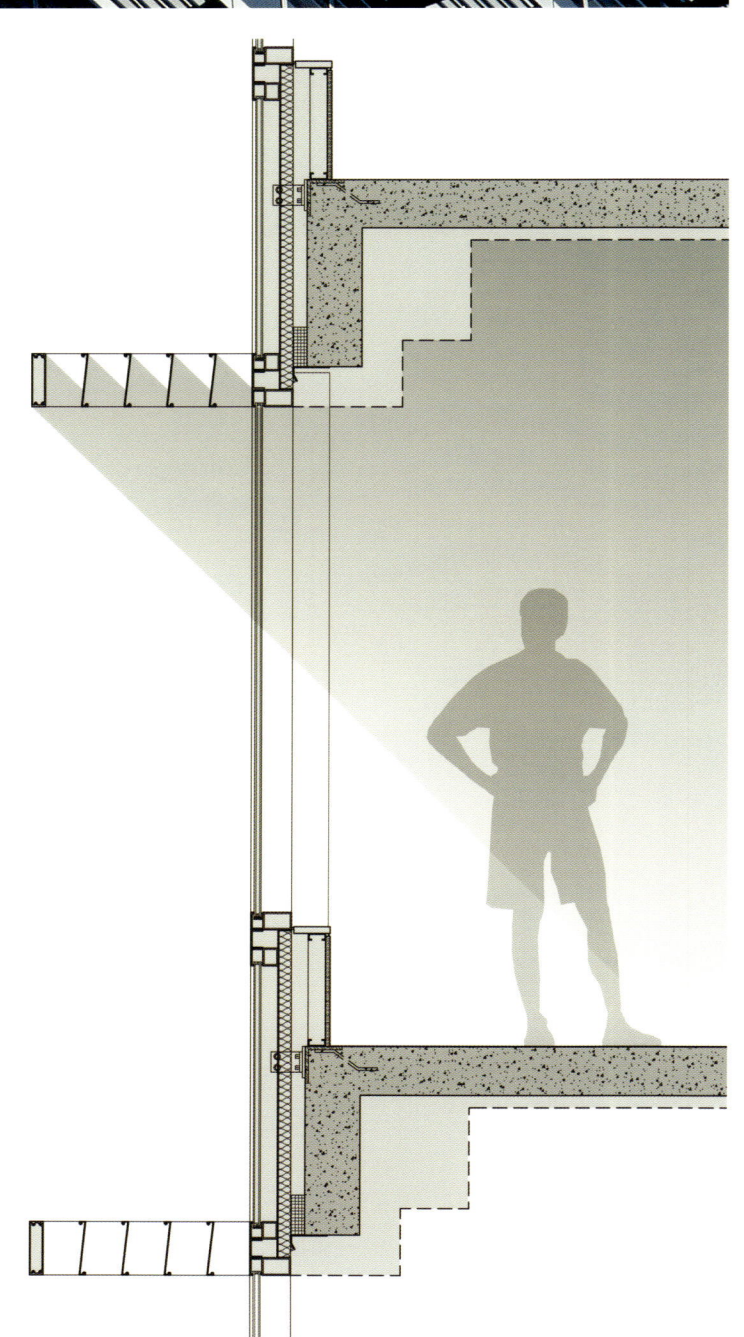

Selected Works

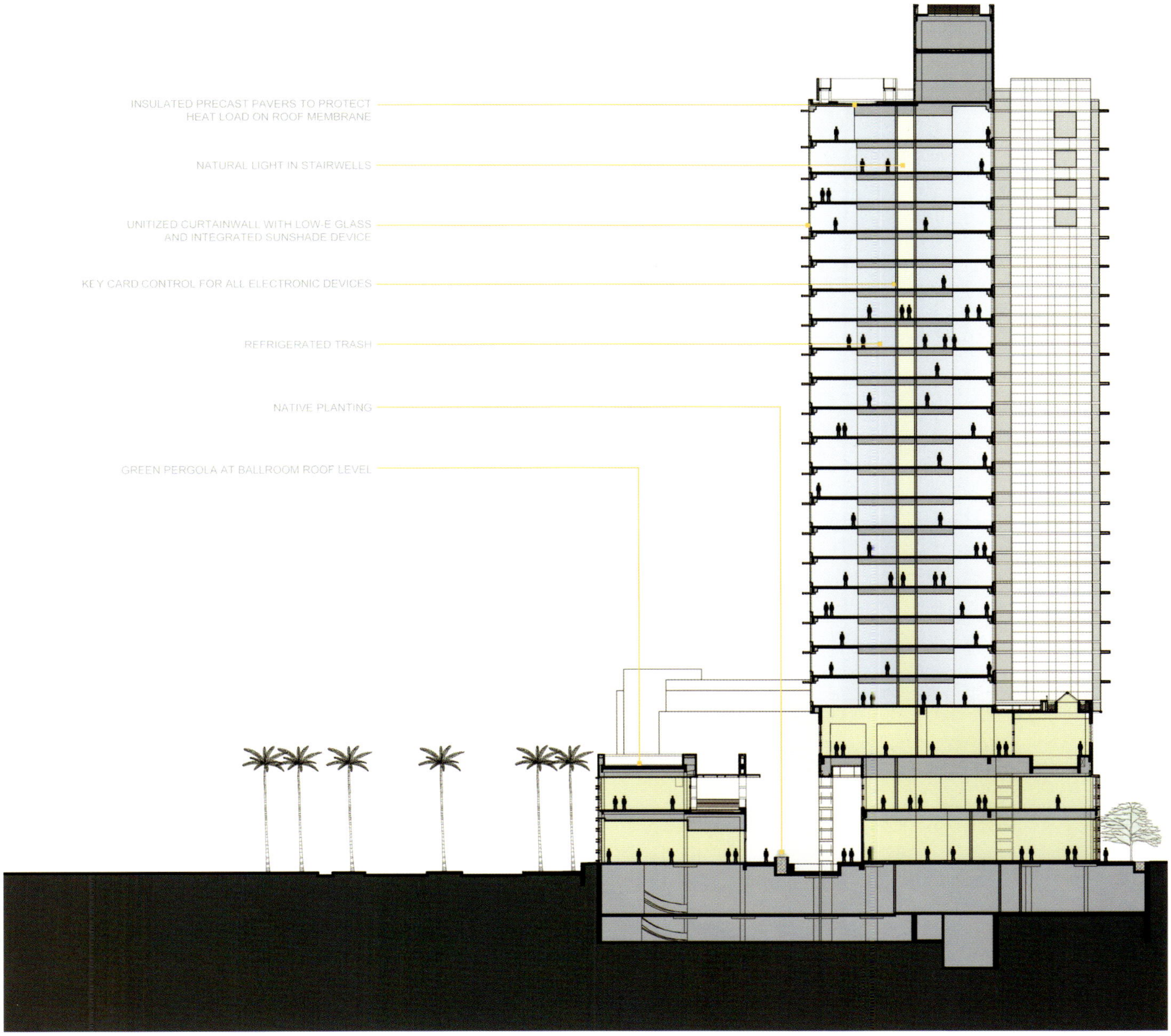

- INSULATED PRECAST PAVERS TO PROTECT HEAT LOAD ON ROOF MEMBRANE
- NATURAL LIGHT IN STAIRWELLS
- UNITIZED CURTAINWALL WITH LOW-E GLASS AND INTEGRATED SUNSHADE DEVICE
- KEY CARD CONTROL FOR ALL ELECTRONIC DEVICES
- REFRIGERATED TRASH
- NATIVE PLANTING
- GREEN PERGOLA AT BALLROOM ROOF LEVEL

*Grand Hyatt São Paulo*

Evanston, Illinois
Design/Completion 1997/2000
Client: Northwestern University
13,000 square feet (1,210 square meters)

# Mary and Leigh Block Museum of Art Expansion

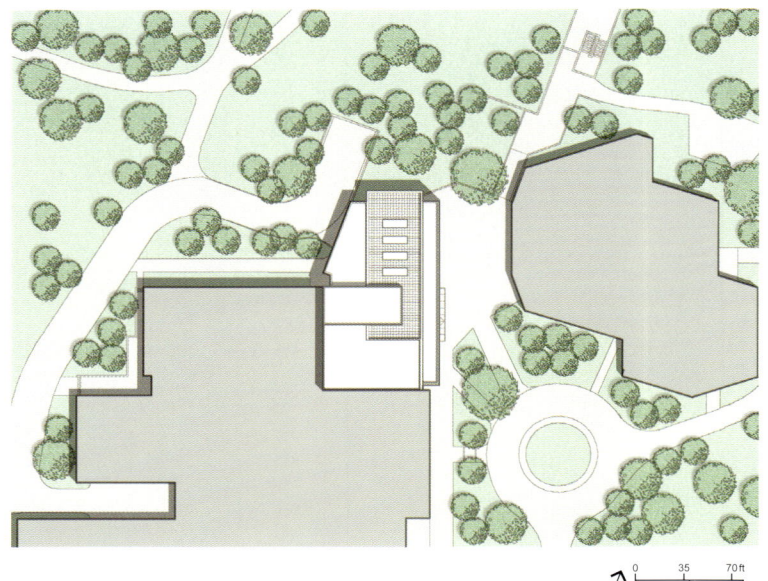

### Site
The museum is located on the main campus of Northwestern University. As part of a group of buildings known as the Arts Circle, it is adjacent to a concert hall and a performing arts center, and has views of Lake Michigan.

### Program
The 13,000-square-foot addition to an existing building includes three exhibition spaces totaling 6,000 square feet, a 160-seat auditorium, administrative offices, a 1,100-square-foot print and drawing center, a digitally wired secondary gallery and classroom, and expanded storage facilities.

### Concept
The museum addition doubles the size of the existing exhibit and educational facility while enhancing the harmony of the Arts Circle. With extensive glass and solid walls of limestone—the predominant material on campus—the addition blends with neighboring buildings while retaining a modernist spirit in its design. The major exhibition space is a floating wing that extends over an open plaza. The resulting portico shelters an important pedestrian thoroughfare and small sculpture court. The stair to the second floor is housed in a two-story glass atrium overlooking Lake Michigan.

### Elements
Concrete structure with limestone, aluminum-and-glass enclosure

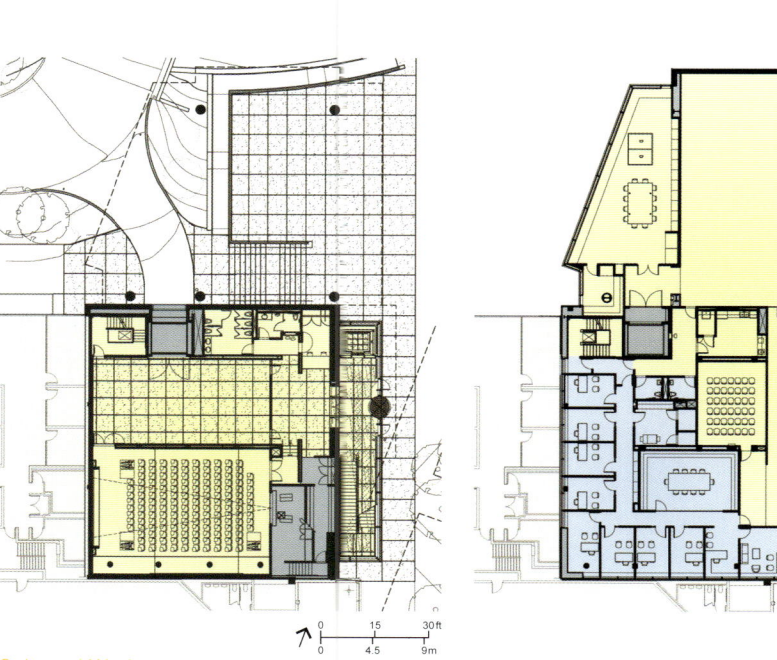

Selected Works

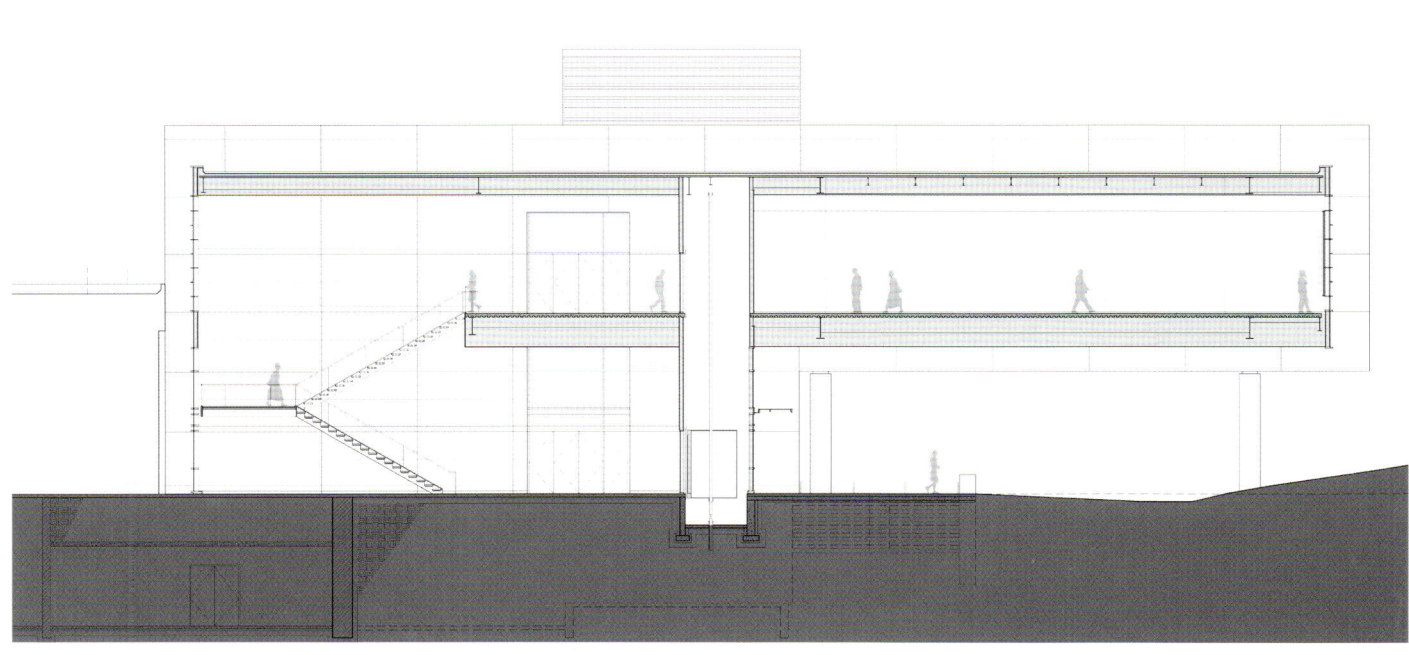

*Mary and Leigh Block Museum of Art Expansion*

*Selected Works*

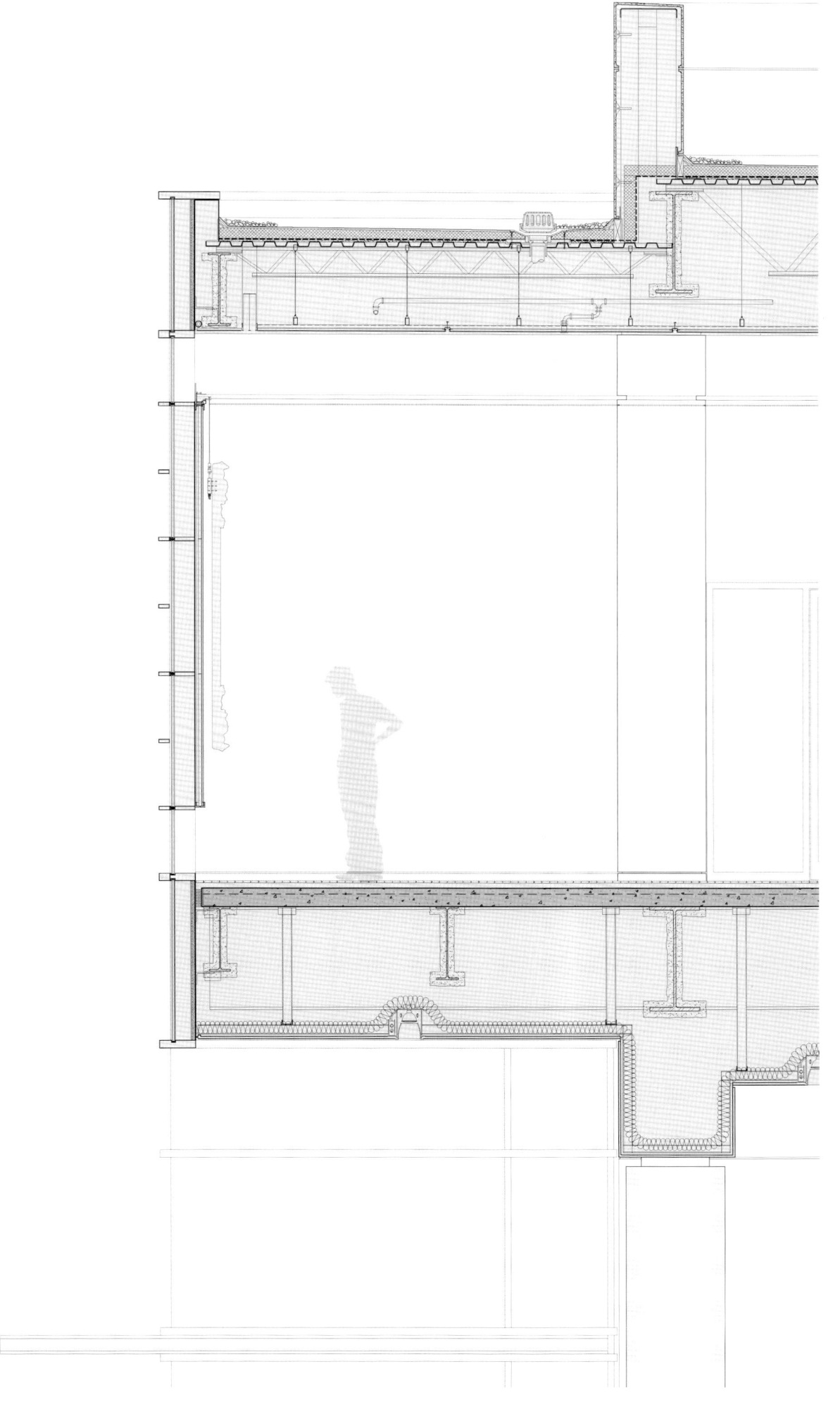

Mary and Leigh Block Museum of Art Expansion

Chicago, Illinois
Design/Completion 1999/2003
Client: Chicago Bears
Owner: Chicago Park District
Additional Parkland: 17 acres (6.88 hectares)
Stadium: 1,600,000 square feet (148,640 square meters)

# North Burnham Park and Soldier Field Redevelopment

### Site
The site is located at the midpoint of Chicago's magnificent 23-mile lakefront park adjacent to the city's Museum Campus and in close proximity to downtown and the convention center.

### Program
Completed in 1924, Soldier Field did not offer the sightlines and seating configurations necessary for today's sporting events and concerts; thus, the stadium had to be completely redesigned and reconstructed. The original Doric colonnades and the lower grandstand façade were retained and restored. The new structure provides seating for 62,000 patrons, 133 luxury skyboxes, and restaurant and club facilities. New underground and surface parking facilities accommodate 5,800 cars.

The redevelopment of North Burnham Park transformed unimproved surface parking into 17 acres of additional green space, with a new boulevard for improved vehicular circulation and a variety of new amenities, including a sledding hill, police memorial, winter garden, and a 20-foot-high, 200-foot-wide water wall commemorating veterans.

### Concept
The primary design challenge was to create a modern facility within the space limitations of the historic colonnades. This feat was accomplished with a unique asymmetrical configuration: club seating and skyboxes on one side of the stadium and grandstand seating on the other. The stadium features a state-of-the-art field of heated natural turf with exceptional drainage. Video scoreboards and modern locker and training facilities have also been provided. The grandstand, with 50-foot cantilevers, utilizes tuned mass dampers to control structural and rhythmic deflections and vibrations.

### Elements
Grandstand supported by structural steel girders with precast concrete risers; state-of-the-art aluminum-and-glass unitized curtain wall system

*The project was a joint venture of two architecture firms: Goettsch Partners, with primary responsibility for the master plan and North Burnham Park project, and Wood + Zapata, with primary responsibility for the architectural design of the Soldier Field stadium.*

*North Burnham Park and Soldier Field Redevelopment*

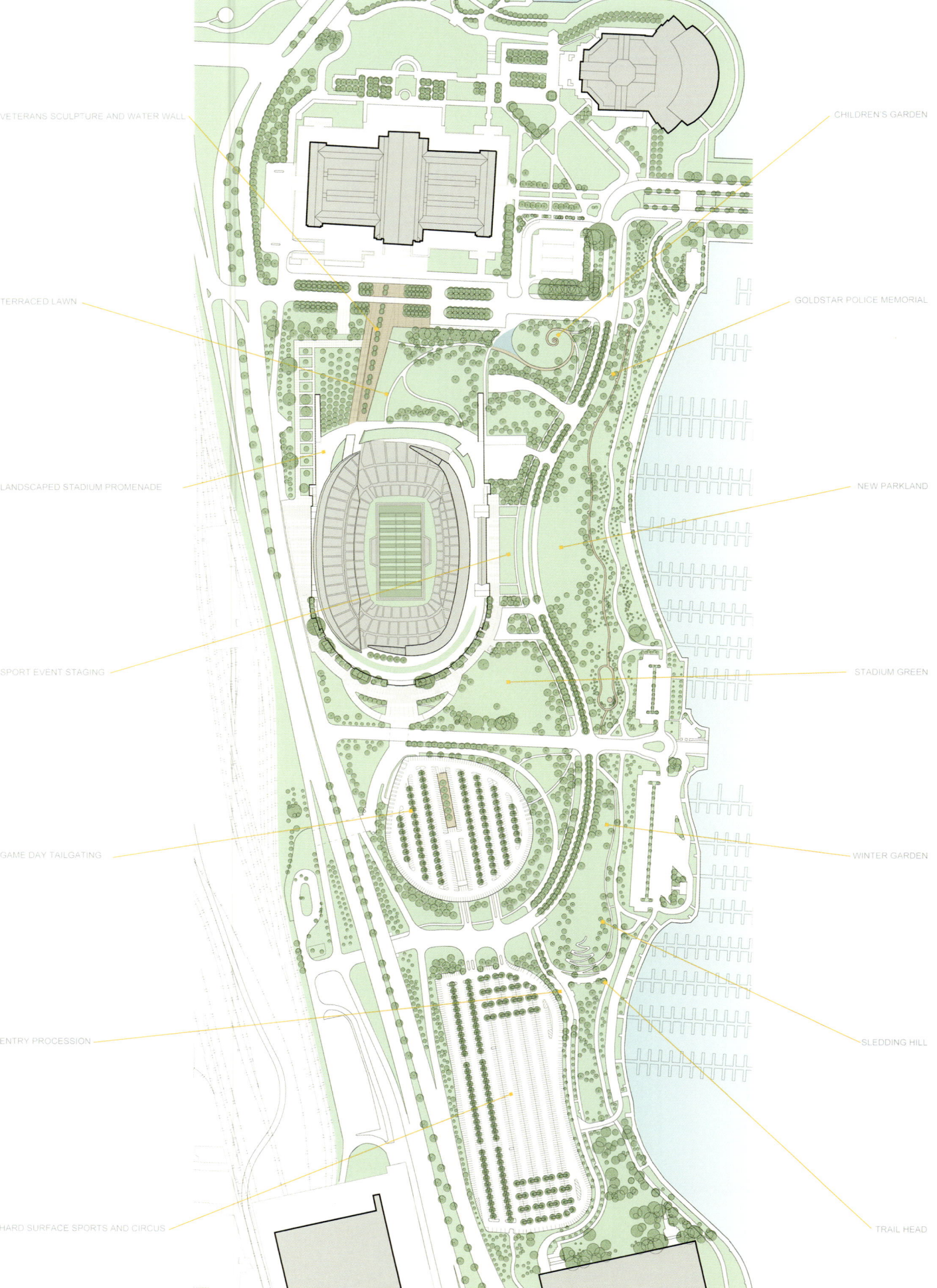

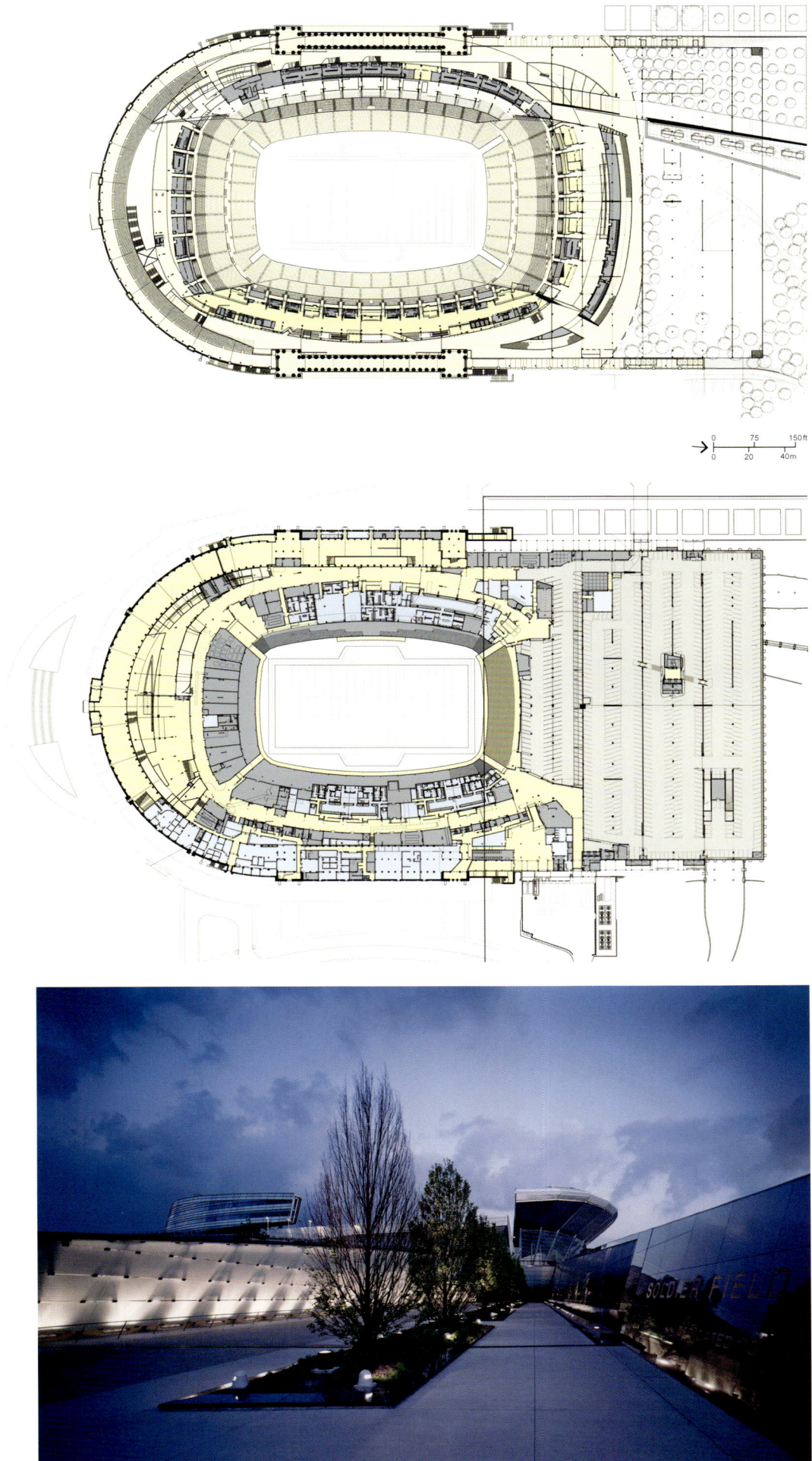

*North Burnham Park and Soldier Field Redevelopment*

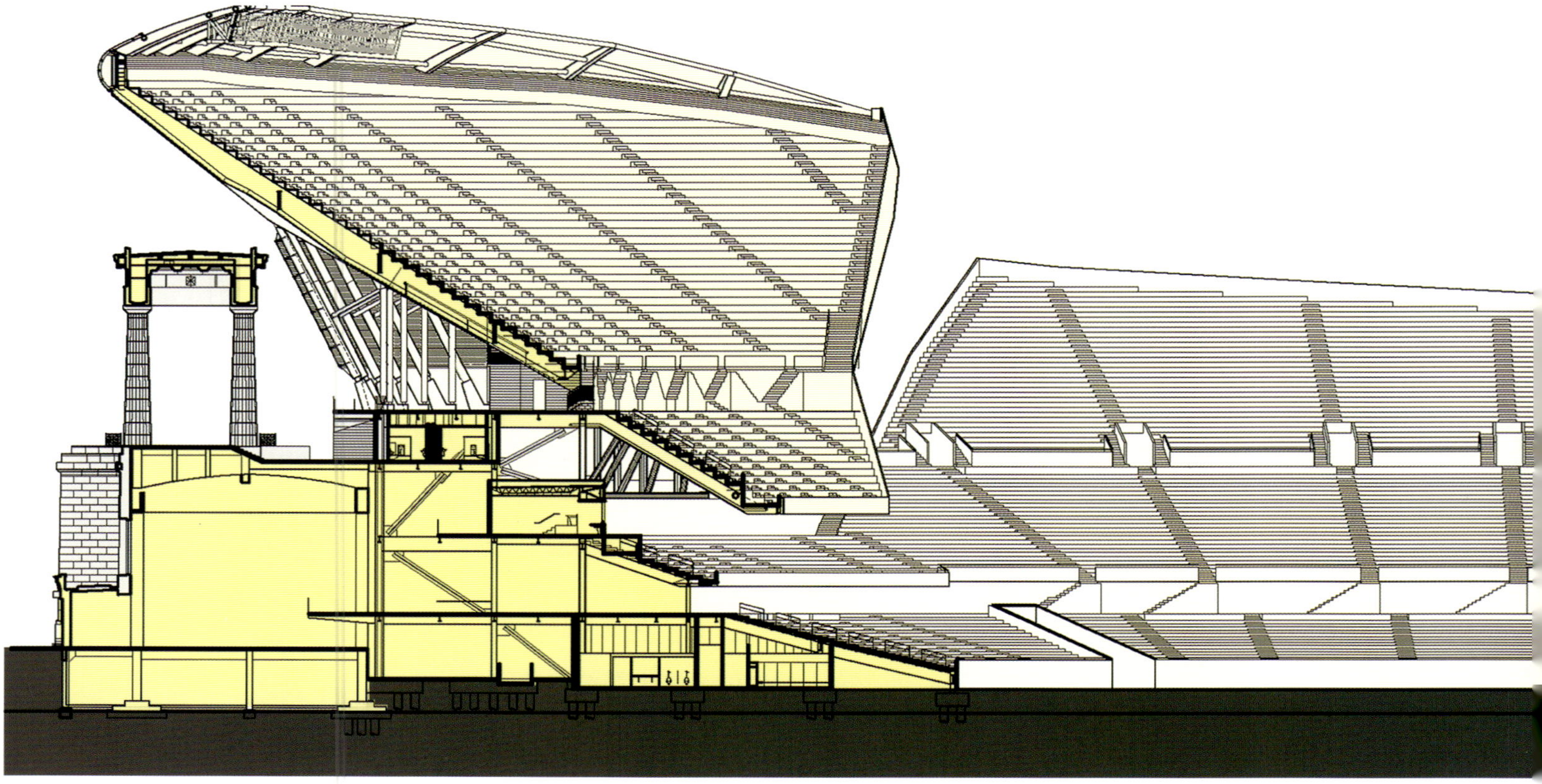

Selected Works

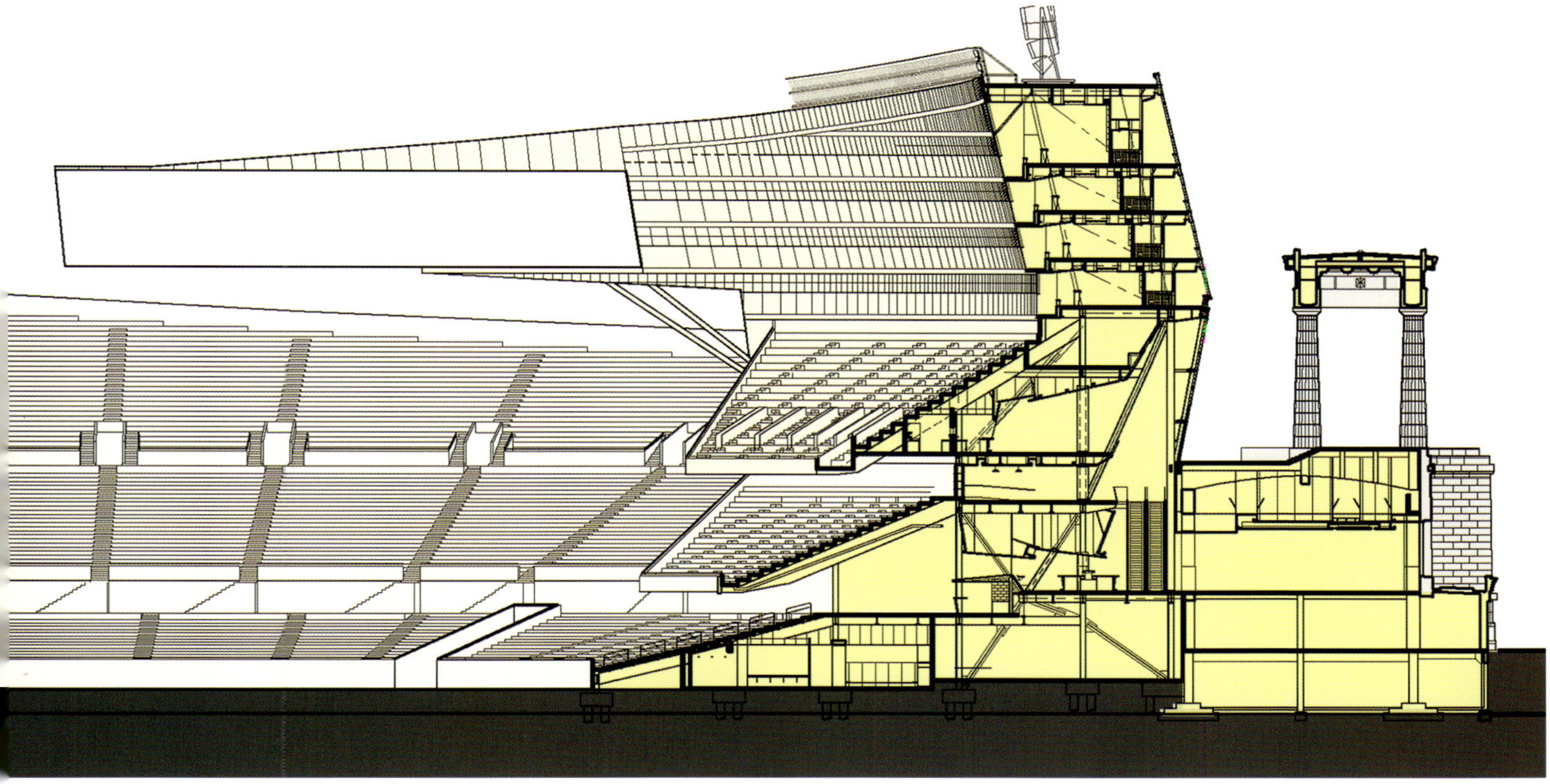

*North Burnham Park and Soldier Field Redevelopment*

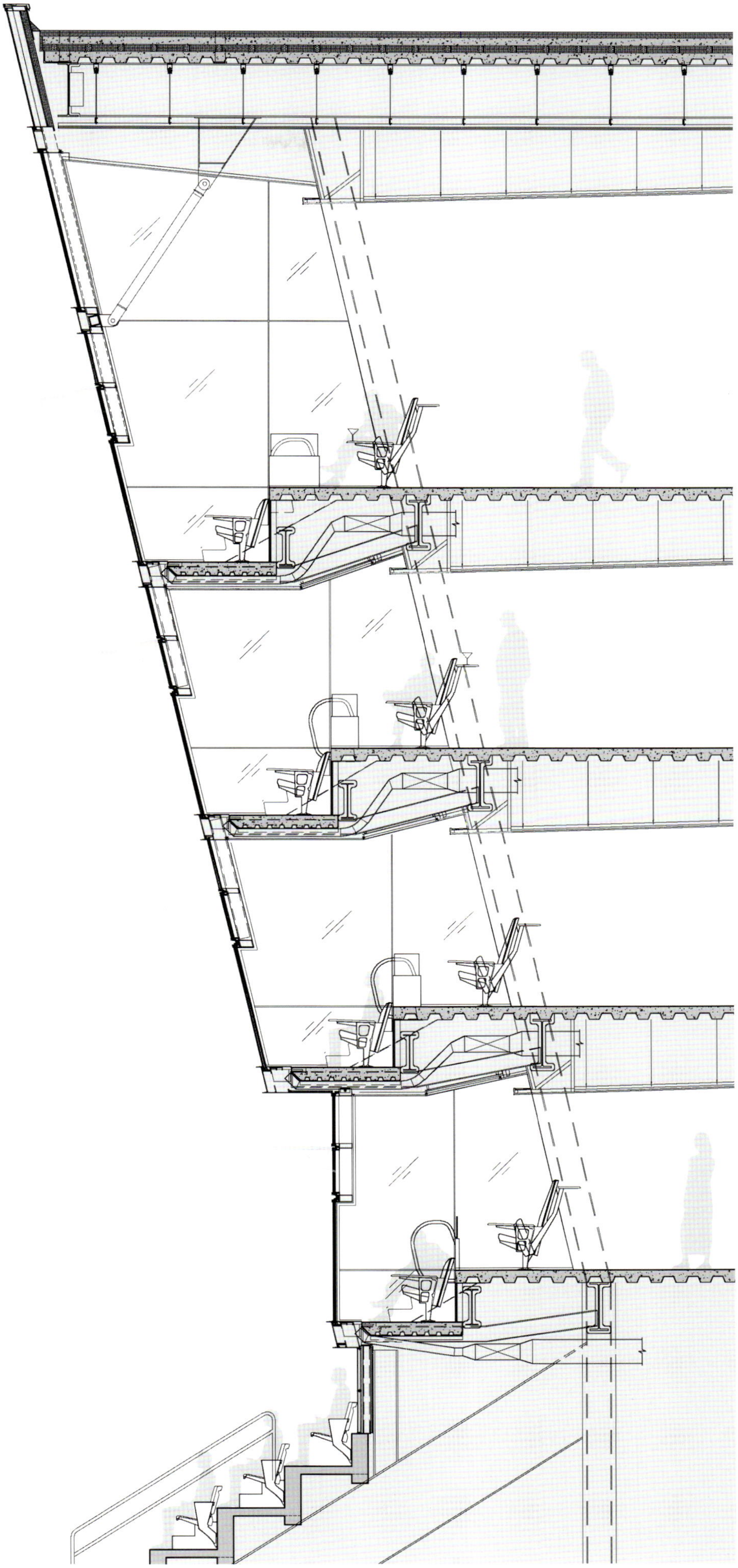

*North Burnham Park and Soldier Field Redevelopment*

# Design Typologies

## Office
- 94 Suzhou International Tower
- 98 SIP Administration Center
- 102 CBS 2 Broadcast Center
- 104 Lujiazui Diamond Tower
- 110 Jenner & Block
- 112 Sunbelt Tower
- 114 Freeborn & Peters
- 116 155 North Wacker and 222 West Randolph

## Hospitality/Residential
- 122 Hyatt Lodge at McDonald's Campus
- 126 Enhance Anting Golf Club Complex
- 128 Grand Hyatt Mumbai
- 132 Ningbo Marriott
- 134 Hyatt Regency Suzhou
- 138 Four Seasons Mumbai
- 140 J.W. Marriott Grand Rapids

## Mixed-Use
- 144 Nanjing International Center
- 150 Greenland Mixed-Use Development
- 152 Product Research and Data Service Center
- 154 Hyatt Regency at Chicony Plaza
- 156 Grand Hyatt Guangzhou
- 158 Ovation Plaza
- 162 Shanghai Caohejing Development
- 164 Bahagia Mixed-Use Development
- 166 Beijing Silvertie Center

## Institutional
- 168 U-505 Submarine Exhibit
- 172 CCS Bard Hessel Museum
- 178 Regenstein Center for African Apes
- 182 Sky Pavilion
- 186 Chicago Tower
- 190 Suzhou Jinji Lake Yacht Club

## Repositioning
- 194 360 North Michigan Avenue
- 198 1 North LaSalle Street
- 200 231 South LaSalle Street
- 204 120 South LaSalle Street
- 208 35 East Wacker Drive

Suzhou, China
Design/Completion 1997/1999
Client: Suzhou Industrial Park Administrative Committee
572,000 square feet (53,140 square meters)

# Suzhou International Tower

### Site
On the edge of the historic city of Suzhou, the Suzhou Industrial Park is a master planned, 24-hour community catering to top electronics and pharmaceutical manufacturing companies. This newly constructed town offers international-quality housing, educational, civic, cultural and recreational facilities for residents and visitors. This government building is located in the first phase of the development's commercial core.

### Program
The building is the administrative center—or city hall—for the first phase of the new town. The 18-story building includes a six-story podium with council chambers, hearing rooms, contact spaces for licensing and public records, and a cafeteria. Above the podium, the tower provides 262,000 square feet of Class A office space. Two floors below grade contain building services and parking for 172 cars.

### Concept
The commission was awarded through an international design competition that called for a contemporary, timeless structure that would be the symbolic and physical center of the first phase of the new development's commercial district. The design maximizes the building height allowed by zoning. The massing clearly expresses the two purposes for which the building is designed: the four-story base provides an expanded footprint for larger spaces required to accommodate the council chambers, meeting facilities and licensing functions; the elliptical tower houses the office functions.

### Elements
Reinforced concrete structural frame, aluminum-and-glass curtain wall system, marble-clad lobby floors and walls

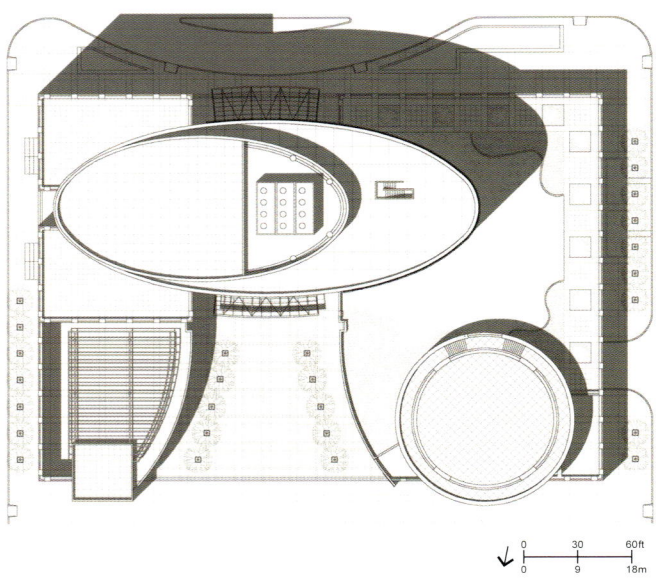

0 30 60ft
0 9 18m

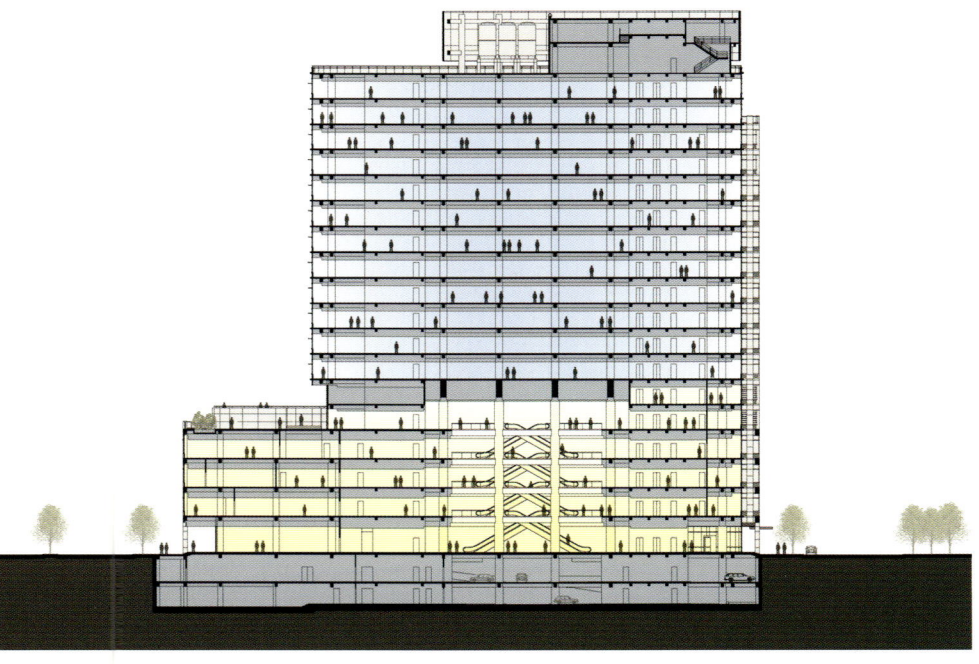

Office

Suzhou, China
Design/Completion 2003/2005
Client: Suzhou Industrial Park Administrative Committee
869,400 square feet (80,770 square meters)

# SIP Administration Center

### Site
The Suzhou Industrial Park (SIP) is a planned community on the edge of the historic city of Suzhou. It is designed to attract leading electronics and pharmaceutical manufacturing companies and their facilities. Confirming the success of the SIP new town, the second phase of the development is now under construction. This building is the featured facility in a six-building governmental center, which was also master planned by the firm.

### Program
The Administration Center—in effect the city hall—is a 21-story office tower with an adjacent three-story podium that houses council chambers, meeting rooms, an auditorium, an exhibition area and a cafeteria. Parking is provided on the lower level. This building replaces the phase one administrative center, Suzhou International Tower, also designed by the firm and completed in 1999.

### Concept
The design challenge was to create a building with a governmental presence that embodies the future aspirations of the SIP. The Administration Center recalls traditional, conservative Chinese government buildings utilizing contemporary details and timeless materials. The predominately stone exterior makes a solid, grand gesture. The introduction of additional glass in the tower's midsection establishes a symmetry and reduces the visual mass of the tower as it appears to hover over the granite base. The curved aluminum-and-glass skylight entry canopy reinforces the building's main entrance and contrasts with the overall building mass.

### Elements
Reinforced concrete structure, unitized curtain wall of granite, aluminum and glass, granite podium and plaza

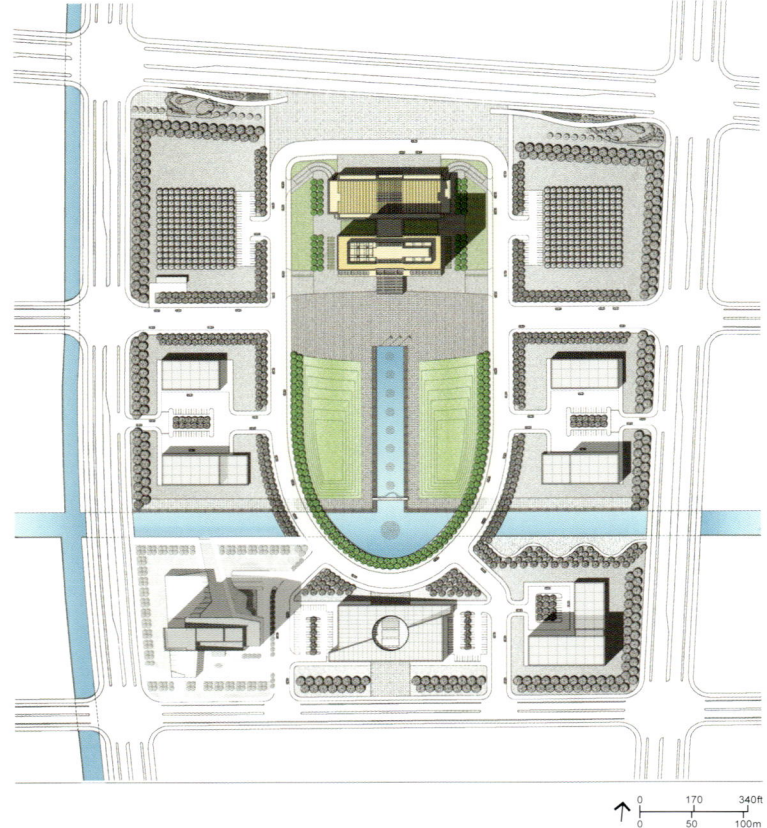

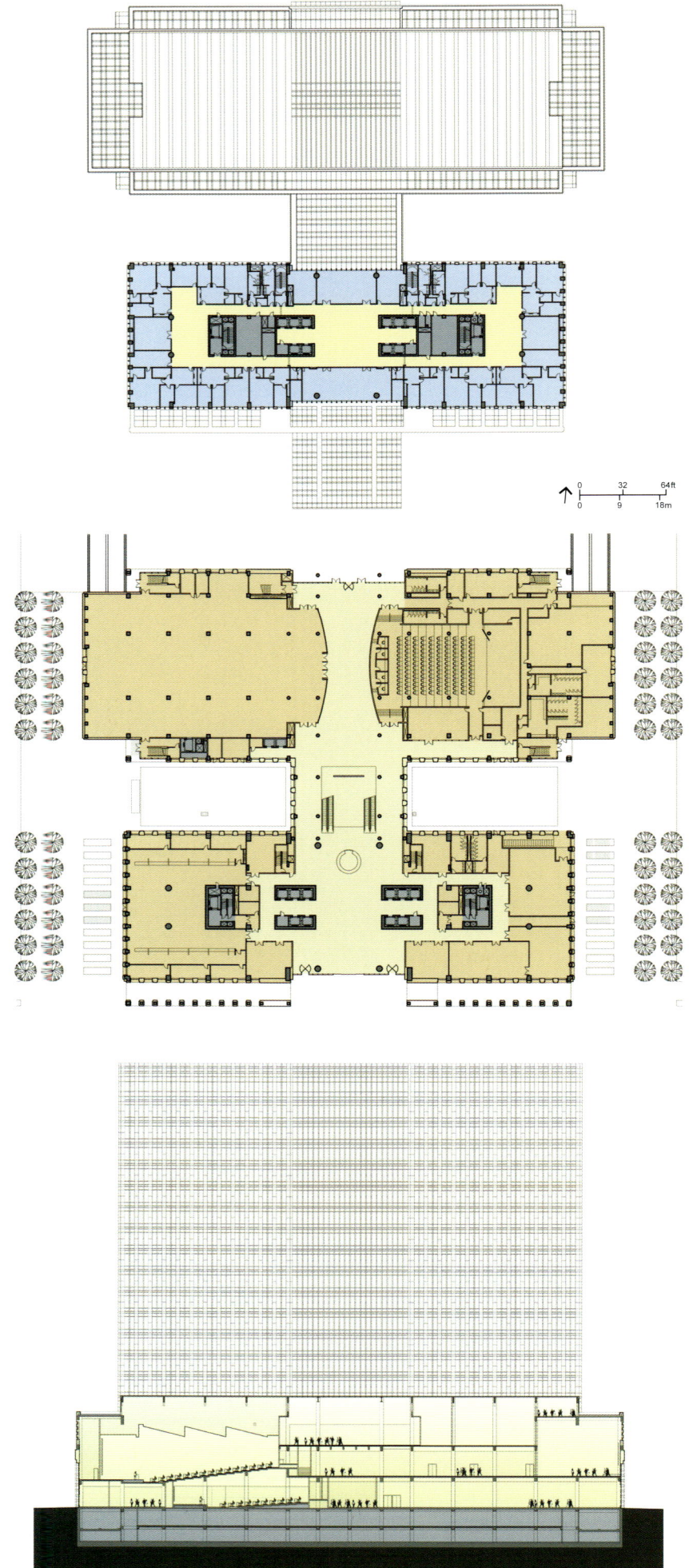

*Office*

*SIP Administration Center*

Chicago, Illinois
Design/Completion 2004/2008
Client: CBS Broadcasting Inc.
100,000 square feet (9,290 square meters)

# CBS 2 Broadcast Center

### Site
Anchoring the corner of a full-block mixed-use complex, CBS Broadcasting will locate a new state-of-the-art broadcast center for its local affiliate, WBBM-TV/CBS 2 Chicago, with a showcase streetfront studio facing Chicago's landmark Daley Plaza.

### Program
CBS 2 will occupy the building's first five floors, comprising approximately 100,000 square feet. The streetfront studio will enable crowds to watch live local news broadcasts as well as other locally produced programs. The studio's corner will feature CBS 2 Weather Control, showcasing the latest weather tracking technology.

The facility will be Chicago's first all-digital, HD-ready facility, utilizing the most up-to-date broadcast technology. In addition to a streetfront studio, a separate production studio with a dedicated control room and green rooms will provide for production of large, long-form programming.

### Concept
Drawing inspiration from the news gathering process and the proportional dynamics of the 16:9 high-definition broadcast "frame," the design's planning embraces the emphasis on the horizontal, sequential nature of storytelling. The project is also inspired by the interrelationship between complementary narratives, the central dynamic of broadcast journalism.

The design embraces the improvisational aspects of collaboration with an emphasis on transparency and visual connection. Glass façades and strategically positioned glazed openings in interior offices and control rooms, combined with low-height open office workstations, maximize accessibility to the available light and view corridors. Additionally, a two-story opening visually links the newsroom operations with the sales staff on different levels of the facility.

### Elements
Raised floor, tailored to each level's specific function; glass with painted-drywall acoustical partitions; carpet tile and vinyl flooring; state-of-the-art digital-broadcast workstations; open-plan furniture systems

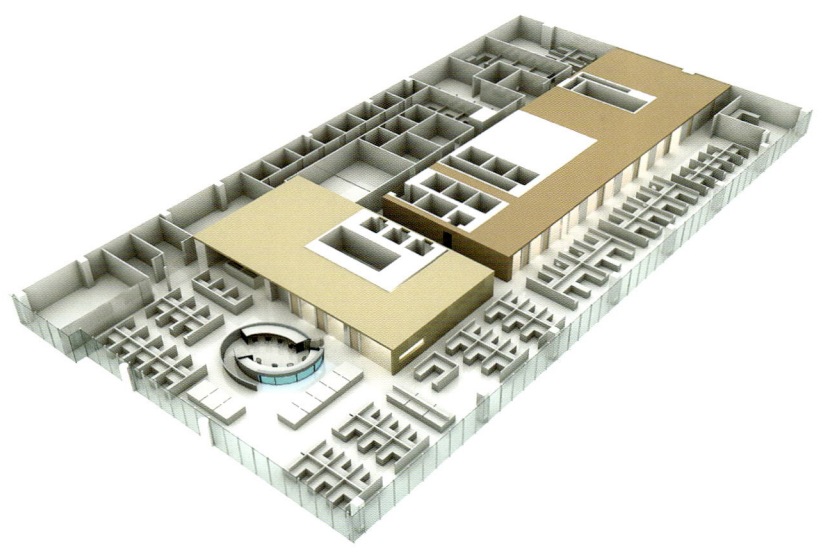

Shanghai, China
Design/Completion 2005/2009
Client: Shanghai Lujiazui Development Co., Ltd.
535,500 square feet (49,750 square meters)

# Lujiazui Diamond Tower

### Site
This office high-rise will be constructed on Century Avenue, the main, 300-foot-wide boulevard in Shanghai's newly developed Pudong area, the primary location for the city's modern office towers.

### Program
Approximately one-half of the building will be occupied by members of the Diamond Exchange, with the remainder available for other tenants. The ground floor will house Diamond Center-related retail; the second floor will include the elevator lobby, exhibition space, and a restaurant.

### Concept
The building is conceived as two rectangular office slabs connected by a skylit atrium with a cable-supported net wall at each end. One tower is dedicated to Diamond Exchange members and designed to provide them with secure transport from their below-grade parking spaces to their offices above. The adjacent tower serves other tenants, with access through an open elevator tower in the center of the atrium.

The ends of the rectangular slabs are clad with horizontal grilles, which provide a monumental surface that disguises the intakes and exhausts of the mechanical system. The curtain wall opposite the atrium uses a series of horizontal fritted-glass screens to reduce glare and minimize the internal heat load.

### Elements
Steel structural frame with concrete shear wall cores; aluminum-and-glass unitized curtain wall; cable-supported glass atrium end walls; exposed, glass-enclosed elevator tower

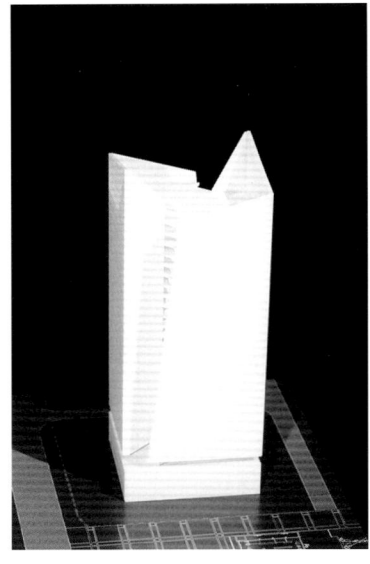

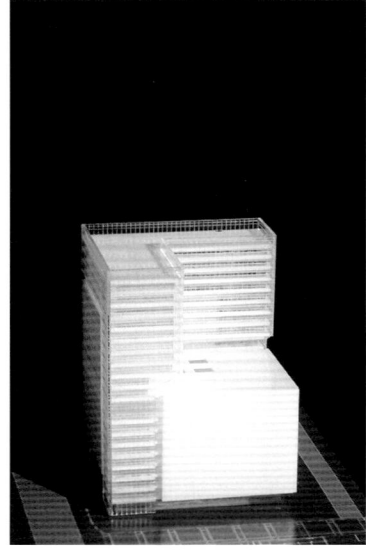
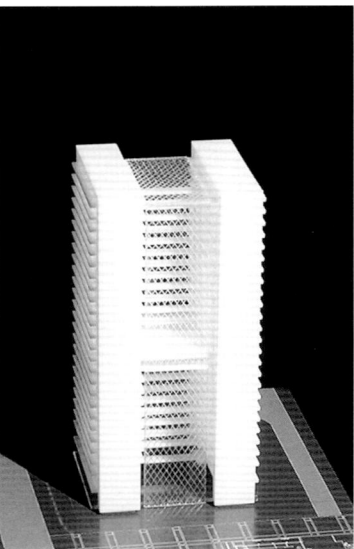

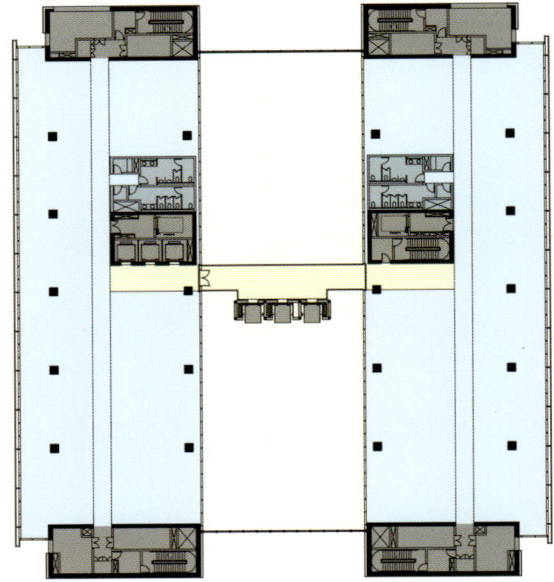

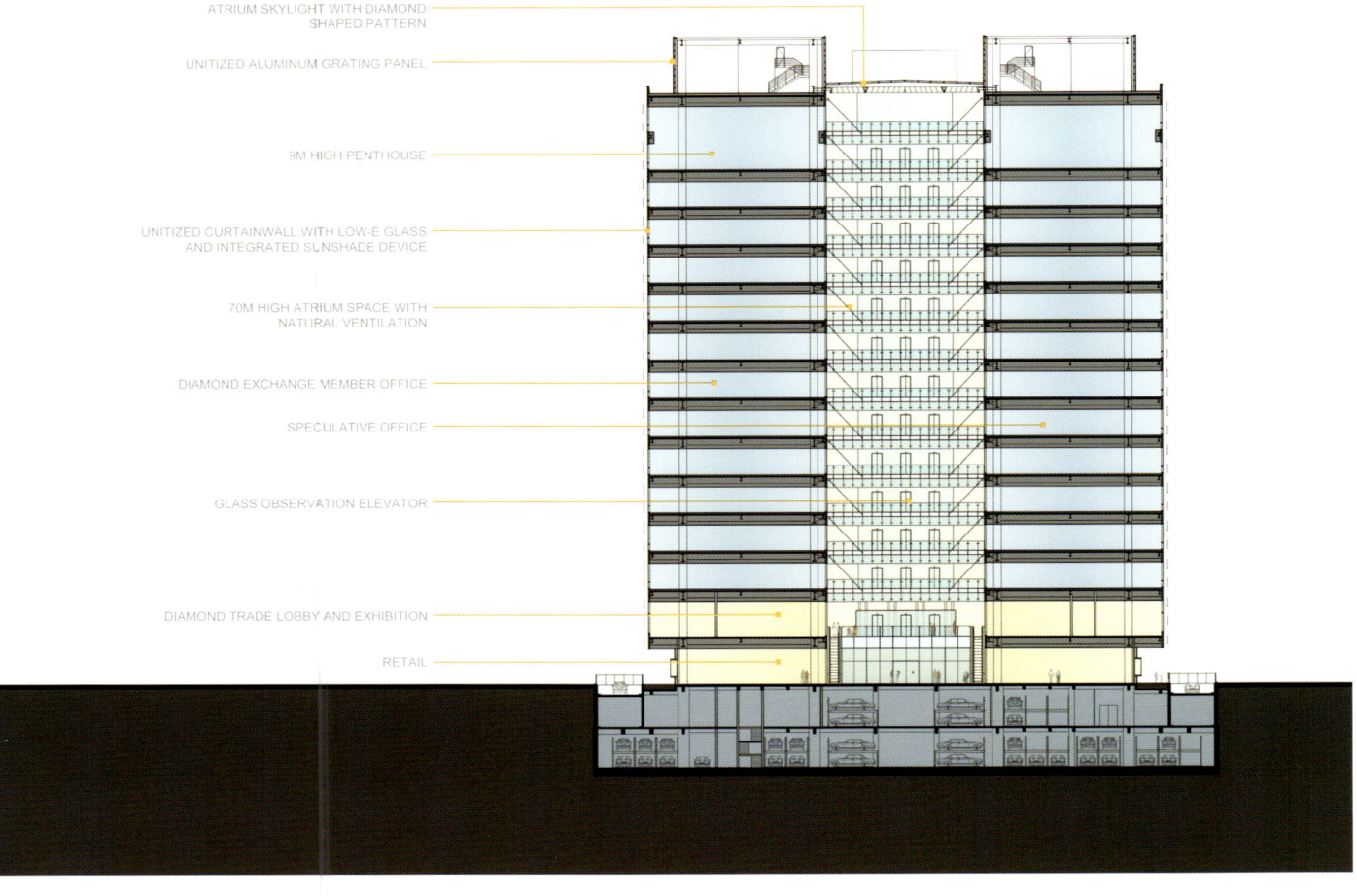

- ATRIUM SKYLIGHT WITH DIAMOND SHAPED PATTERN
- UNITIZED ALUMINUM GRATING PANEL
- 9M HIGH PENTHOUSE
- UNITIZED CURTAINWALL WITH LOW-E GLASS AND INTEGRATED SUNSHADE DEVICE
- 70M HIGH ATRIUM SPACE WITH NATURAL VENTILATION
- DIAMOND EXCHANGE MEMBER OFFICE
- SPECULATIVE OFFICE
- GLASS OBSERVATION ELEVATOR
- DIAMOND TRADE LOBBY AND EXHIBITION
- RETAIL

*Office*

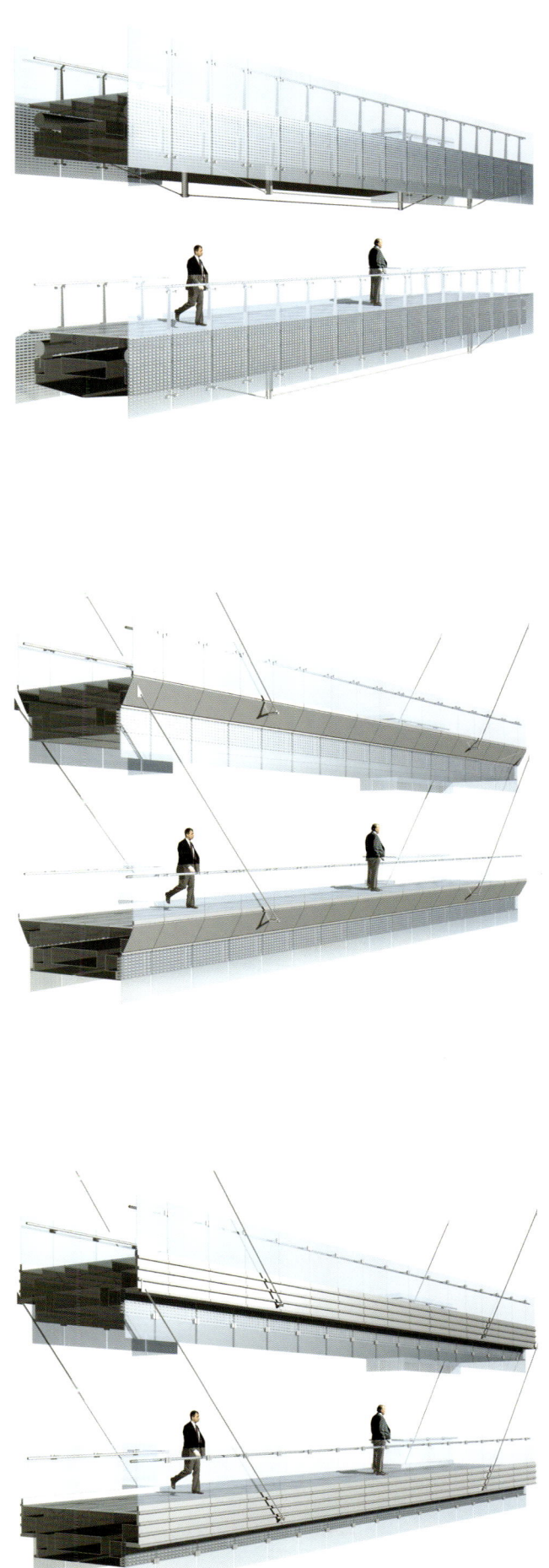

*Lujiazui Diamond Tower*

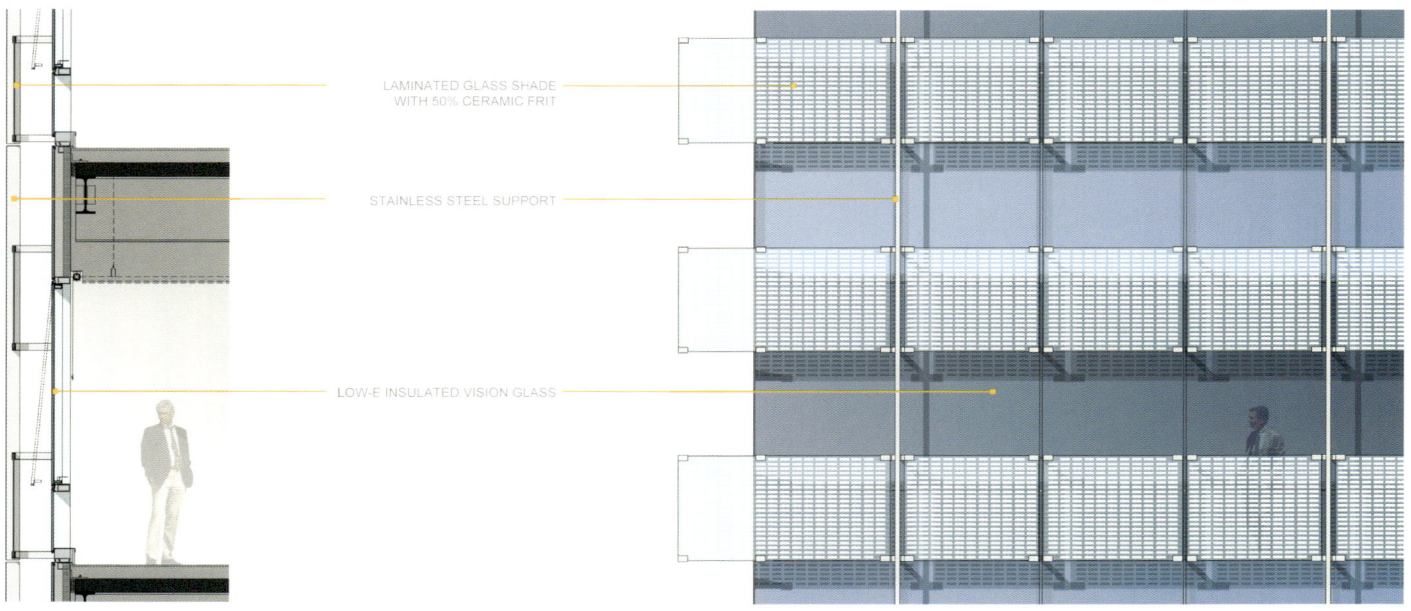

LAMINATED GLASS SHADE
WITH 50% CERAMIC FRIT

STAINLESS STEEL SUPPORT

LOW-E INSULATED VISION GLASS

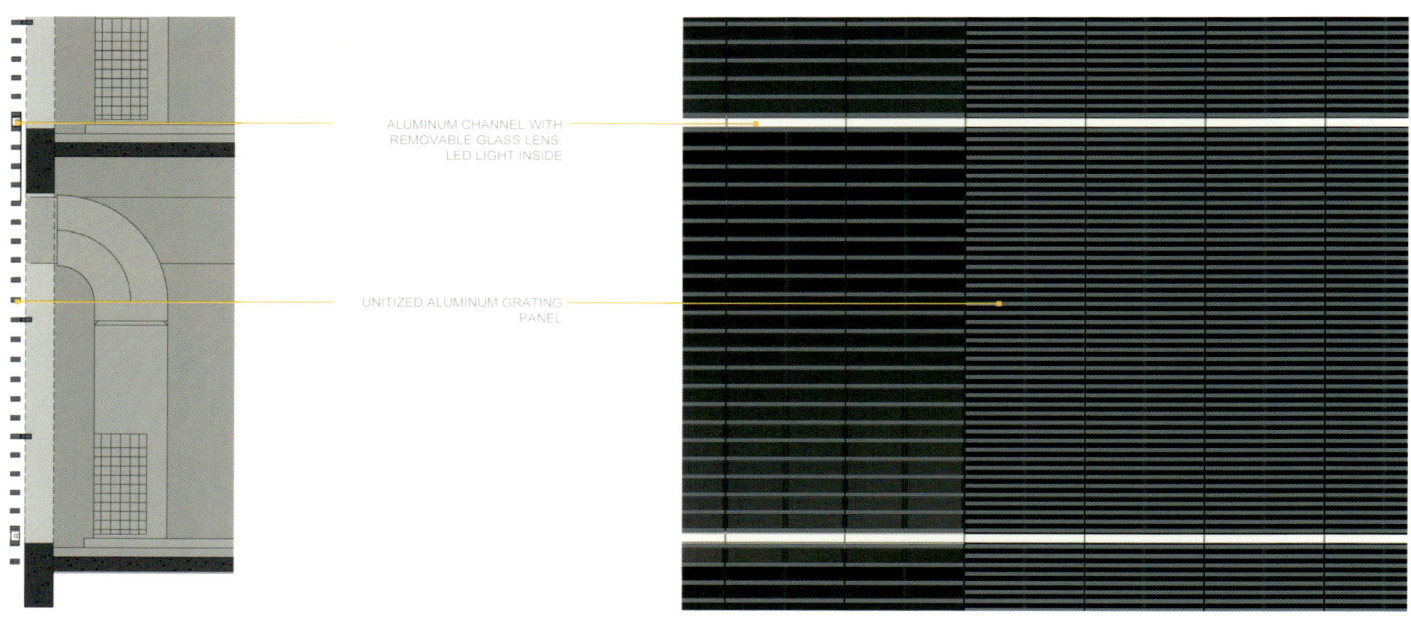

ALUMINUM CHANNEL WITH
REMOVABLE GLASS LENS
LED LIGHT INSIDE

UNITIZED ALUMINUM GRATING
PANEL

*Office*

*Lujiazui Diamond Tower*

Chicago, Illinois
Design/Completion 2005/2009
Client: Jenner & Block LLP
375,000 square feet (34,800 square meters)

# Jenner & Block

### Site
The new Chicago offices of this national law firm will occupy the top floors of a new 1,100,000-square-foot office high-rise in Chicago's River North neighborhood. Building amenities include a health club, cafeteria, and white-tablecloth restaurants.

### Program
Jenner & Block's 14 office floors will accommodate a highly collaborative work environment with a high-performance information technology platform for approximately 500 attorneys and 600 support staff. Attorneys anchor the high-rise floors, with administrative teams occupying space in the tower's mid-rise. The building's top floor houses a technologically advanced conference center with double-height spaces and panoramic city views for client meetings and frequent social and pro-bono functions.

### Concept
The design objective is to create an environment that facilitates a nimble, high-performance culture while enabling a collaborative and highly interactive work process. Spatially, the design integrates these objectives through the extensive use of glass to create layers of transparency throughout the space—from floor-to-ceiling glass attorney office façades to translucent glazed conference walls.

The typical attorney office floor is organized by a flexible, modular planning design, allowing for interchangeable blocks of secretarial and paralegal work sites with case room clusters. These internal support spaces are conceived as demountable assemblies, allowing for rapid reconfiguration to meet the dynamic demands of fluid caseload requirements.

### Elements
Glazed and acoustical partitions, carpet flooring, articulated ceiling planes, custom glass and millwork assemblies, state-of-the-art digital meeting technologies and communication tools, stone flooring, inset carpets, specialty ceilings and custom lighting

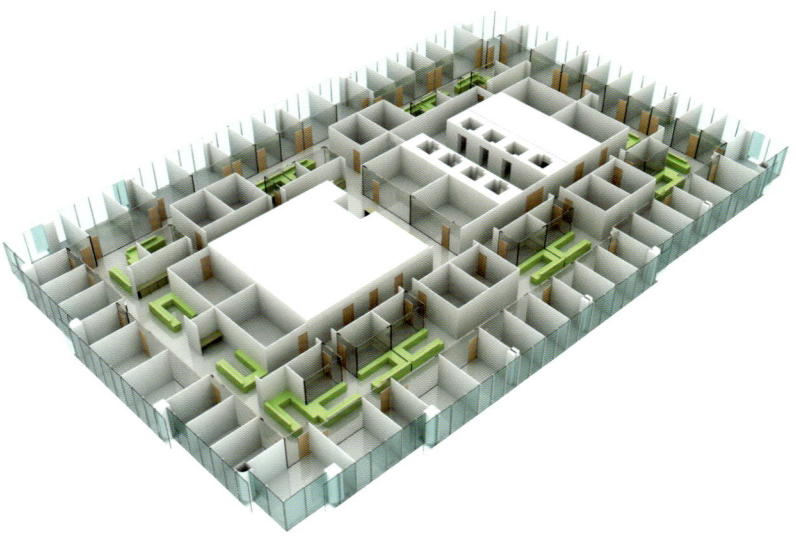

Chicago, Illinois
Design 2001
Client: Sunbelt Management Co.
1,200,000 square feet (111,480 square meters)

# Sunbelt Tower

## Site
The proposed office tower is located in downtown Chicago near Michigan Avenue, just north of the Chicago River.

## Program
The 42-story building provides 1,200,000 square feet of multi-tenant office space.

## Concept
The building is designed for tenants who require flexible, open floor plates, the latest data and communication services as well as tenant-dedicated systems for emergency power and supplemental cooling. Maximum efficiency is achieved on the typical office floor with 45-foot column-free space between the core and exterior wall.

The column-free spaces on each side of the core are slightly shifted in opposite directions and vary in height to provide a distinctive skyline profile for the building. Each floor features eight column-free corner offices. A large public arcade under the building connects to adjoining prime retail streets.

## Elements
Reinforced concrete core with perimeter structural steel frame, unitized aluminum-and-glass curtain wall

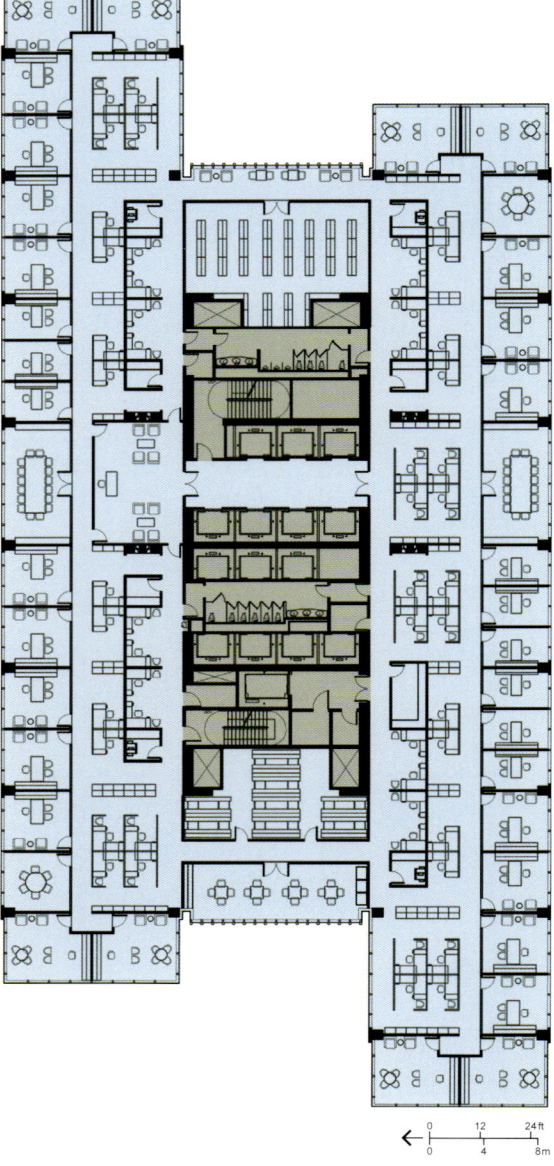

Chicago, Illinois
Design/Completion 2005/2007
Client: Freeborn & Peters LLP
60,000 square feet (5,570 square meters)

# Freeborn & Peters

### Site
Freeborn & Peters occupies six floors of a 65-story 1,300,000-square-foot office tower, the sixth tallest building in Chicago and the 12th tallest in the United States. A central feature of the facility is a three-story central atrium that anchors the existing conference center and library facilities.

### Program
In order to improve the effectiveness of the collaborative work spaces within the practice, the client determined that the environment surrounding the existing three-story atrium needed to be strategically reconfigured to improve its effectiveness and future flexibility. Central to this concept is the integration of collaborative meeting and audiovisual technologies into all work spaces.

### Concept
The extension of the vertical stairwell within the atrium by three additional floors reinforces the atrium's role in the office design. The reception floor is moved to the base of the atrium, thus centering the space vertically within the practice's overall occupancy within the tower.

All conference rooms are reconfigured in size and capacity to reflect current and anticipated usage patterns. Interactive meeting technology is integrated into all six surfaces of a conference environment. Network connections are accessed through the floor and via a wireless network with ceilings containing projection and audio equipment.

The wall planes enclosing the new conference environments are conceived of as smart, interactive yet translucent surfaces. Laminated glass façades double as smart board writing surfaces as well as light screens. Light enters from all sides making the atrium, already a hallmark within the building, a more dynamic gathering place and the centerpiece of a rejuvenated spatial experience.

### Elements
Custom laminated-glass panels in aluminum frames, custom millwork technology walls, stone and carpet flooring, specialty ceilings, custom lighting

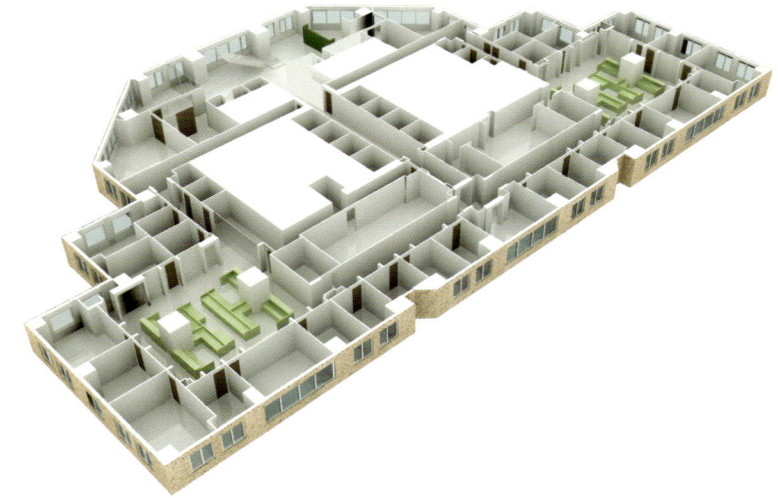

Chicago, Illinois
Design/Completion 2006/2010 (155 North Wacker), 2011 (222 West Randolph)
Client: The John Buck Co.
155 North Wacker: 1,400,000 square feet (130,060 square meters)
222 West Randolph: 1,038,000 square feet (96,430 square meters)

# 155 North Wacker and 222 West Randolph

### Site
These two proposed office towers are sited across the street from each other in Chicago's West Loop district, conveniently located near mass transit and the expressways.

### Program
The 52-story 155 North Wacker building provides 1,125,000 square feet of multi-tenant office space and features a 45-foot-high lobby, a ground-floor restaurant, a second-floor conference center and a third-floor fitness facility. Loading docks and parking for 200 cars are located two floors below grade; a bridge connects the building to additional parking in an adjacent garage. 222 West Randolph is a 44-story multi-tenant building with 763,000 square feet of office space and seven floors of parking for 500 cars at its base.

### Concept
The two office high-rises are designed for tenants who require flexible, open floor plates, advanced data and communication services, and individual emergency power and auxiliary cooling systems. Maximum planning efficiency is achieved on the office floors with 45-foot, column-free spaces between the central service core and exterior wall.

The towers are planned as individual buildings, each on its own half-block site, featuring landscaped plazas that face one another. Together, these smaller plazas establish a large, inviting urban space straddling one of the city's main north–south arterials. Considered in conjunction with other existing and planned public spaces along the east-west corridor, the plazas help connect areas west of the train stations to the lake with a series of parks and other activity nodes.

Building on the sustainable design initiatives of previous projects, 155 North Wacker has already received Silver-level pre-certification in the LEED Green Building Rating System® for core and shell development. Once completed, the building will likely pursue formal certification for LEED-CS Gold. The 222 West Randolph project is also being approached from a sustainable design perspective and, in the process, will address the criteria for LEED certification.

### Elements
Reinforced concrete core, perimeter structural steel frame, unitized aluminum-and-glass curtain wall, glass lobby enclosure, marble cladding on the elevator core walls and lobby floor

*Office*

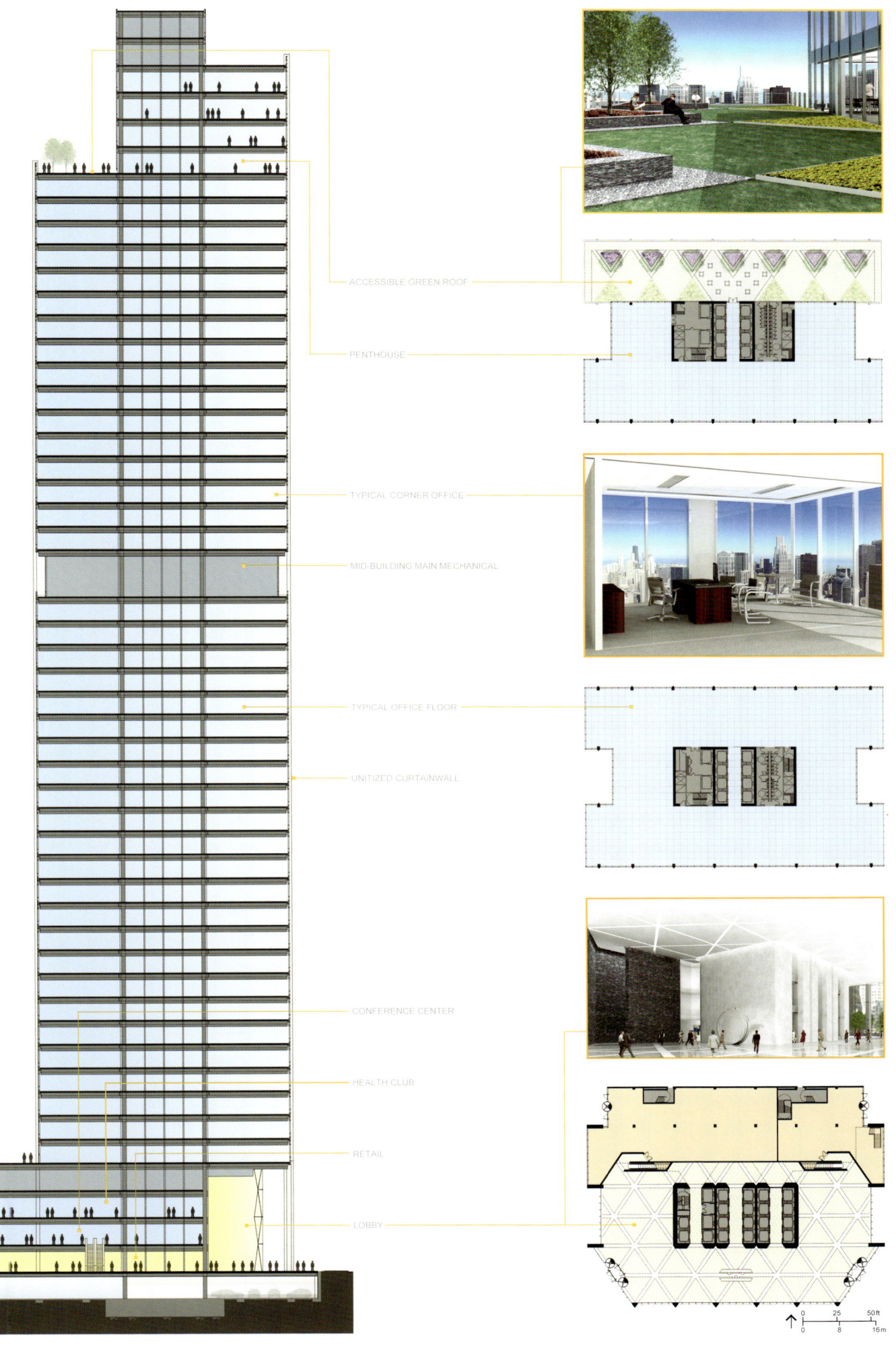

*155 North Wacker and 222 West Randolph*

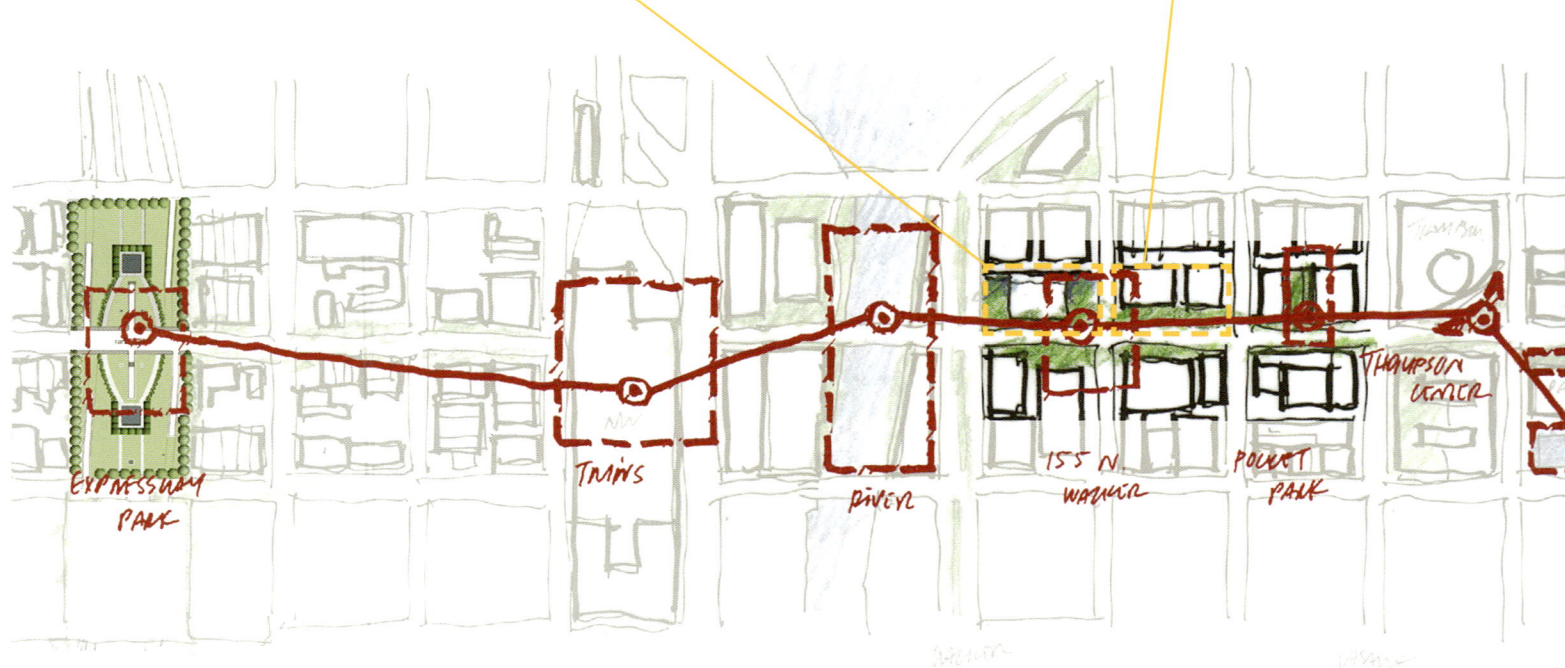

Office

155 North Wacker and 222 West Randolph

Oak Brook, Illinois
Design/Completion 2002/2005
Client: McDonald's Corporation
200,000 square feet (18,580 square meters)

# Hyatt Lodge at McDonald's Campus

### Site
The building is located on the heavily wooded corporate campus of McDonald's Corporation in the western suburbs of Chicago.

### Program
Originally designed by the firm in 1985 to accommodate McDonald's trainees and other corporate guests, the full-service hotel is operated by the Hyatt Corporation and is now also open to the general public. To compete with other facilities in the area, the hotel's interiors and amenities needed an update. The remodeling includes 225 guest rooms, two ballrooms, 10 meeting rooms, a themed bar, café and restaurant, and a fitness center and spa.

### Concept
The lodge is carefully set in an existing forest of mature trees and is designed to maximize continuous views of the landscape. The U-shaped building wraps around a rare, 200-year-old Ohio Buckeye tree, creating an inviting forecourt. Several terraces overlook an adjacent lake, over which a curved, covered walkway connects the lodge to the company's training center. Natural materials such as wood and stone are revealed throughout the main floor with its lounge and grand fireplace. The lounge, restaurant, meeting spaces and guest rooms include simple, contemporary furnishings that complement the hotel's updated amenities. A color palette of earth tones reinforces the lodge-like design.

### Elements
Stone and wood

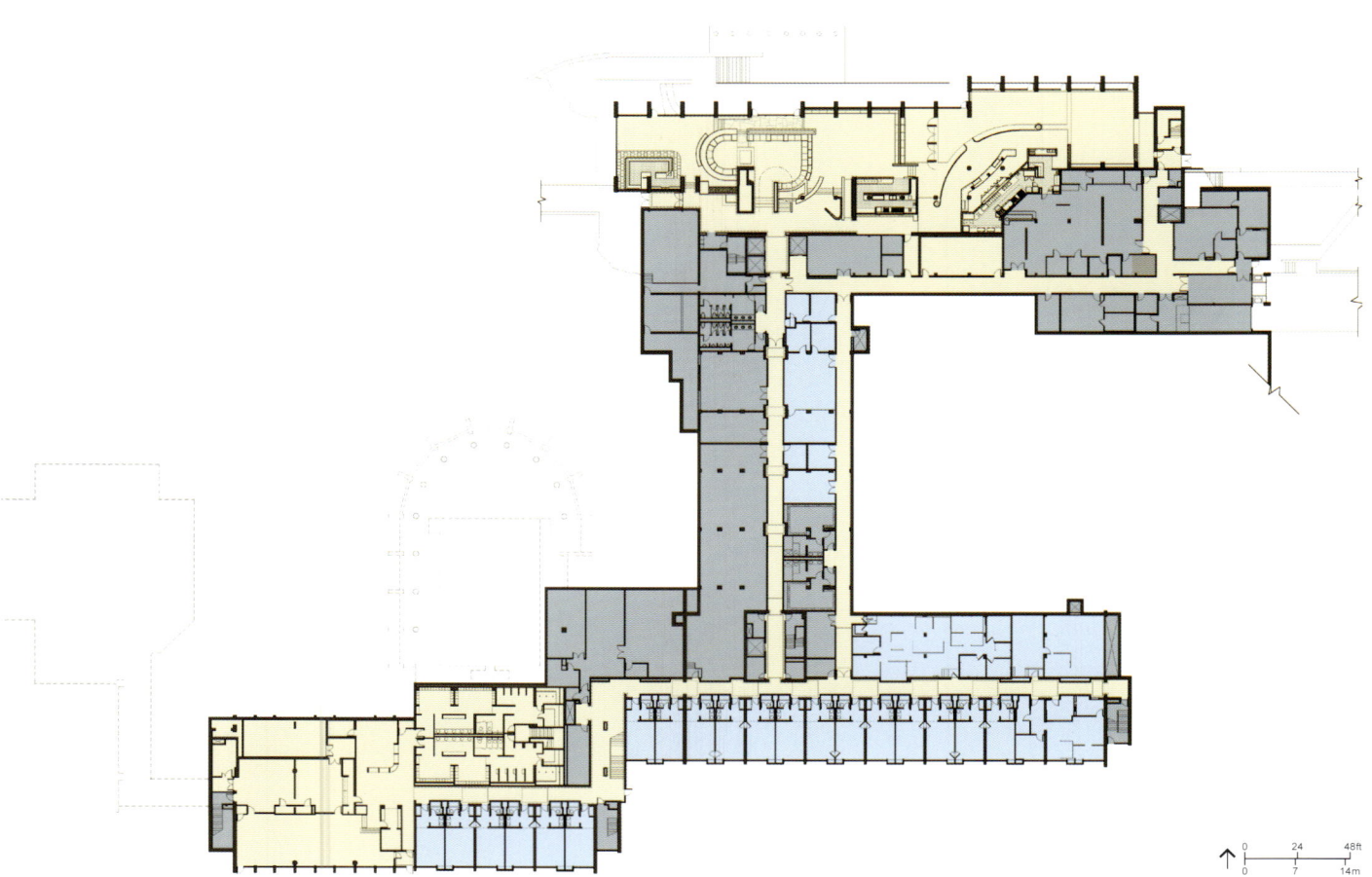

Hospitality/Residential

Shanghai, China
Design/Completion 2004/2006 (Phase 1), 2008 (Phase 2)
Client: Enhance Holdings
484,000 square feet (45,000 square meters)

# Enhance Anting Golf Club Complex

### Site
The business hotel and golf complex is located on the outskirts of Shanghai in a planned development known as International Automobile City.

### Program
Featuring a world-class 18-hole golf course designed by Robert Trent Jones Jr., the project includes a 350-room, five-star Crowne Plaza hotel with a conference center, ballroom, 150 serviced apartments, a golf clubhouse, spa and fitness facilities, and a separate restaurant structure. Parking is provided for 300 cars.

### Concept
The development is designed to provide a resort environment, with a large entry courtyard, low-rise buildings, and terraces and formal lawns all integrated into the landscape. The first building to be completed is the clubhouse, sitting at the highest point of the site overlooking the golf course. Guests and visitors enter the building from the courtyard and are led to a dramatic, 26-foot-high glass atrium. A glass curtain wall provides the restaurant and bar, adjacent to the atrium, with uninterrupted views of the entire golf course. Lower-level locker rooms offer direct course access.

In the second phase, a hotel, serviced apartment building, and restaurant and bar structure will complete the complex. Also clad in granite and glass, these structures share an orientation toward the golf course. The hotel and serviced apartment wings connect to the conference center through a glass-enclosed walkway. The stand-alone dining and entertainment complex is adjacent to the street and easily accessible to other visitors and residents of International Automobile City.

### Elements
Reinforced concrete structure clad in granite and glass; public areas of clubhouse feature unique all-glass enclosure

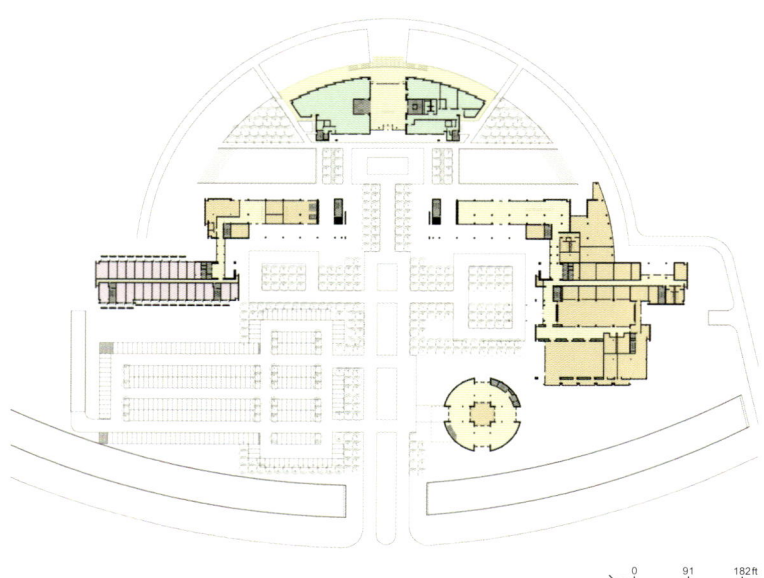

Hospitality/Residential

Mumbai, India
Design/Completion 1996/2004
Client: Unison Hotels Ltd.
1,200,000 square feet (111,480 square meters)

# Grand Hyatt Mumbai

### Site
Mumbai is India's second-largest city and its primary financial center and commercial port. The 10-acre development is located 20 minutes south of the city's international airport.

### Program
This five-star facility includes 547 hotel guest rooms, 147 serviced apartments, a business center, health spa, fitness center, pool, and 108,000 square feet of retail. Because of its proximity to the airport, the structure could not be more than six stories tall, and local mandates required that 15 percent of the site remain open. To attract major conferences and customary weeklong wedding celebrations, the hotel project includes a 900-seat grand ballroom, meeting rooms, four restaurants, an entertainment center, and below-grade parking for 1,000 cars.

### Concept
Challenging zoning requirements called for an ambitious design to meet the expectations of sophisticated international travelers. The courtyard complex with a large, landscaped garden in the middle is modern yet timeless, with subtle local and cultural references. Each component complements the others while retaining a distinct identity and a clear separate entrance. The main building, with its deep porte-cochère, has a curved façade of banded glass and aluminum that stands in subtle contrast to the stone-clad wings.

### Elements
Reinforced concrete structural frame clad with granite, aluminum-and-glass window system

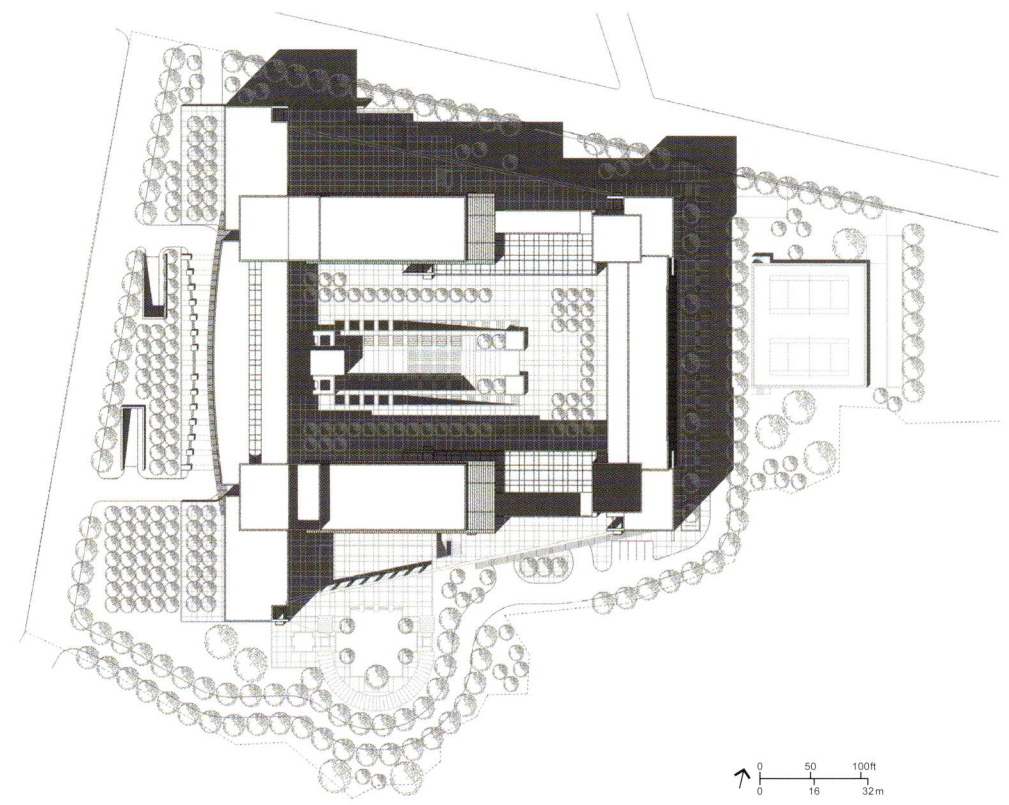

*Grand Hyatt Mumbai*

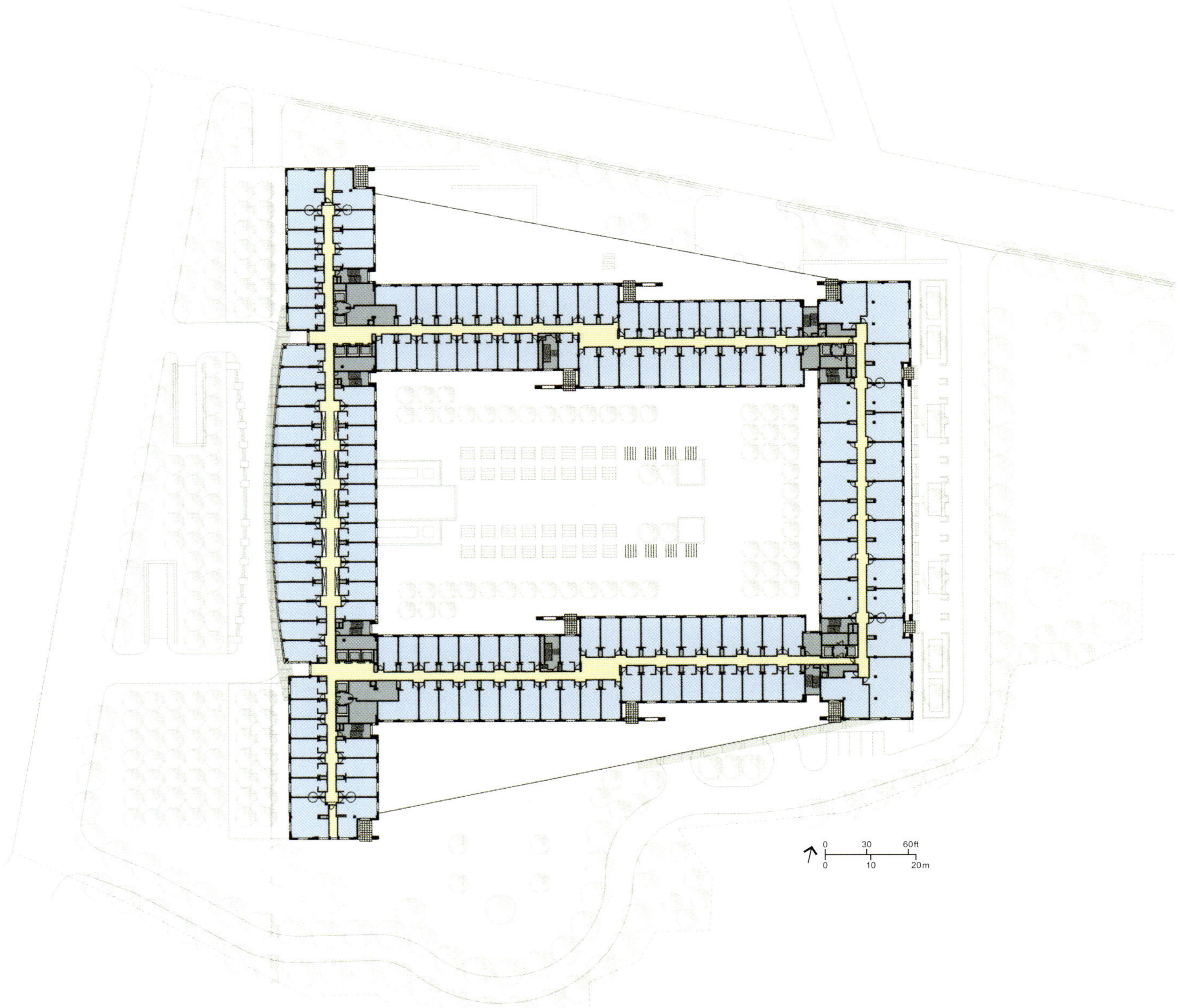

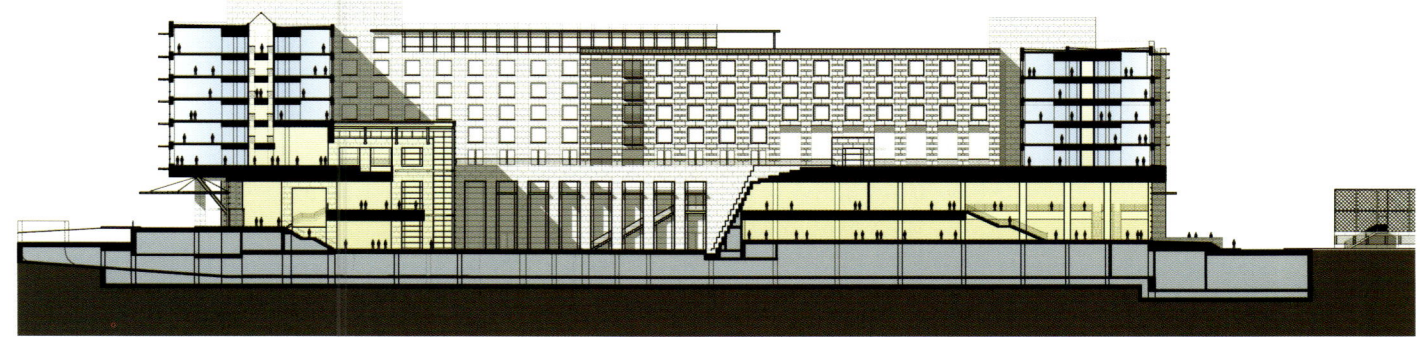

*Hospitality/Residential*

Grand Hyatt Mumbai

Ningbo, China
Design Competition 2004
Client: Ningbo Haichen Investment Co.
904,000 square feet (84,000 square meters)

# Ningbo Marriott

### Site
The hotel and office complex is adjacent to the established urban core of Ningbo, a city of more than five million people that is emerging as a financial center for entrepreneurs.

### Program
The mixed-use development comprises a 38-story tower and 54,000-square-foot podium. The tower includes 18 floors of office space and 14 hotel floors. The podium houses support functions for the hotel, including a ballroom, meeting rooms, restaurants, and a fitness center. Below-grade parking accommodates 417 cars.

### Concept
The new mixed-use tower and base were designed to integrate two old British school buildings that will be converted, expanded and incorporated into the complex as a retail center. The triangular tower was designed to maximize views and provide a focal point for the redevelopment of the riverfront.

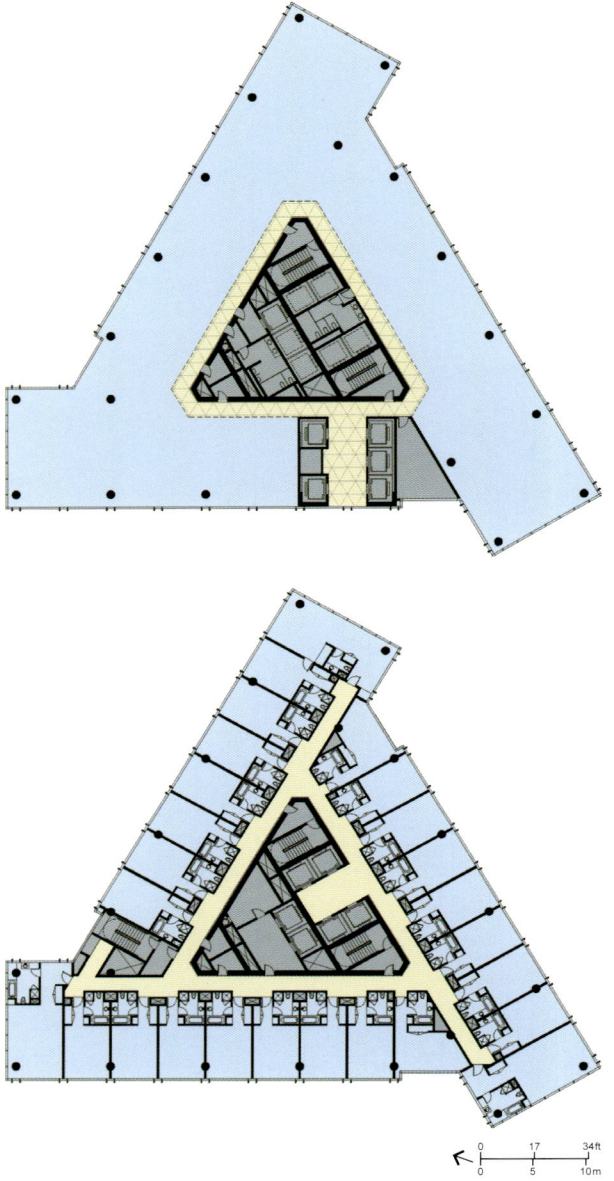

Suzhou, China
Design/Completion 2004/2009
Client: Genway Housing Development Group Co. Ltd.
1,550,000 square feet (144,000 square meters)

# Hyatt Regency Suzhou

### Site
On the edge of the historic city of Suzhou, the Suzhou Industrial Park is a fully planned development designed to attract state-of-the-art electronics and pharmaceutical manufacturing facilities. This complete and newly constructed town offers international-quality housing, educational, civic, cultural and recreational facilities for residents and visitors. The hotel complex is adjacent to the new exhibition center and a large recreational lake with a well-developed promenade.

### Program
The complex comprises two towers and two podiums. A Hyatt Regency hotel with 434 guest rooms is housed in one tower, with a ballroom, meeting rooms, a fitness center, and spa. In the second tower, a Hyatt Residences property provides 390 serviced apartments, and a 161,500-square-foot retail component caters to guests. Parking for 430 cars is provided below grade.

### Concept
The project plan is based on a system of concentric and interlocking curvilinear forms. The development has a relatively low density (FAR 2.88) on a large site. The two 21-story high-rise components were designed as U-shaped forms pushed to the perimeter of the site to allow for a large interior garden space. The two high-rise elements are raised and supported by a three-story podium forming a bridged entry for each tower. Each tower has an atrium with exposed elevators and single-loaded guest room corridors that look onto the garden, creating a resort-like atmosphere. Granite-clad podium components house various hotel, food, beverage, and retail functions.

### Elements
Reinforced concrete structural frame, aluminum-and-glass curtain wall, granite-clad podium

Hyatt Regency Suzhou

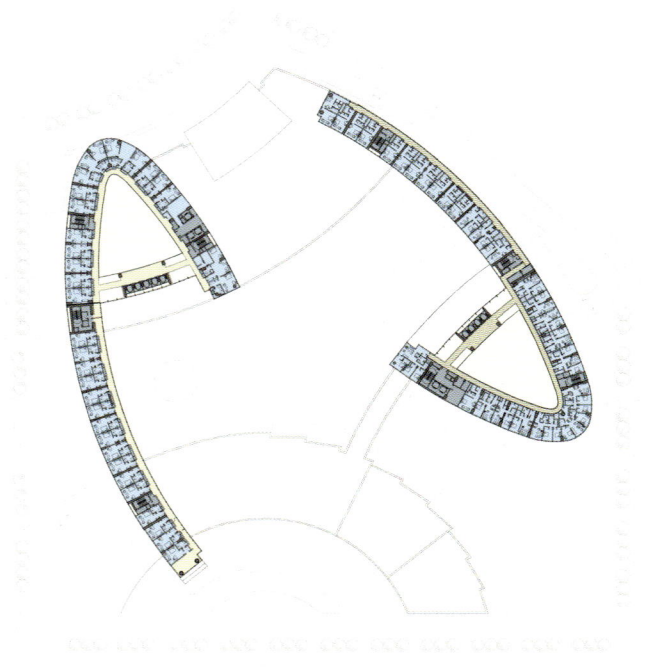

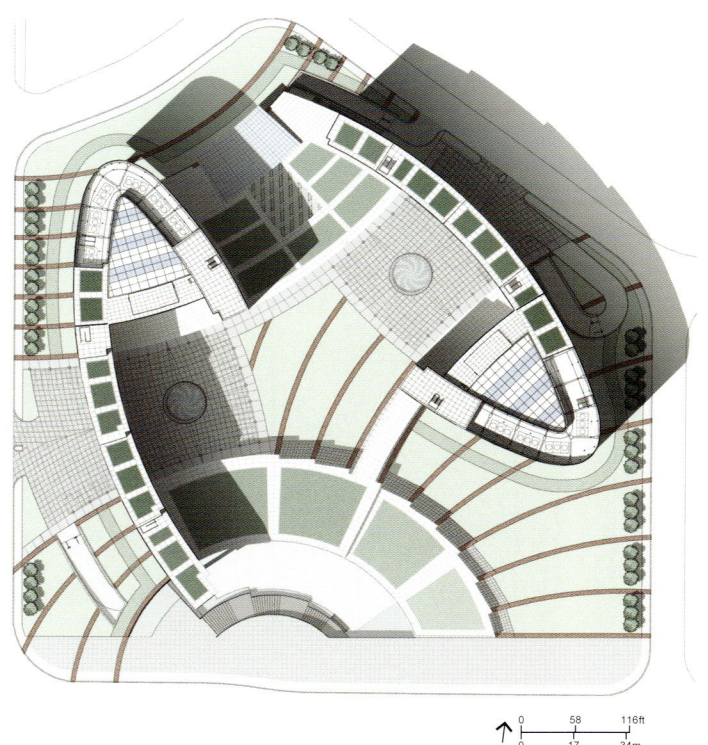
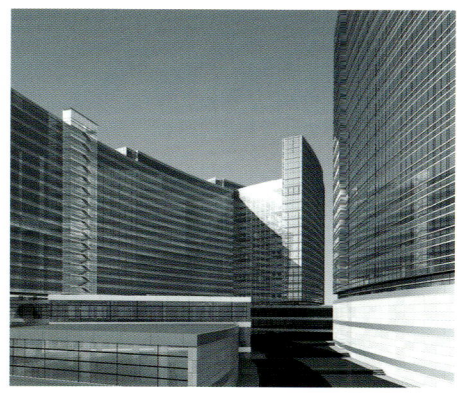

*Hospitality/Residential*

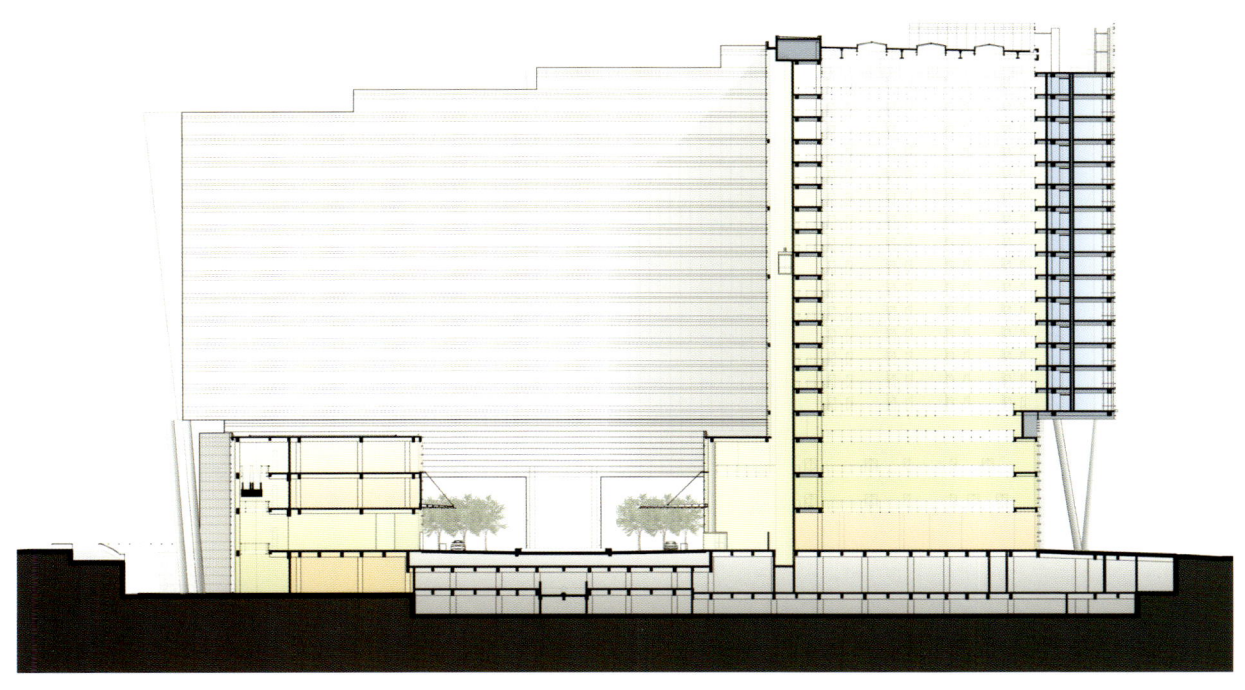

*Hyatt Regency Suzhou*

Mumbai, India
Design/Completion 2001/2006
Client: Magus Estates and Hotels Pvt. Ltd.
253,000 square feet (23,500 square meters)

# Four Seasons Mumbai

### Site
Formerly known as Bombay, the city of Mumbai is India's second-largest city and the primary financial center and commercial port. The hotel is located in the old manufacturing district near downtown, an area undergoing revitalization.

### Program
The first Four Seasons property in India, this 33-story hotel is positioned as a premier destination for business travelers. The 253,000-square-foot project includes 188 guest rooms, two restaurants, four meeting rooms and a business center, a pool, fitness center, and spa.

### Concept
The project's design was driven by converging influences: its luxury status, the emphasis on landscaping, and many principles of Vastu, a spiritual science of architecture that is particularly important in India. The result is a sleek tower of granite and glass that befits a five-star hotel.

In keeping with Vastu, the building is properly oriented to the sun, and its highest point, a spire that serves as the hotel's antenna, is positioned at the southwest corner. Refuge floors mandated by the building code are placed at intervals on the front and back elevations. These refuge floors appear as balconies on the façade, providing visual contrast to the smooth curtain wall of non-reflective glass. An attached, three-story building with a floor-to-ceiling glass façade contains a restaurant and rooftop pool.

The hotel is designed to be an oasis within a densely populated district. Views from the guest rooms, restaurants and meeting facilities focus on beautifully landscaped gardens that also serve as function areas.

### Elements
Concrete structural frame; exterior enclosure of aluminum, glass and granite

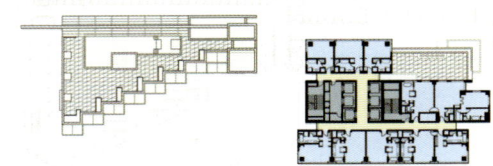

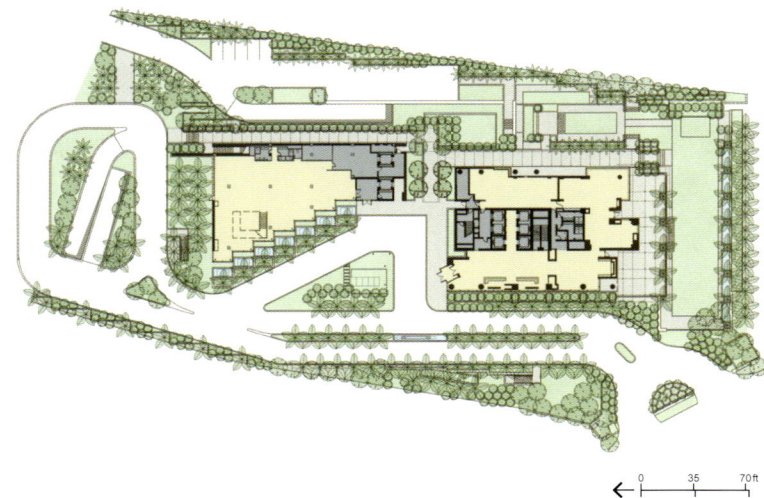

Grand Rapids, Michigan
Design/Completion 2004/2007
Client: Alticor Inc.
350,000 square feet (32,520 square meters)

# J.W. Marriott Grand Rapids

### Site
The building is sited along the east bank of the Grand River near the Amway Grand Plaza Hotel and the DeVos Place Convention Center.

### Program
The 24-story hotel complex includes 340 guest rooms, a 13,000-square-foot ballroom, business suites and meeting rooms, a restaurant, health club, and indoor pool. A rooftop helipad provides access for exclusive guests, and a separate parking structure accommodates 500 cars.

### Concept
The new hotel supports Grand Rapids' growing convention and tourism business. The elliptical form and full-height atrium of the tower optimize its riverfront location and orientation to the sun. The structure's unique shape also preserves the views of a neighboring condominium building, a requirement of the project. Guest rooms are located around the perimeter of the high-rise to provide panoramic views.

The tower has a crystalline quality that stands out on the city's developing skyline yet is compatible with the Amway Grand Plaza Hotel, directly to the north and owned by the same company. The building base connects to and reinforces the river walkway system of Grand Rapids. An attached low-rise podium to the east contains the ballroom and meeting facilities. Its horizontal composition and precast concrete and aluminum façade contrast with the tower. Two steel-and-glass bridges link the hotel to the parking garage as well as the skywalk to the convention center.

### Elements
Tower with a concrete structure and aluminum-and-glass curtain wall system; podium with a steel structure, precast concrete cladding, aluminum panel system, aluminum-and-glass window system

Hospitality/Residential

*J.W. Marriott Grand Rapids*

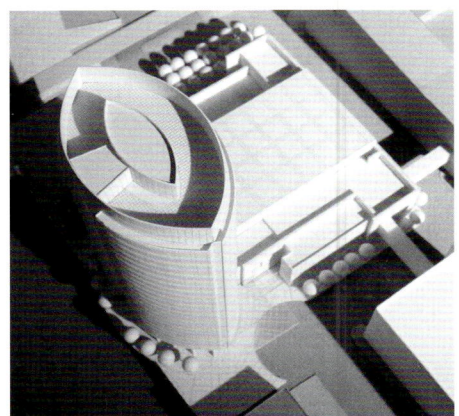
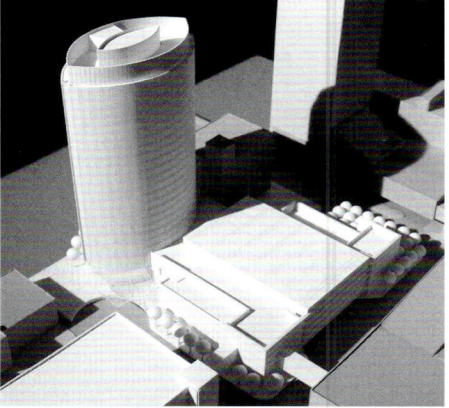
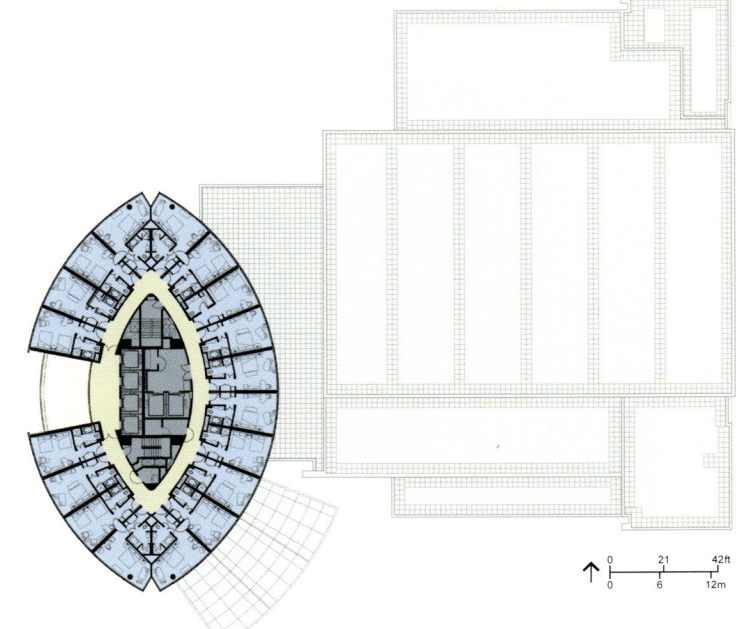
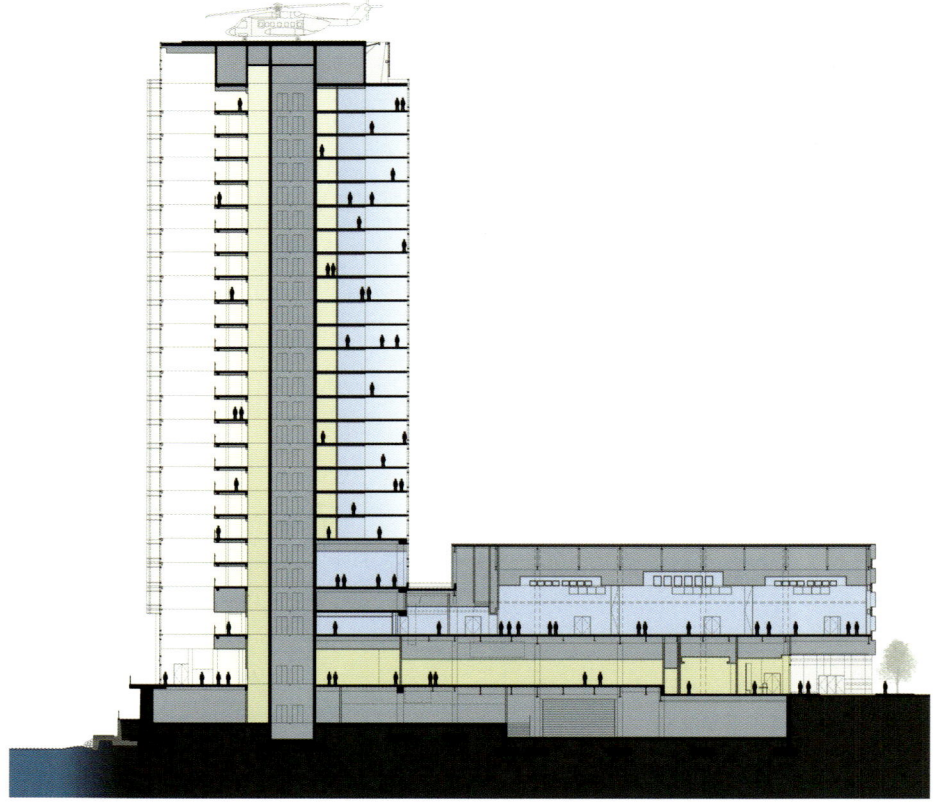

Hospitality/Residential

*J.W. Marriott Grand Rapids*

Nanjing, China
Design/Completion 2003/2007 (Phase 1), 2009 (Phase 2)
Client: Nanjing International Group Ltd.
4,445,000 square feet (412,950 square meters)

# Nanjing International Center

### Site
This mixed-use project is located on a major boulevard in downtown Nanjing, facing an exhibition center, a large park that includes Xuanwu Lake, and Purple Mountain, one of the city's most significant landmarks.

### Program
The two-phased development provides 4,445,000 square feet designed to accommodate a number of different functional components. The first phase consists of an eight-story, 950,000-square-foot retail podium with two towers: a 35-story office and hotel tower and a 38-story residential condominium tower. Phase two consists of a 1,050-foot-tall tower with offices, a hotel and condominiums, as well as an adjacent podium for hotel amenities and parking.

### Concept
This very complex project is organized so that each programmatic component can function independently, each with a separate entry and direct access to the large underground parking structure. The eight-story retail podium with a continuous 900-foot-long street-level arcade is slightly curved, creating a large public plaza at the center of the site. Within the retail podium, a 90- by 90-foot, eight-story skylit atrium fills the space with natural light.

Each of the three towers varies in plan and height, yet each has a similar enclosure consisting of a granite base out of which an aluminum-and-glass form emerges. Each tower has two angled, saw-toothed façades in order to maximize views of Purple Mountain.

### Elements
Reinforced concrete structural frame with an aluminum-and-glass curtain wall system; retail podium clad in granite

*Mixed-Use*

Mixed-Use

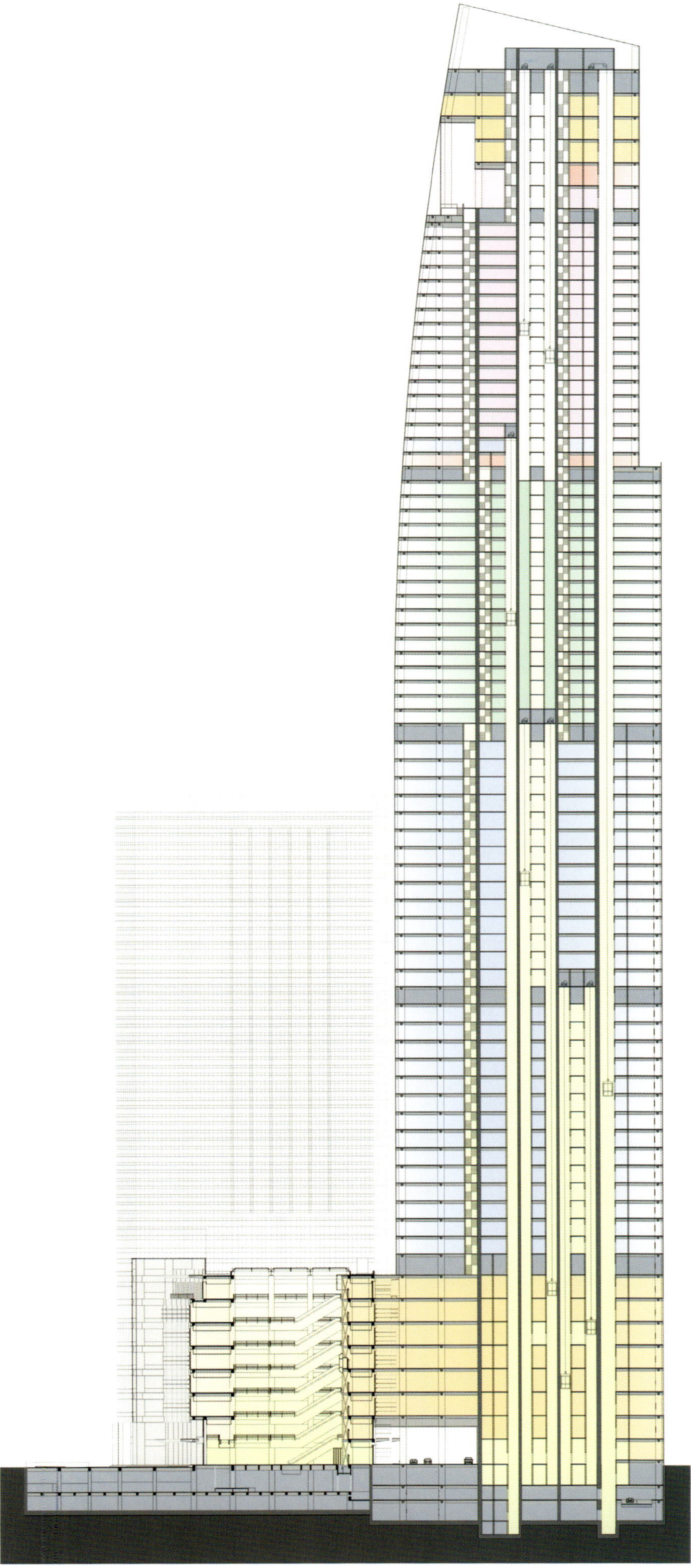

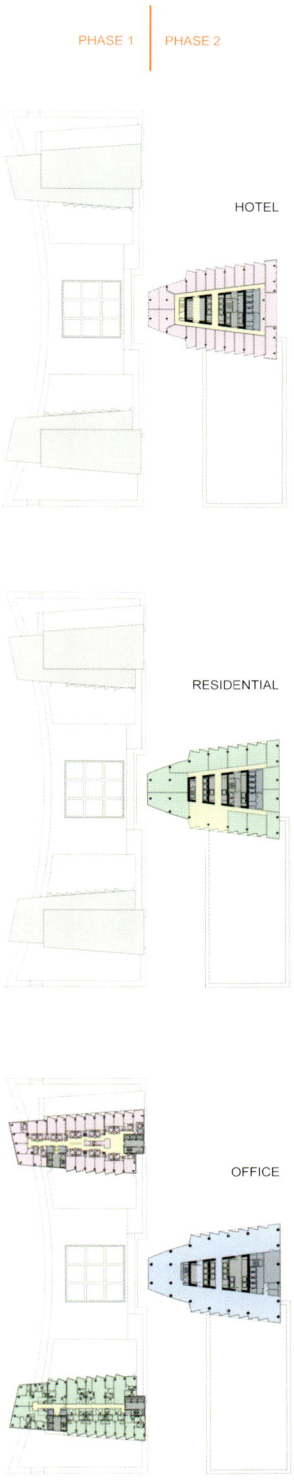

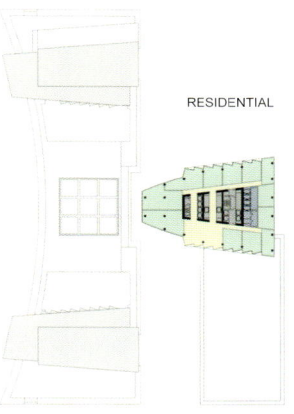

PHASE 1
PHASE 2
HOTEL
RESIDENTIAL
OFFICE

0
80
160ft
0
24.5
49m



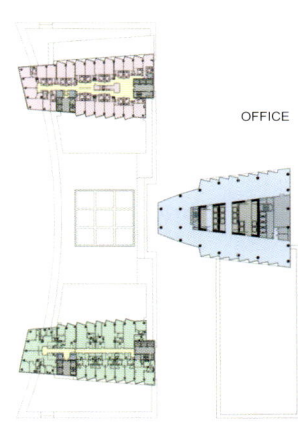

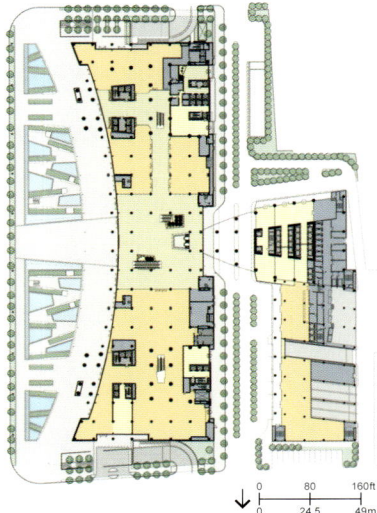

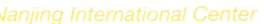

*Nanjing International Center*

Mixed-Use

Nanjing International Center

Xi'an, China
Design/Completion 2004/2007
Client: Shanghai Greenland Co.
2,174,000 square feet (202,000 square meters)

# Greenland Mixed-Use Development

### Site
This mixed-use project is part of a large urban development on the outskirts of Xi'an, a city in western China with a population of more than six million.

### Program
The project consists of five high-rise buildings, each with a three-story retail base and two levels of below-grade parking. Two of the buildings provide offices above a shared retail podium, two have serviced apartments, and the fifth is a 384-room Holiday Inn.

### Concept
One of the major features of the development is a large park. Using the park as a reference point, an entry portal was established by the inclined faces of the apartment buildings. The five buildings relate to each other through alignment, roof slope, and exterior cladding that is different in scale but similar in the use of materials. A unified landscape plan was created to enhance the cohesiveness of the development.

### Elements
Reinforced concrete structure; high-rise floors enclosed with unitized aluminum curtain wall with energy-efficient glass; podium enclosed with aluminum panels; horizontal and vertical trusses support four-story glass walls and glass roofs in entrance lobbies; granite floors and glass elevators and handrails in retail components

*Greenland Mixed-Use Development*

Shanghai, China
Design Competition 2005
Client: Shanghai Futures Exchange
866,000 square feet (80,500 square meters)

# Product Research and Data Service Center

### Site
The complex is located on a suburban site southwest of Shanghai.

### Program
This product research, and data service complex is composed of office, research, and training areas, as well as a fitness center, dining facility, and a housing component. Parking for 300 cars and 450 bicycles is also included.

### Concept
The design objective was to create a complex that would provide an urban rhythm to the long streetscape area that adjoins the site. A series of modern buildings and courtyard elements are linked to a pedestrian spine that connects all the buildings and forms the primary east–west axis. An organic, sweeping gesture defines the more secluded southern portion of the site, optimizing solar exposure and unobstructed views to the landscape. On the north side, the main point of entry is a glass-enclosed, light-filled pavilion that has secure access to the spine and can accommodate large groups of people. The data center, located directly to the west of the transparent entry pavilion, employs a contrasting solid expression.

The office component is split into two buildings with a shared courtyard. Typical office floors are topped by high-rise office towers that are linked by a sky bridge. The education and dining components, located to the south of the spine, are light-filled, two-story spaces that have direct access to outdoor plazas and views of the landscape. In the landscape design, water serves as a wayfinding device throughout the complex, and all programmatic components are provided with visual access to green space and natural light.

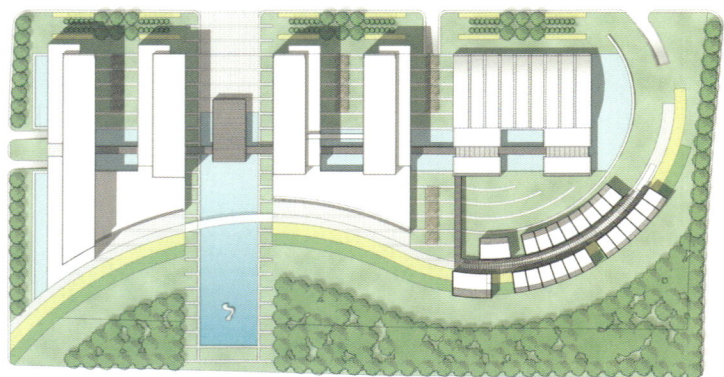

*Product Research and Data Service Center*

Chengdu, China
Design/Completion 2005/2007
Client: Chicony
2,005,000 square feet (186,300 square meters)

# Hyatt Regency at Chicony Plaza

### Site
This 37-story project occupies a full city block adjacent to a vibrant public plaza in the central business district of Chengdu.

### Program
The mixed-use development integrates a 12-story shopping center with a 25-story Hyatt Regency hotel. Together, they provide 1,200,000 square feet of retail space, 450 guest rooms and supporting hotel amenities.

### Concept
The project is designed to maximize program-specific relationships within the existing urban context. By asymmetrically stacking the hotel tower above the retail podium, the design helps integrate the building's mass with its surroundings. The orientation of the podium entry to the north creates an ideal relationship with the active urban plaza. The hotel tower, sited to the south, provides all rooms with unobstructed views and abundant natural light. The two primary masses of podium and tower are unified by a series of stepped gardens that are accessible from the hotel's sky lobby, ballrooms, and dining facilities.

Cantilevered glass volumes activate the base of the building, broadcasting digital media to passersby. These contemporary "retail awnings" provide a continuous rhythm of canopies for pedestrians while further organizing the podium's extensive signage and advertising needs.

### Elements
Reinforced concrete structure; transparent and "milky white" opaque glass; computerized lighting and graphics animate the façades

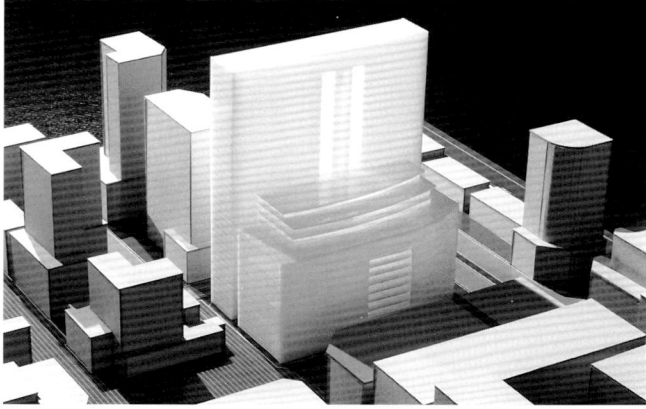

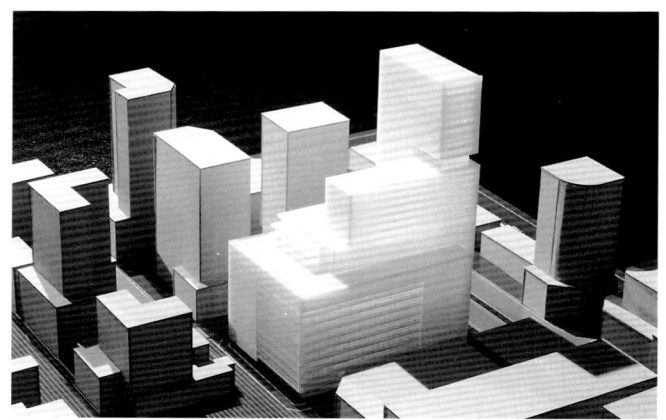

*Hyatt Regency at Chicony Plaza*

Guangzhou, China
Design/Completion 2004/2007
Client: Guangzhou R&F Properties Co., Ltd.
915,000 square feet (85,000 square meters)

# Grand Hyatt Guangzhou

### Site
The complex is located on a 2½-acre site next to a park in Guangzhou's rapidly growing Pearl River mixed-use satellite development.

### Program
The third-largest city in China with a population of seven million, Guangzhou is experiencing an explosion of business travelers and tourists. The 915,000-square-foot complex features a 400-room, five-star hotel in one tower and 215,000 square feet of office space and restaurants in another. The towers are joined by a podium that contains a 14,000-square-foot ballroom with a floor-to-ceiling height of 22 feet. On-site parking for 325 cars is provided below grade.

### Concept
Planning guidelines in the area dictated a dual-tower massing. The hotel high-rise features a unique top-down design. The lobby and registration desk are at the top of the 24-story tower, connected by a sky bridge to food and beverage facilities in the adjacent office tower.

Forming a V on the site, the triangular buildings project a business-like presence along the street and open up to the park on the opposite side. Clad in local stone with a unitized aluminum-and-glass curtain wall, the towers capitalize on expansive views of the city. Notably, while the towers are the same height, the hotel has 18 floors and the office building has 15. With carefully planned fenestration, this difference is virtually unnoticeable on the façade.

The elevated, glass-enclosed podium supported by tree-like steel braces houses the main ballroom. This component creates a breezeway between the two towers and links the street and the park.

### Elements
Reinforced concrete core, unitized aluminum-and-glass curtain wall, local stone

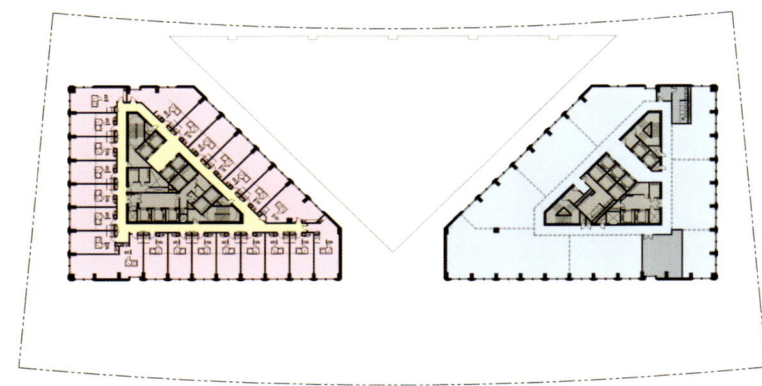

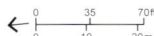

Grand Hyatt Guangzhou

Milwaukee, Wisconsin
Design/Completion 2005/2009
Client: Irgens Development Partners, LLC
1,050,000 square feet (97,550 square meters)

# Ovation Plaza

### Site
The mixed-use tower is located on the northern edge of Milwaukee's central business district adjacent to the Milwaukee River. The area is known as Juneau Town after Solomon Juneau, a founder of the city, and was the location for the original settlement that became Milwaukee.

### Program
The tower contains several interrelated functions including office, a business hotel, condominiums, retail, and parking. The building is directly connected to the Marcus Center for Performing Arts to the south of the project by a skyway bridge.

### Concept
The form of the building is derived from two influences: the program and the site. The programmatic elements and their unique spatial requirements establish the varying floor plates. The existing site provides the other conceptual generator.

Milwaukee has two urban grid systems slightly askew from one another; the zone between the river and the major north–south connection of Water Street is where the two systems are reconciled. As the project falls within this intermediary zone, its form is manipulated by the grid shift. This shift translates into more than just a formal exercise, as the building's massing creates an identity for the project within its surrounding context, and provides the building occupants with unencumbered view corridors east to Lake Michigan and south across the river to Milwaukee's downtown.

### Elements
Reinforced concrete core with perimeter structural steel frame, unitized aluminum-and-glass curtain wall, precast concrete with perforated metal panel cladding at garage enclosure

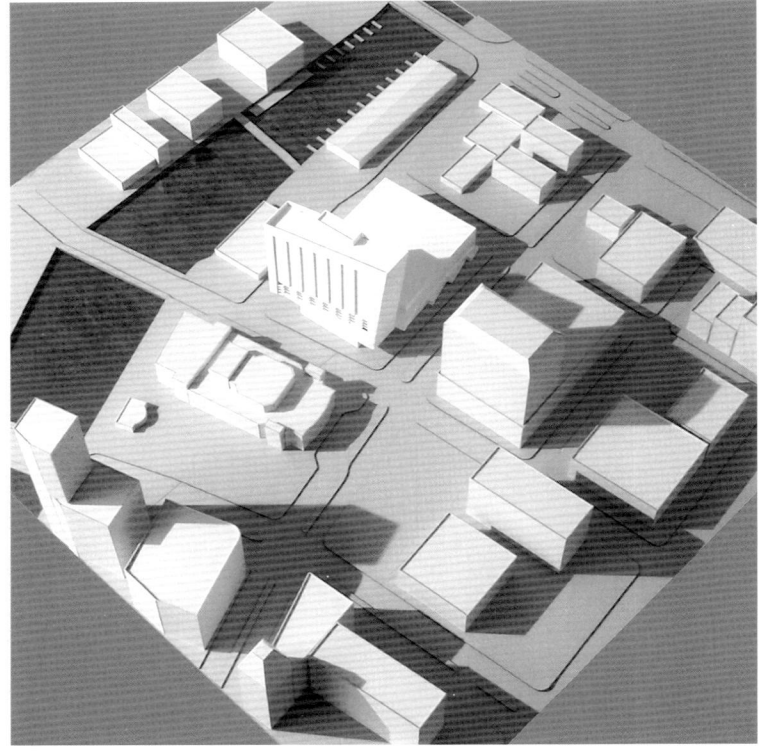

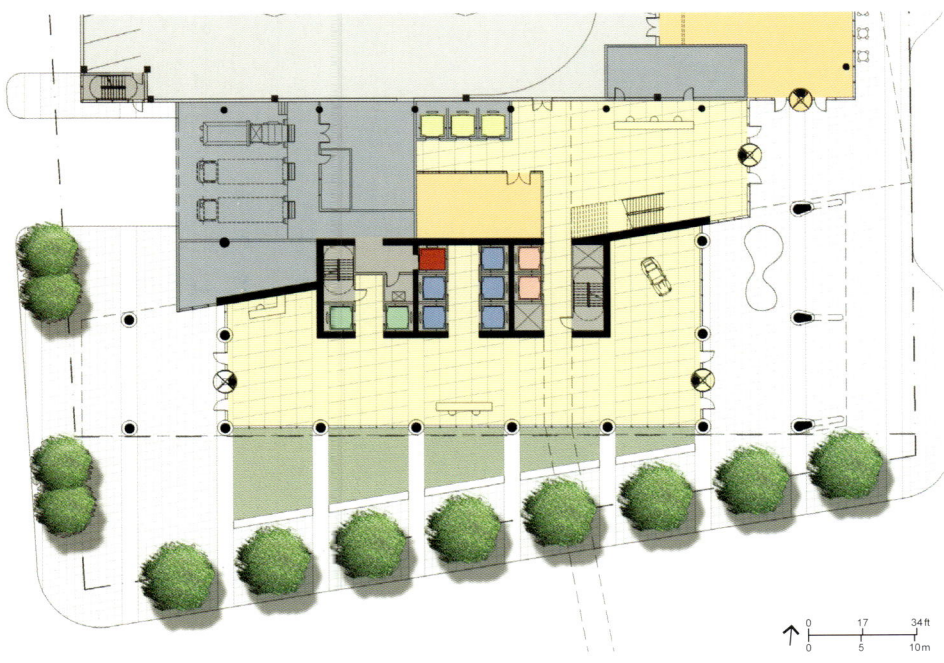

*Mixed-Use*

OFFICE

RESIDENTIAL

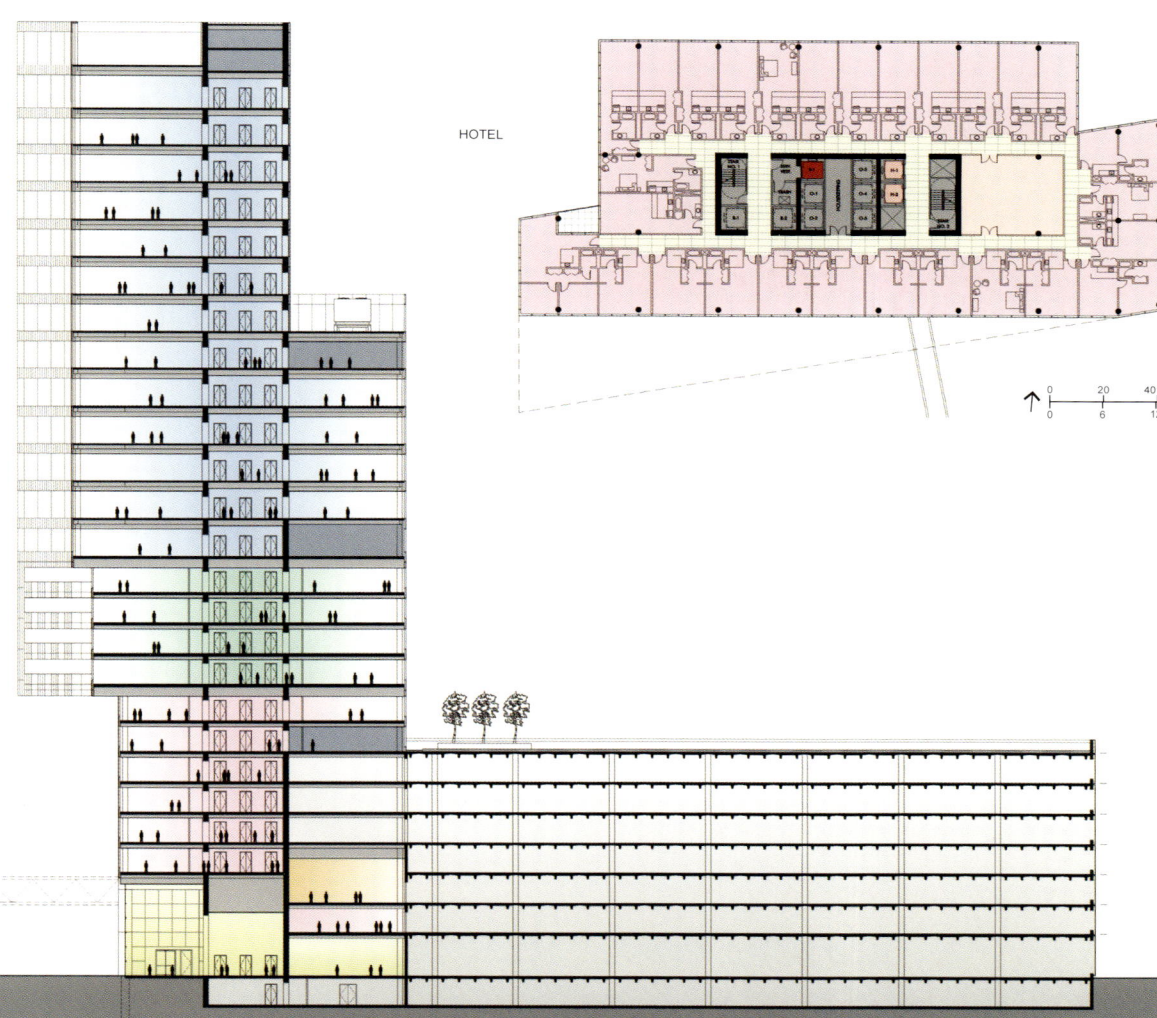

HOTEL

161

Ovation Plaza

Shanghai, China
Design Competition 2006
Client: Caohejing Hi-Tech Park
3,371,000 square feet (313,220 square meters)

# Shanghai Caohejing Development

### Site
Located southwest of downtown Shanghai and adjacent to a planned underground rail system, the project occupies two parcels totaling 22 acres of a larger five-parcel development.

### Program
The mixed-use project includes two office towers comprising 1,202,000 square feet, a 601,500-square-foot retail mall, a 121,000-square-foot fitness and community center, and six mid-rise buildings with 1,068,000 square feet of office space. Despite its significant size, the complex has set aside 7.4 acres of green space.

### Concept
The master plan for the two parcels creates two distinctly different developments that remain unified through shared elements. The public programs of fitness and retail establish an architectural language that links the two parcels, and also serve as the organizing agents for future development.

Twin office towers dominate the main parcel. Not only are the asymmetrical towers shaped to maximize southern exposure, they are located to establish a strong axial relationship to future rail stations at the southwest corner of the site. Topped by sky gardens and clad with intelligent skins, the towers form a ceremonial gateway to the overall development. A skybridge joins the towers and offers inspiring views of the surroundings. Reinforcing the axial relationship at the pedestrian level is the skylit retail atrium. Activated by a fabric of circulation bridges, this atrium connects the four-level shopping center with the future subway station.

On the second parcel, six mid-rise headquarters buildings, envisioned as a "necklace of jewels," are strategically arranged to expand view corridors and maximize solar exposure. Descending in height from north to south, the buildings are organized along a sweeping access road. Each building maintains a powerful street presence while creating more intimate two-story lobby spaces to the south. Individual drop-off zones are protected by the network of second-level pedestrian bridges that originate from the shared fitness complex.

### Elements
Reinforced concrete structure, metal panels, unitized glass systems, wood louvers for sun shading, computerized lighting for retail podium, long-span steel truss work for atrium and bridge

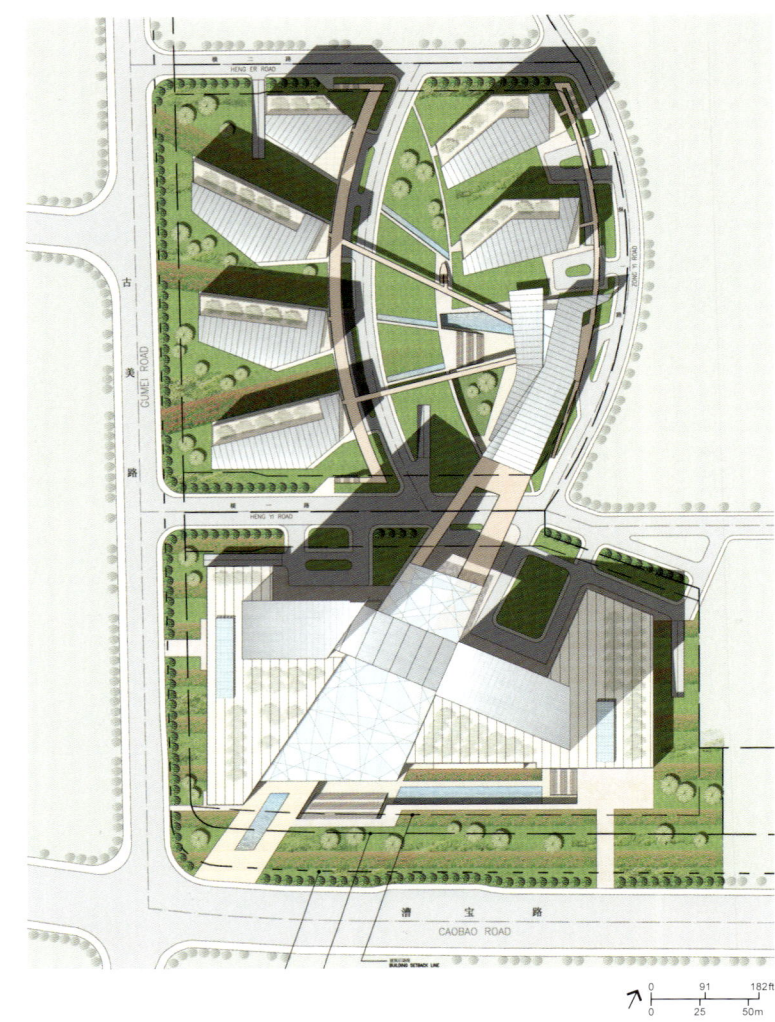

*Shanghai Caohejing Development*

Kuala Lumpur, Malaysia
Design Competition 2005
Client: Bahagia Investment Corp.
1,147,000 square feet (106,560 square meters)

# Bahagia Mixed-Use Development

### Site
The complex is adjacent to the city's convention center and a large park, near other major hotels and skyscrapers.

### Program
The mixed-use development consists of a hotel with 350 guest rooms, retail, restaurants, and banquet and meeting rooms; 150 luxury residential apartments; and 211,000 square feet of office space. A parking structure for 750 cars in the base supports all three functions.

### Concept
The architectural concept for the building was to utilize a central core for structure and vertical transportation that serves all components: parking, office, hotel, and condominiums. The exterior curtain wall is similar for all four functions. However, because the hotel and condominium components cannot efficiently use the deep space between the core and exterior wall, large portions of the building were carved out, providing a unique typical floor with single-loaded corridors and views to an elevated internal courtyard.

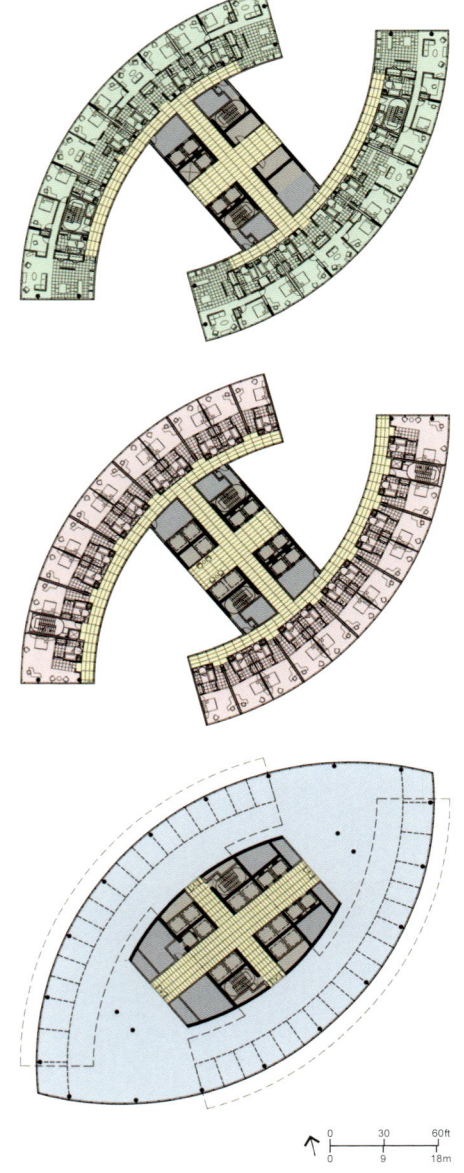

Mixed-Use

Beijing, China
Design Competition 2001
Client: China Silver Tai Investment Co.
3,444,000 square feet (320,000 square meters)

# Beijing Silvertie Center

### Site
The 8-acre hotel and office complex is located on Changan Road, one of the most important streets in the central business district of Beijing.

### Program
The mixed-use development comprises four buildings including a Grand Hyatt hotel with 550 guest rooms and complete banquet, ballroom, and meeting facilities; 430,000 square feet of serviced apartments; 1,300,000 square feet of Class A office space; and 217,000 square feet of retail. Parking for 1,570 cars is also provided, the majority of which is below grade.

### Concept
The design approach was to create a major mixed-use development that is a convincing ensemble in its own right but also becomes an important addition to the fabric of the city. The competition called for four buildings to house the office, hotel, apartment, and retail spaces. The buildings have a common aesthetic language with similar, yet not identical, curtain wall systems. These cohesive systems unify the structures while different shapes and heights set them apart.

The office towers step back from the front of the site, creating a large, angled garden in the middle of the complex. The hotel's elliptical shape draws attention to the largest component on the site and is counterbalanced by the other towers' rectilinear forms.

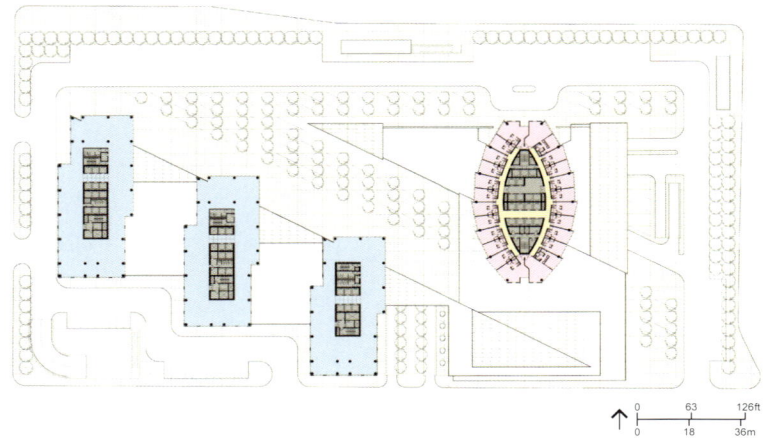

Chicago, Illinois
Design/Completion 2001/2005
Client: Museum of Science and Industry
32,000 square feet (2,970 square meters)

# U-505 Submarine Exhibit

## Site
The structure is 40 feet below the northeast lawn of Chicago's Museum of Science and Industry.

## Program
After being on display outside the museum for 50 years, the German U-505 submarine was severely corroded. Conserving the 700-ton artifact—listed on the National Register of Historic Places—was paramount. The climate-controlled, underground pavilion fully displays the submarine and protects it from further deterioration. The 27,000-square-foot addition includes interactive exhibits, a theater and a wall commemorating American sailors from World War II. Renovations were made to 5,000 square feet of adjacent space.

## Concept
The museum's objective was to insert this structure without compromising the historic significance of the original building—one of only a few remaining from the 1893 World's Fair. To meet this goal, the addition was placed below grade, a uniquely appropriate setting for a submarine.

The design recalls World War II-era submarine pens and dry docks, with exposed concrete walls and arched steel girders. Visitors can now walk around the submarine's entire perimeter; a series of ramps provides cantilevered observation points and access on two levels.

The structure's unique form responds to the shape of the submarine and the physical forces of the site underground. The angled design resulted in a structure that is approximately 10 feet wider at the roof. Because the top of the exhibit space is broader, major features such as the conning tower, periscopes, and artillery can be viewed easily, and spaciousness is achieved within the enclosure. The arched, structural steel roof girders support up to 7 feet of soil above and could be erected more quickly than a concrete structure after the submarine was lowered into place.

## Elements
Exposed concrete frame and foundation, structural steel girders

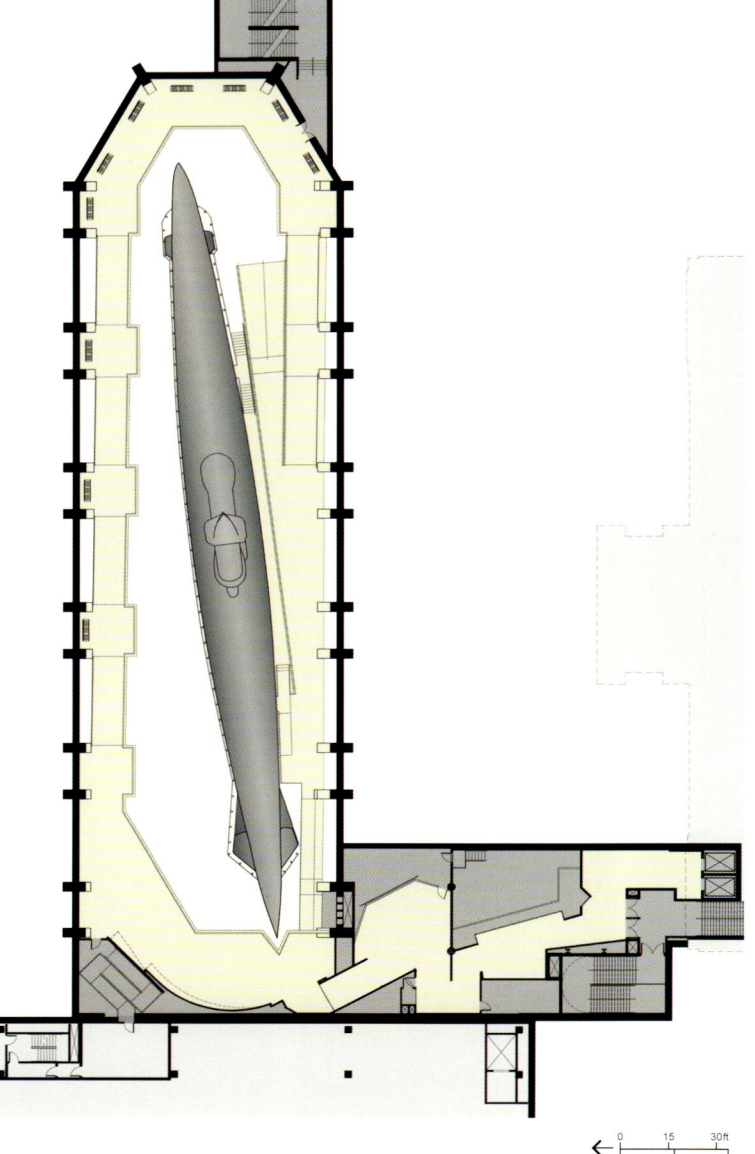

Institutional

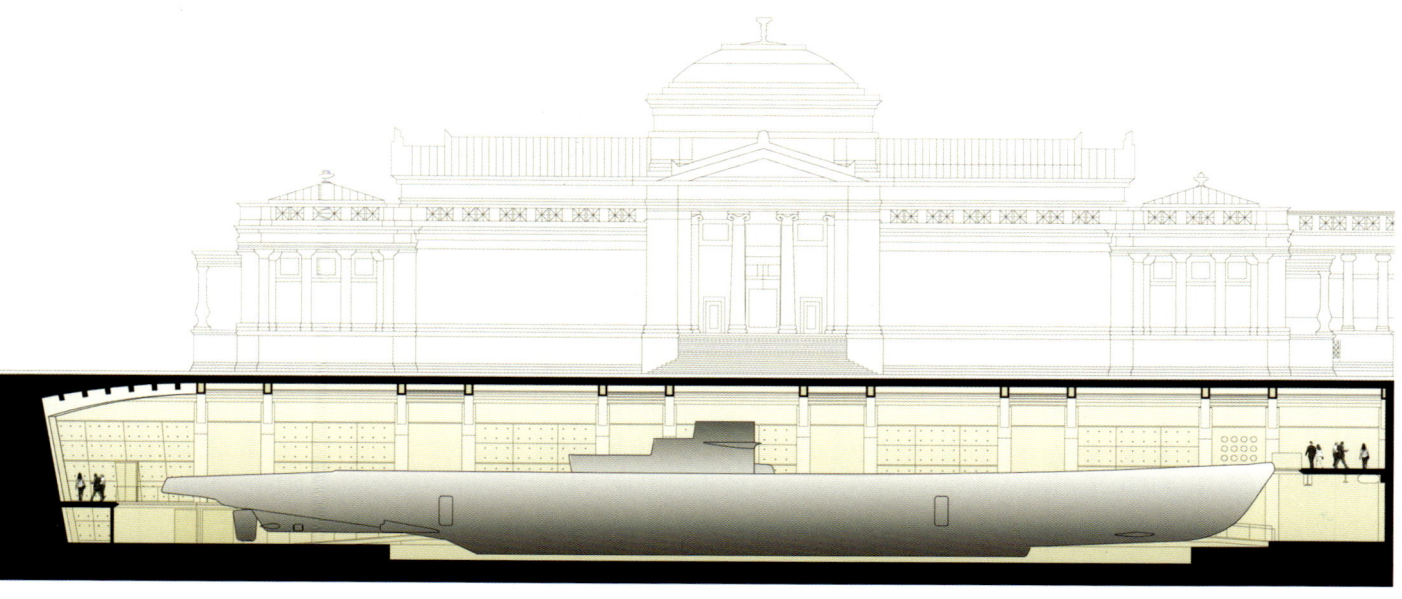

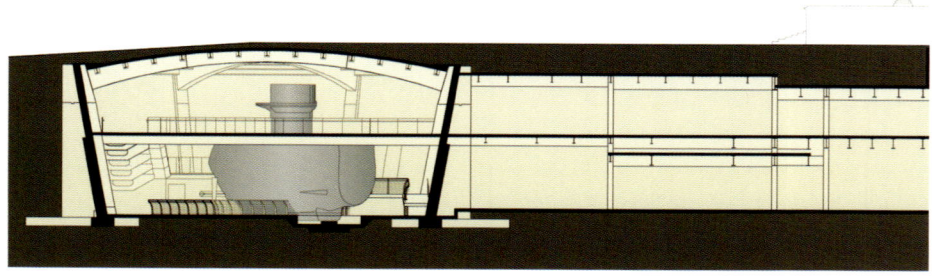

*Institutional*

U-505 Submarine Exhibit

Annandale-on-Hudson, New York
Design/Completion 1990/1992 (Original Building), 2004/2006 (Expansion)
Client: Bard College
Original Building: 38,000 square feet (3,530 square meters)
Expansion: 20,000 square feet (1,860 square meters)

# CCS Bard Hessel Museum

### Site
The campus of Bard College is a pastoral 500-acre setting adjacent to the Hudson River and the Catskill Mountains in upstate New York.

### Program
The original 38,000-square-foot building, initially called the Center for Curatorial Studies (CCS), brought four distinctly different but related functions together into a single architectural composition: galleries for the exhibition of art, a library and teaching wing, a scholar and faculty wing, and a fully conditioned storage space. In 2001, the decision was made to build additional galleries for the exclusive exhibition of work from the Marieluise Hessel Collection, a private collection of modern art.

### Concept
The goal of the museum is to provide a contemplative atmosphere in which to study curatorial sciences related to contemporary art. The gallery design establishes a distinctive, modern aesthetic consistent with the museum's educational mission. Programmed spaces for display, teaching, and study are expressed through massing, scale, and composition. Exhibition facilities include a foyer gallery, two large galleries, a gallery for video art, and one for prints and drawings.

The terra cotta exterior of the new galleries relates to the masonry enclosure of the original building. Pronounced, angled skylights fill the new permanent collection gallery with natural light. The new and original buildings are joined by a clear, inviting entry fronting a landscaped plaza.

### Elements
Terra cotta rain screen exterior enclosure; insulated metal panel cladding; window system with integrated, motorized solar shades; exhibit lighting; state-of-the-art HVAC environmental controls

*Center for Curatorial Studies*

174

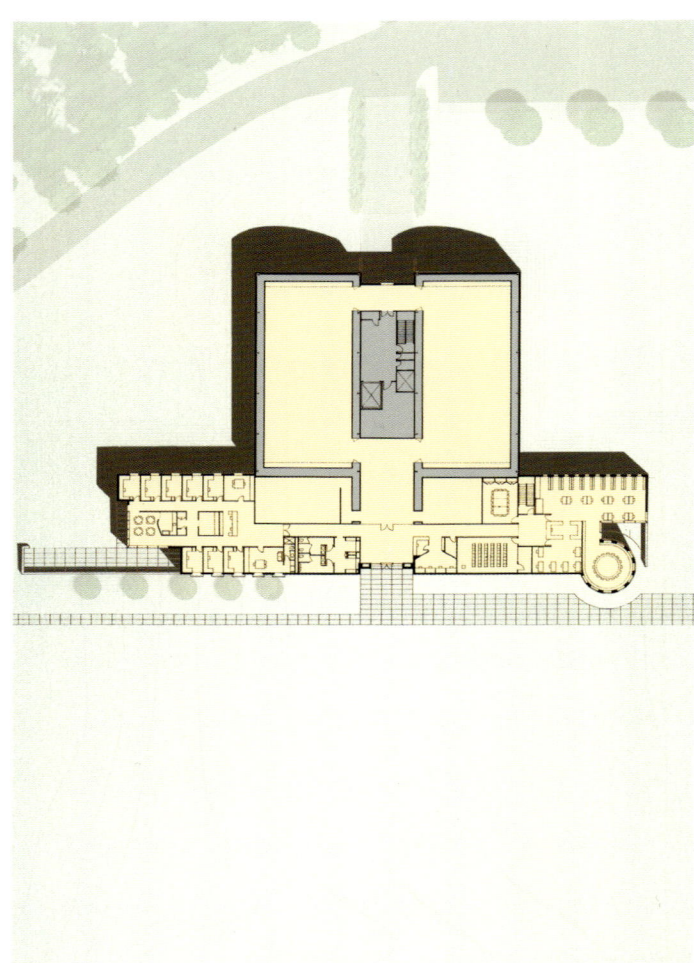

Phase One

Institutional

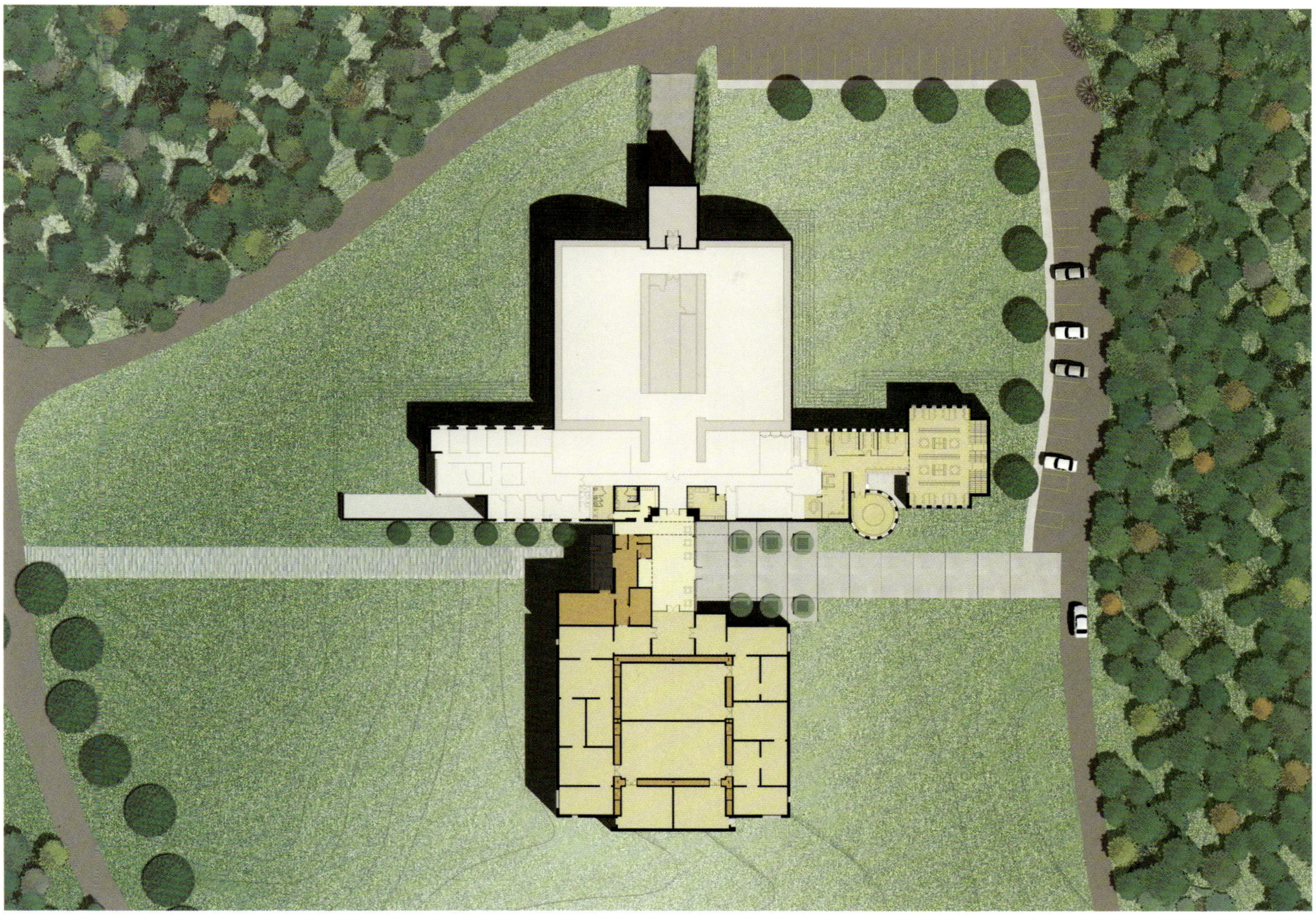

Expansion

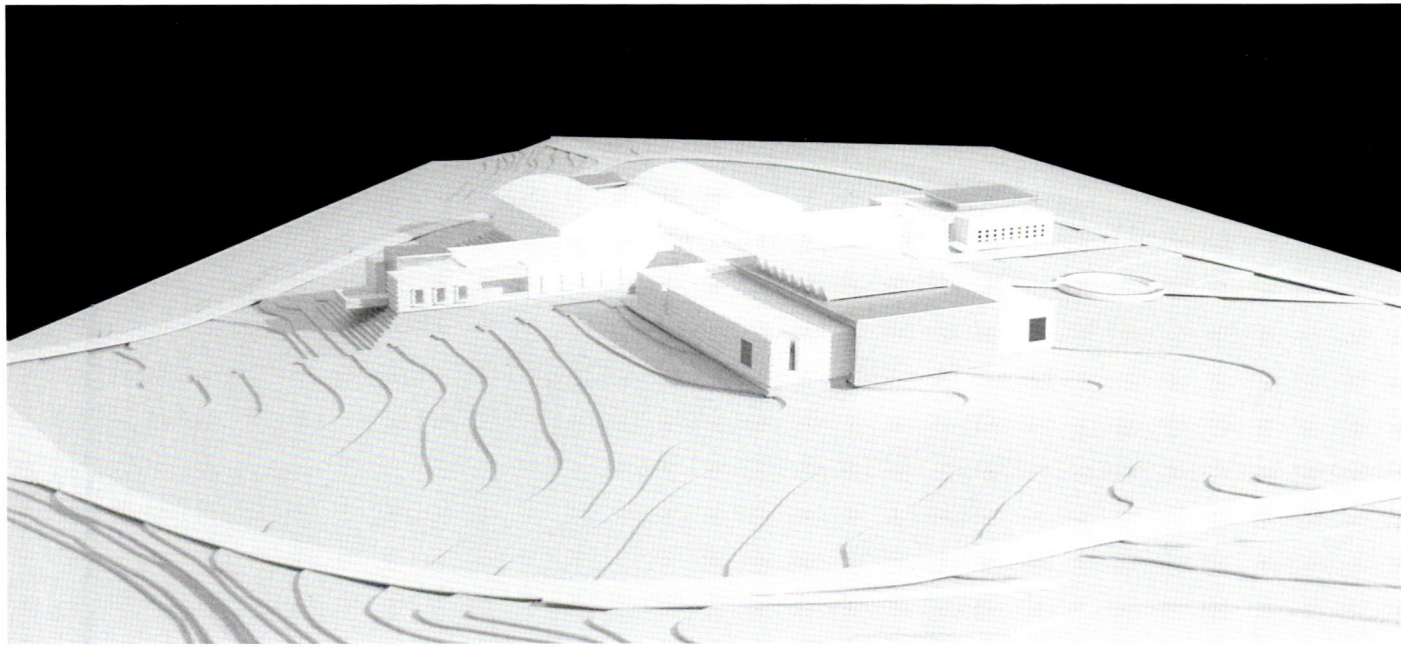

Center for Curatorial Studies

*Institutional*

*Center for Curatorial Studies*

Chicago, Illinois
Design/Completion 2000/2004
Client: Lincoln Park Zoo
Building: 27,000 square feet (2,510 square meters)
Outdoor Environments: 25,000 square feet (2,320 square meters)

# Regenstein Center for African Apes

### Site
This center for African apes is part of a free public zoo in Lincoln Park just north of Chicago's central business district and adjacent to Lake Michigan.

### Program
The facility includes a two-story, 27,000-square-foot building and 25,000 square feet of connected outdoor environments. Three feature exhibit spaces simulate African habitats, and a lower level accommodates medical and food-preparation facilities and a holding area. The rear of the building supports the zoo's leading research and conservation facility, formally known as the Lester E. Fisher Center for the Study and Conservation of Apes.

### Concept
At the forefront of zoo building design, the ape house is a sustainable, visitor-friendly structure that provides a naturalistic setting within an urban zoo. Integrally heated laminated glass walls 18 feet high by 32 feet wide with movable glass partitions allow the chimpanzees and gorillas to roam freely between their indoor and outdoor spaces. Animal-activated devices for food, water, and heat, and discreet, escape-proof mesh screens create a comfortable and stimulating home for the animals. "Nose-to-nose" viewing alcoves separate visitors from the apes with extremely clear, 1½-inch-thick sloping glass panels. Throughout the facility, visitors remain at or below the apes' eye level, a non-threatening position that helps the animals feel more at ease.

The building's brick and limestone façade respects existing zoo buildings and creates a neutral palette against which the animals' dark coats stand out. Sustainable features include a green roof, a skylight that refracts the sun in the summer and reflects it into the building in the winter, and an exposed concrete interior that provides an efficient thermal retainer for nighttime cooling. A moat that is a barrier to animal escape also serves as an on-site stormwater reservoir.

### Elements
Reinforced concrete structural frame, exposed limestone and brick exterior, aluminum-and-glass window system, laminated glass on exhibits

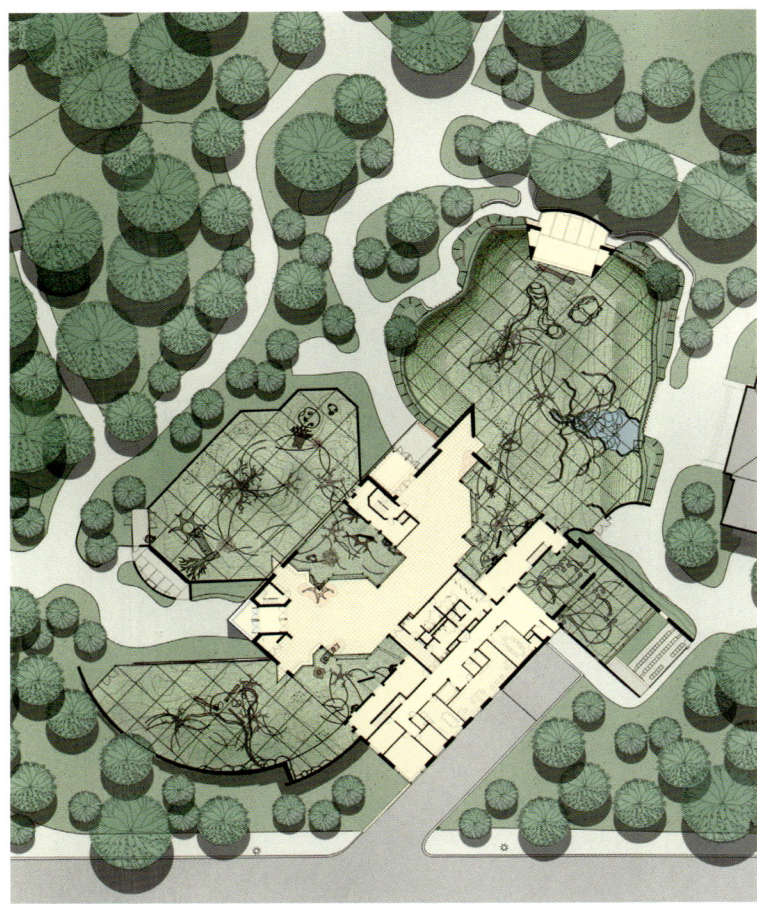

Institutional

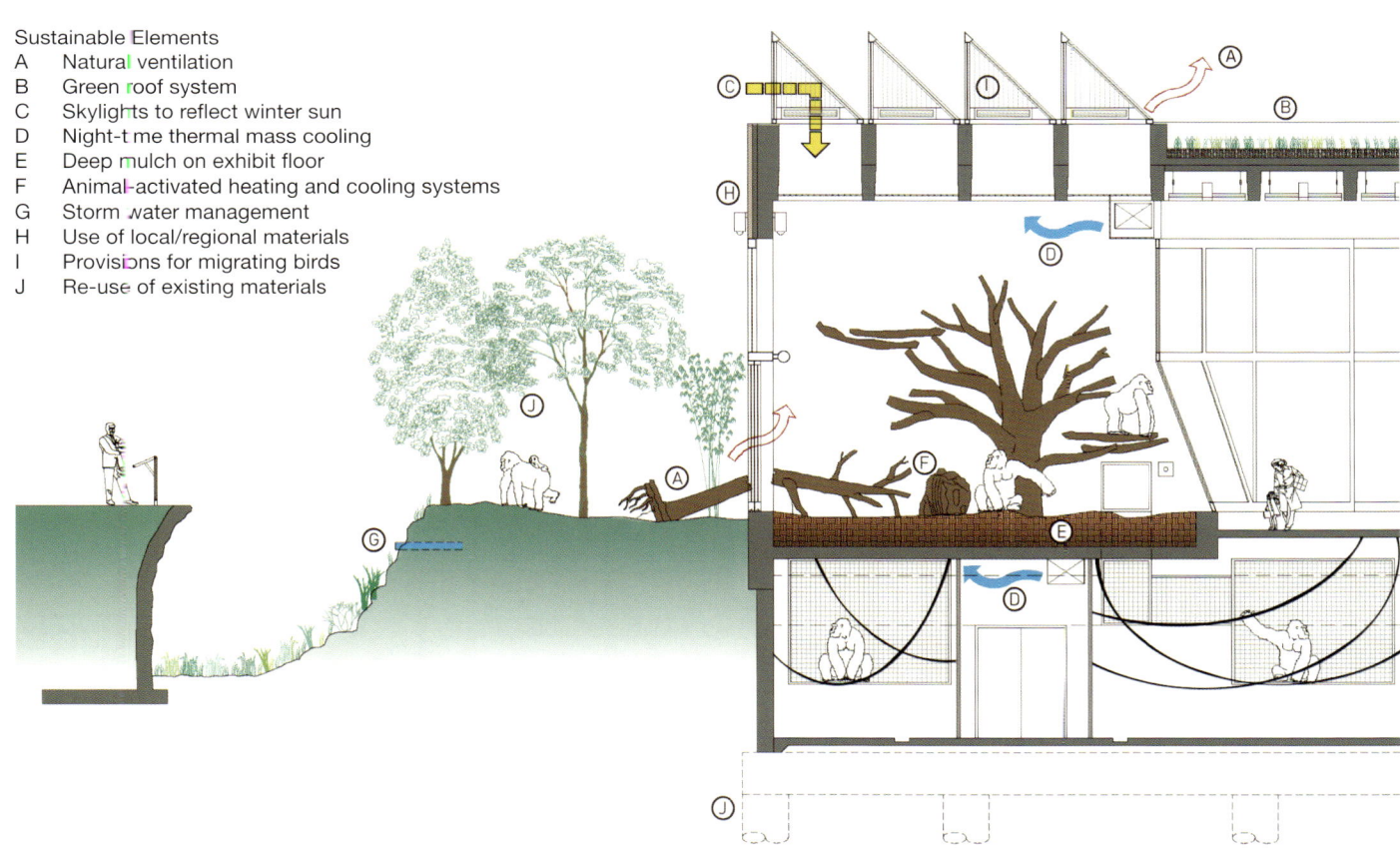

Sustainable Elements
A   Natural ventilation
B   Green roof system
C   Skylights to reflect winter sun
D   Night-time thermal mass cooling
E   Deep mulch on exhibit floor
F   Animal-activated heating and cooling systems
G   Storm water management
H   Use of local/regional materials
I   Provisions for migrating birds
J   Re-use of existing materials

Regenstein Center for African Apes

Chicago, Illinois
Design/Completion 1993/1999
Client: Adler Planetarium & Astronomy Museum
Addition: 64,000 square feet (5,950 square meters)
Existing Building/Renovation: 96,000 square feet (8,920 square meters)

# Sky Pavilion

### Site
The Adler Planetarium is located on a peninsula that defines the easternmost point of Chicago's Museum Campus, with spectacular views of Lake Michigan and the Chicago skyline.

### Program
The 64,000-square-foot expansion of the existing building contains a 190-seat theater, exhibit spaces, and a restaurant, public winter garden, and education center. The original building plan, including a 1970 underground addition, was reorganized, historic relief sculptures were restored, and the museum's historic original entrance was reopened. Parkland and a lakefront pedestrian promenade were created when a parking lot was removed, improving outdoor activity around the planetarium and providing a link to the Museum Campus.

### Concept
In an effort to maintain the integrity and prominence of the original 1930 Art Deco landmark structure, the pavilion addition sits primarily below ground. The dynamic, semi-circular building radiates outward from the existing planetarium dome with a glass reveal skylight integrating old and new. Only the structure's sloping glass roof is visible as it wraps 180 degrees around the existing building. The technologically sophisticated multi-layer roof and glass wall provide unprecedented views of the sky and lake while filtering daylight and reducing the heat load.

Granite from the original building was used to clad the base of the addition although the slabs are laid up horizontally rather than vertically, in subtle contrast to the existing building. The interior is open, with interactive exhibits designed to make astronomy more accessible to visitors.

### Elements
Aluminum-and-glass skylight system, custom structural steel skylight framing, granite to match the original building

Sky Pavilion

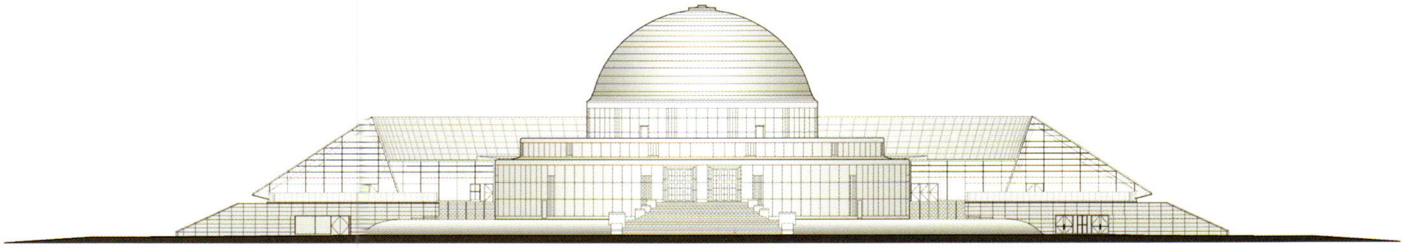

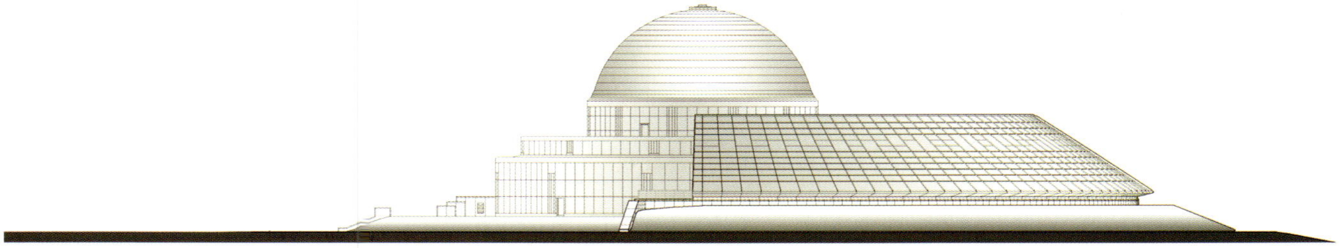

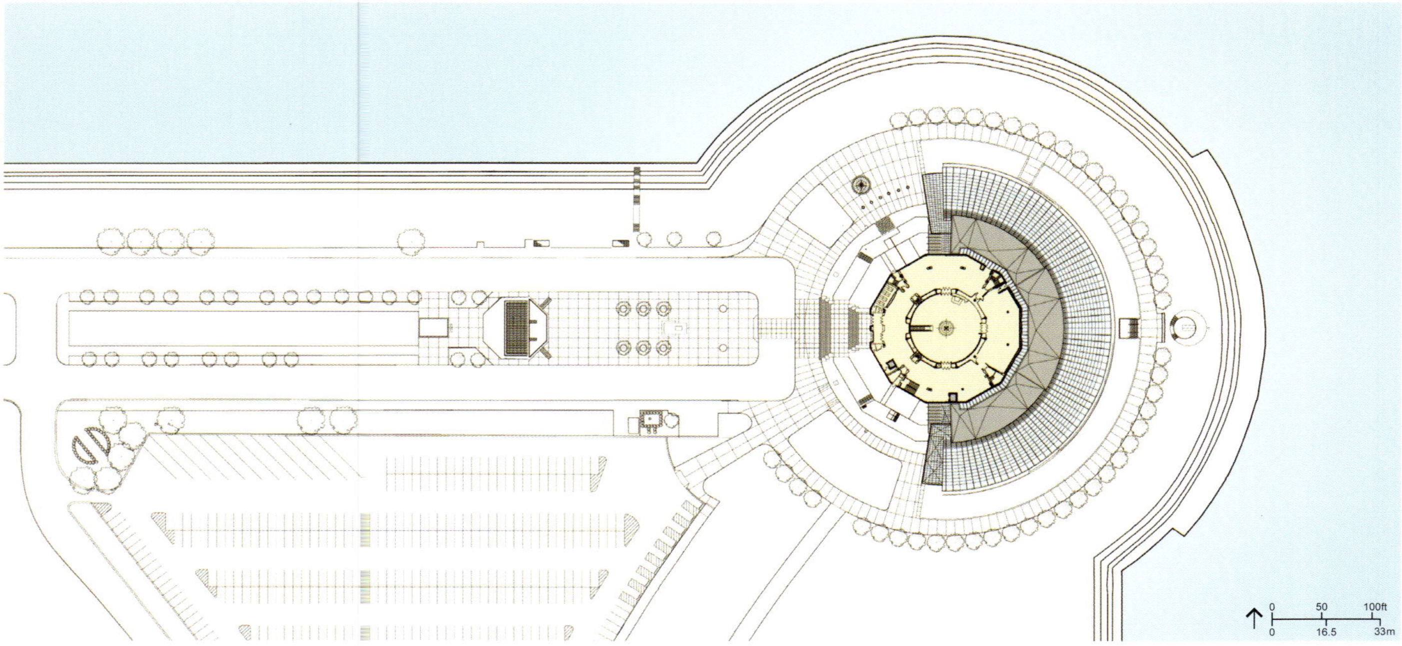

*Institutional*

*Sky Pavilion*

Chicago, Illinois
Design/Completion 2003/2011
Client: A consortium of the Staubach Co.,
Creative Real Estate Services and Walsh Construction
500,000 square feet (46,500 square meters)

# Chicago Tower

### Site
The structure is sited on Chicago's lakefront, southeast of downtown in close proximity to the McCormick Place convention center, Soldier Field, and three of the city's most popular museums.

### Program
The tower will rise from a podium building that will house a reception center, exhibition space, and retail facilities. The tower itself will provide a multi-level observation deck as well as the technology to support multiple forms of wireless communications and broadcast antennas extending to 2,000 feet.

### Concept
To date, most observation decks and transmitting antennas have been the result of the adaptive reuse of portions of existing tall buildings. As such, the observation and transmitting functions have been seriously compromised. Chicago Tower, by contrast, is specifically designed for these uses.

The tower's observation deck is intended to enhance the visitor experience, with the world's fastest passenger elevators providing access to a series of observation floors. The highest level will be an outdoor deck 1,600 feet above the ground; the lowest level will have a glass floor. In between, additional floors will feature more observation levels as well as a bar, restaurant, and conference facilities.

The tower's transmitting capabilities will accommodate all modes of wireless communication, including HDTV signals at 2,000 feet along with cellular, PC services, microwave transmission, Wi-Fi, and public-safety wireless services. At the ground level, the broadcast facility will be supported by a fully redundant emergency power supply. Ample below-grade service space with direct connection to generous riser space is fully accessible at all levels of the tower.

### Elements
Poured-in-place concrete structure clad with fiberglass panels to provide a finished surface that is also transparent to transmitting equipment; tuned mass damper to control horizontal movement induced by wind loads; world's fastest elevators, at approximately 38 miles per hour; heavy emphasis on life safety, with four stair towers and areas of refuge every 220 feet

Chicago Tower

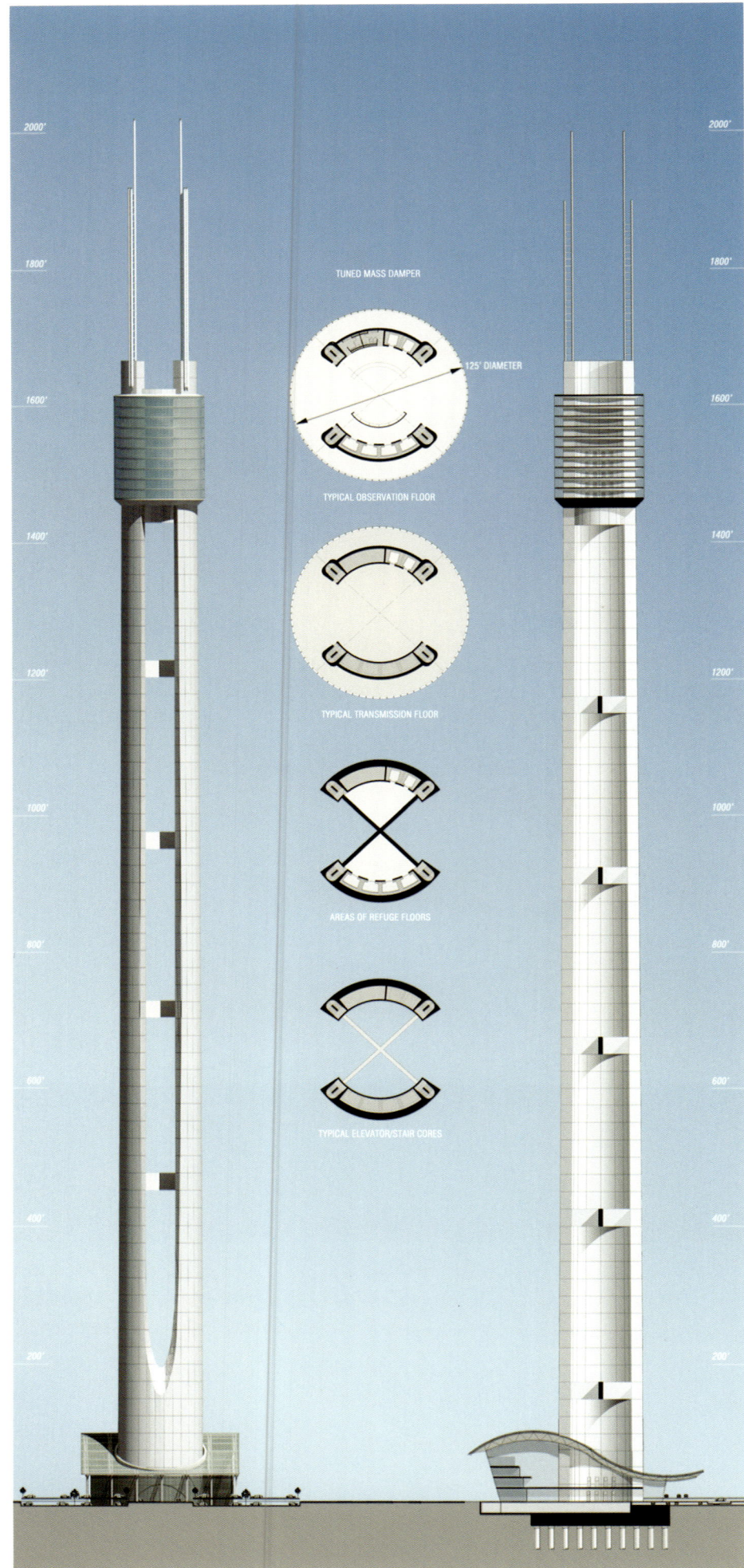

*Institutional*

*Chicago Tower*

Suzhou, China
Design/Completion 2005/2007
Client: Suzhou Industrial Park Conglomerate
136,500 square feet (12,680 square meters)

# Suzhou Jinji Lake Yacht Club

### Site
The yacht club is located on Jinji Lake, within the Suzhou Industrial Park and a short distance from four other projects designed by the firm: Suzhou Genway Tower, Suzhou International Tower, the SIP Administration Center, and the Hyatt Regency Suzhou. The club sits directly adjacent to a slip area for 50 boats.

### Program
The building contains diverse functions related to the recreational needs of the yacht club, including a restaurant with private dining, a bar, retail, hotel suites, a fitness center with locker rooms, and a conference facility.

### Concept
The building's design is the direct result of the programmatic elements being influenced by the site. To the north, an ordered system of paths and plazas gives way to the gentle curves of the lakefront. The yacht club responds to this context with rectilinear façades fronting the pathways and more sculpted, gradual arcs facing the water.

Without resorting to mimicry, the building's forms and details recall boat building, expressing the underlying structural frame while providing dynamic interior space in which to observe the activity on the lake. The building's main volume is raised in order to preserve views of the lakefront for pedestrians along the pathways.

### Elements
Concrete structure, aluminum-and-glass enclosure with a hardwood screen

Suzhou Jinji Lake Yacht Club

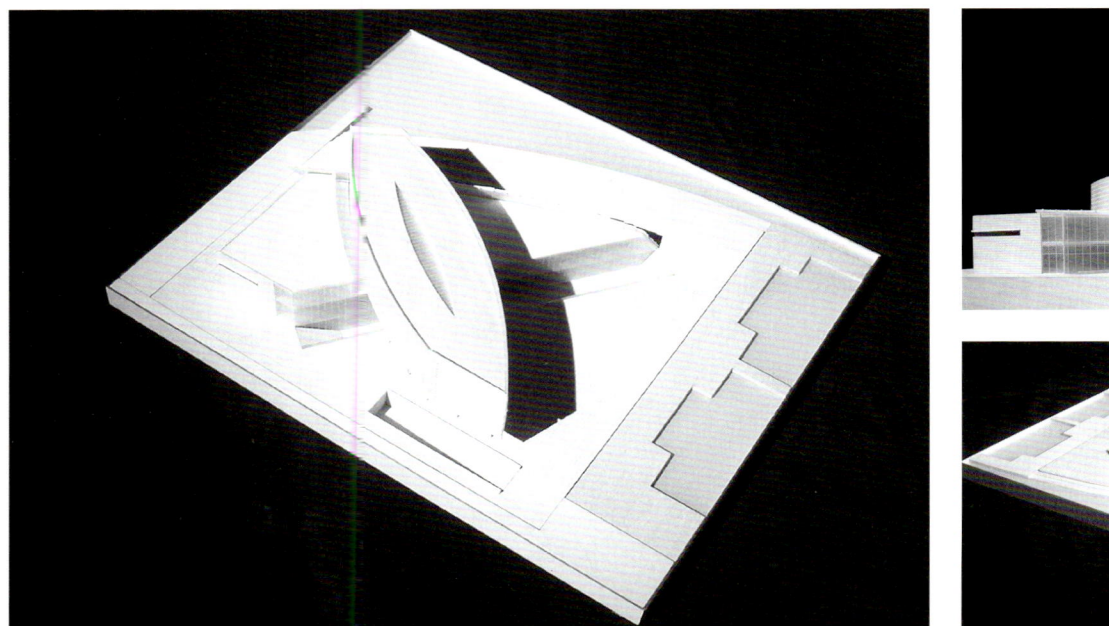
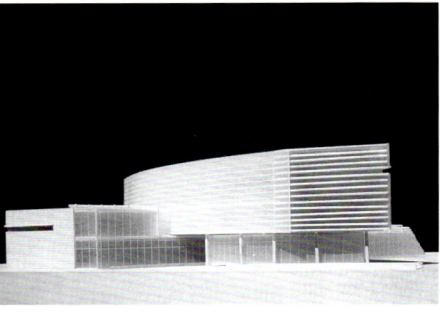

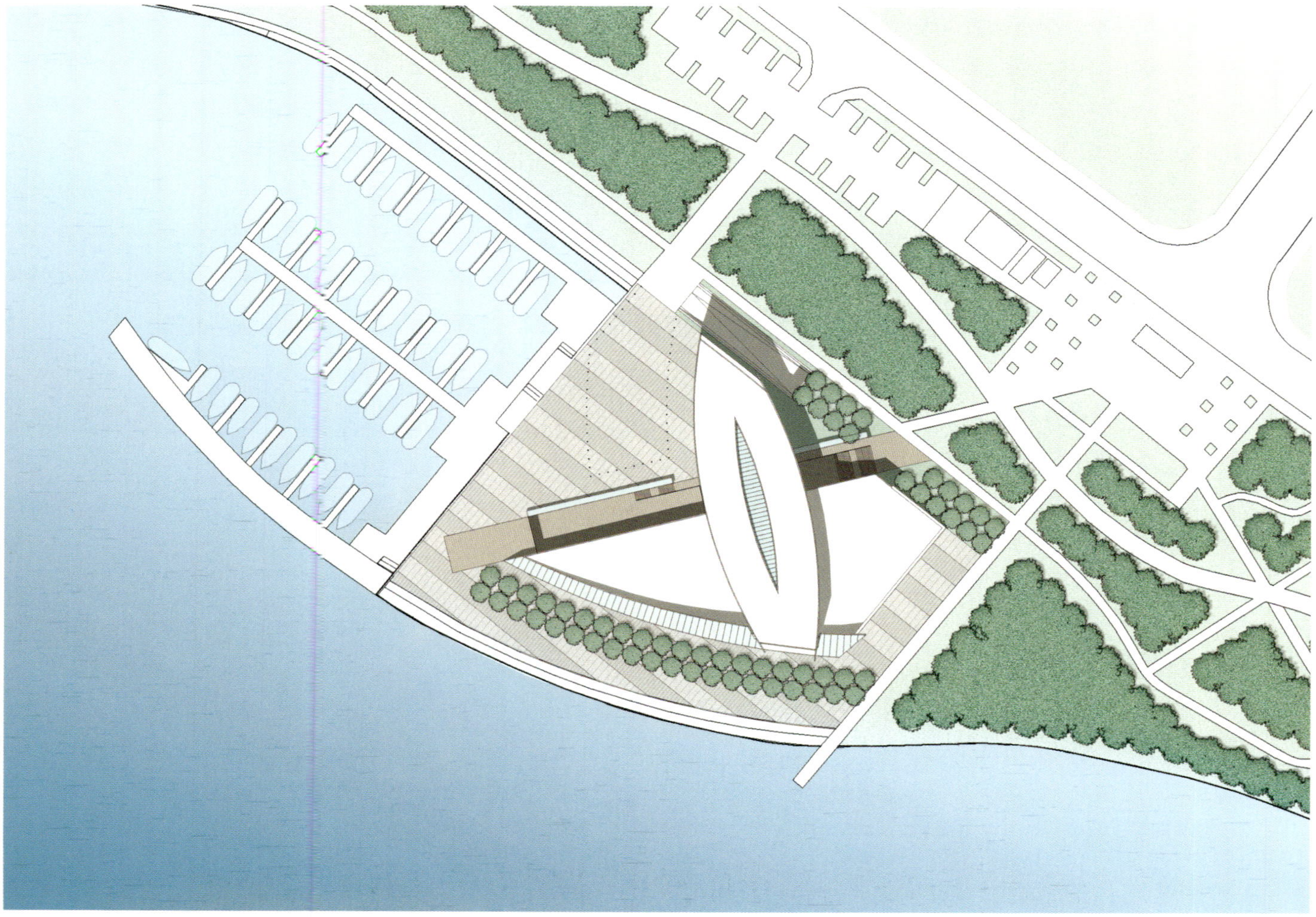

*Institutional*

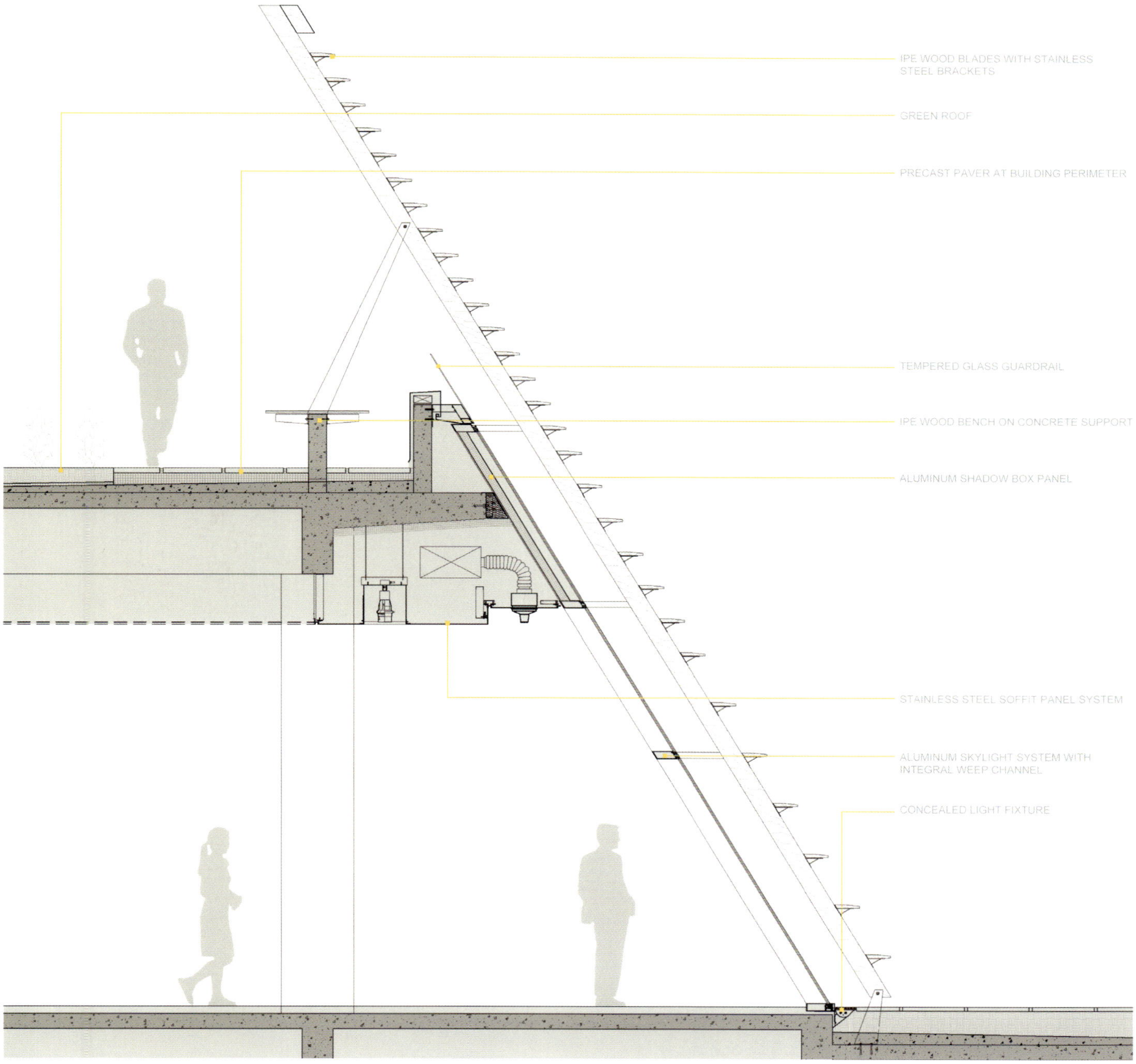

193

- IPE WOOD BLADES WITH STAINLESS STEEL BRACKETS
- GREEN ROOF
- PRECAST PAVER AT BUILDING PERIMETER
- TEMPERED GLASS GUARDRAIL
- IPE WOOD BENCH ON CONCRETE SUPPORT
- ALUMINUM SHADOW BOX PANEL
- STAINLESS STEEL SOFFIT PANEL SYSTEM
- ALUMINUM SKYLIGHT SYSTEM WITH INTEGRAL WEEP CHANNEL
- CONCEALED LIGHT FIXTURE

*Suzhou Jinji Lake Yacht Club*

Chicago, Illinois
Design/Completion 1999/2001
Client: MB Beitler
250,000 square feet (23,230 square meters)

# 360 North Michigan Avenue

### Site
The original London Guarantee and Accident Building, built in 1923, is located at the corner of Michigan Avenue and Wacker Drive, one of Chicago's most recognized intersections overlooking the Chicago River.

### Program
After an unsympathetic 1960s remodeling and years of deferred maintenance, a new owner wanted to return the historic building to its original prominent stature while adding modern building systems. The revitalization plan included restoring the original domed rotunda and marble lobby, new elevators, electrical services, floor-by-floor dedicated mechanical rooms, and the installation of a fiber-optic backbone. On the upper floors, elevator lobbies, corridors, and bathrooms were renovated, and basic tenant design standards were developed.

### Concept
Alfred S. Alschuler's stunning Beaux-Arts building had been damaged during a 1960s "modernization" project. The glass and cast-iron entry was replaced with an unadorned granite slab façade and stainless steel doors. The once-soaring, 30-foot-high rotunda of ornamental plaster had been concealed with acoustical ceiling tiles for so long that only the building's engineer and architectural historians knew that it existed.

To reclaim the building, the architects studied original drawings, remnants of ornamental plaster, and digitally enhanced photographs from the 1920s to recreate details that had been lost or destroyed. Detailed pencil sketches of more than two dozen patterns were scanned into CAD software to create composite photo renderings and detailed drawings for artisans and pattern makers to use in reproducing the ornamentation. Metal and plaster finishes were scraped back to determine historical color palettes, and a 6- by 10-foot bronze plaque depicting Chicago's first white settlers was discovered in storage and reinstalled above the entryway.

### Elements
Restored cast ornamental metal entry, ornamental plaster rotunda, marble floor and walls

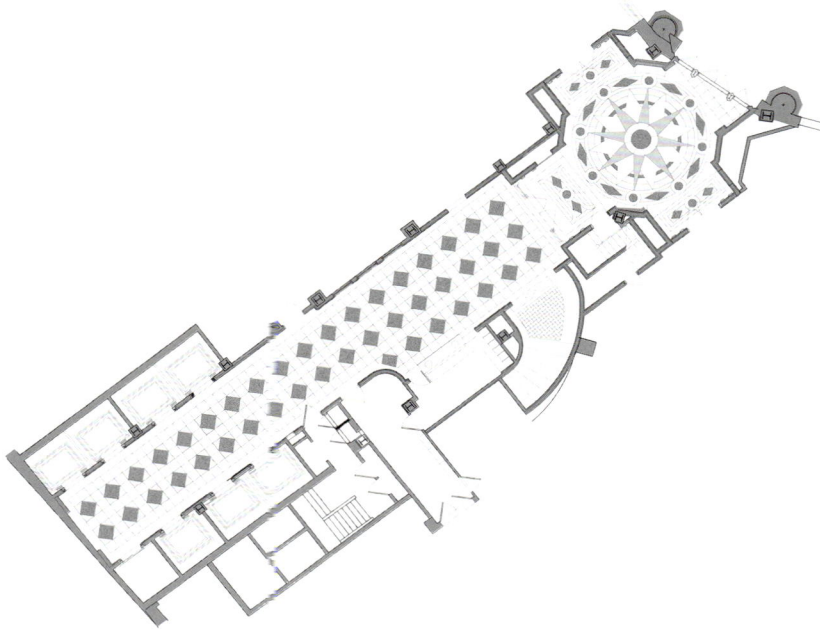

*Repositioning*

360 North Michigan Avenue

Chicago, Illinois
Design/Completion 1999/2002
Client: Douglas Elliman-Beitler
480,000 square feet (44,600 square meters)

# 1 North LaSalle Street

### Site
The office building sits in a prime location in the city's financial center.

### Program
The 49-story landmark by Vitzthum & Burns had endured benign neglect with no significant long-term improvements for many years. This renovation included the lobby, main entry, and storefronts. The elevator system and cabs were modernized, and the mechanical, electrical, plumbing, and fire protection systems were upgraded. In addition, corridors and toilet rooms on the office floors were renovated, and tenant design standards were developed.

### Concept
When 1 North LaSalle Street opened in 1930, it was one of the foremost examples of the Art Deco style. A carefully planned renovation has restored its notable design elements and repositioned the building for a more exclusive market.

In the lobby, existing marble floors, walls, borders, and bases were repaired, and elevator doors and lighting were refinished and restored to the original finishes. New elevator cabs were created to harmonize with the restored lobby. The exterior storefront windows were replaced with new cast aluminum storefronts that closely match the proportions of the original building design.

### Elements
Bronze, marble, glass, and aluminum

Chicago, Illinois
Design/Completion 1991/1996
Client: Jones Lang LaSalle
Owner: Bank of America
1,000,000 square feet (92,900 square meters)

# 231 South LaSalle Street

### Site
This historic 21-story building is located in Chicago's financial district at the foot of LaSalle Street, near the Chicago Board of Trade and the Federal Reserve Bank of Chicago.

### Program
Bank of America (then Continental Bank) wanted to recapture the grandeur of its interior spaces and upgrade its infrastructure. In phases that spanned four years so that the bank's operations would not be disrupted, the entire building was renovated floor by floor, a new building core was put in place, and the two-story, 45,000-square-foot main banking hall was restored.

### Concept
Completed in 1924, the building is noted for its two-story grand banking hall—a peristyle of tall Ionic columns, an elaborate coffered ceiling, and marble floors. Over the years, the grand hall had lost its luster, and disjointed departmental build-outs lacked the coherence and efficiency the bank needed. The infrastructure rehabilitation included a complete floor-by-floor demolition of all existing systems and the establishment of a new central core that includes mechanical, electrical and fire protection systems, telephone and fiber optics, toilet rooms and elevators. Each floor features two new compact building cores; large, flexible open-plan work spaces; and common conference and entrance areas. Private offices and additional conference rooms are located at the four corners of the building.

To reclaim the beauty of the banking hall, ornamental plaster was reconstructed, marble walls and floors were refurbished, and a mural by Jules Guerin depicting banking practices around the world was restored. In addition, a new lighting system was designed to accentuate the historic character of the space.

### Elements
Ornamental plaster and marble

231 South LaSalle Street

Chicago, Illinois
Design/Completion 1995/1998
Client: The Lurie Co.
610,000 square feet (56,670 square meters)

# 120 South LaSalle Street

### Site
This landmark office building is located in the heart of Chicago's financial district.

### Program
Work included a full first-floor lobby renovation and the complete modernization of the elevator, electrical, telephone and data, HVAC, and security systems. New exterior windows were installed, and a connection to the adjacent parking garage and loading dock was developed. Elevator lobbies, corridors, and toilet rooms were renovated on multi-tenant floors.

### Concept
The building, originally designed by Graham, Anderson, Probst & White in 1926, needed to be significantly updated in order to attract new tenants with improved planning efficiencies and reduced operating and maintenance costs. The primary design challenge was to modernize the building without compromising its historic features. Most apparent in the renovation of the lobby and elevator cabs, this challenge was resolved with design solutions that are sympathetic to the building's classical façade and intact historic second-floor banking hall.

More than 2,500 windows were replaced; those surrounding the light court were expanded to accommodate a flexible planning module and introduce more interior light. In addition, the underutilized light court was restored to its original intent by removing insensitive mechanical additions and installing a landscaped deck that is accessible from the major tenant's conference, training and cafeteria floor.

### Elements
Steel frame, clay-tile arch, exterior enclosure of limestone and terra cotta with punched windows

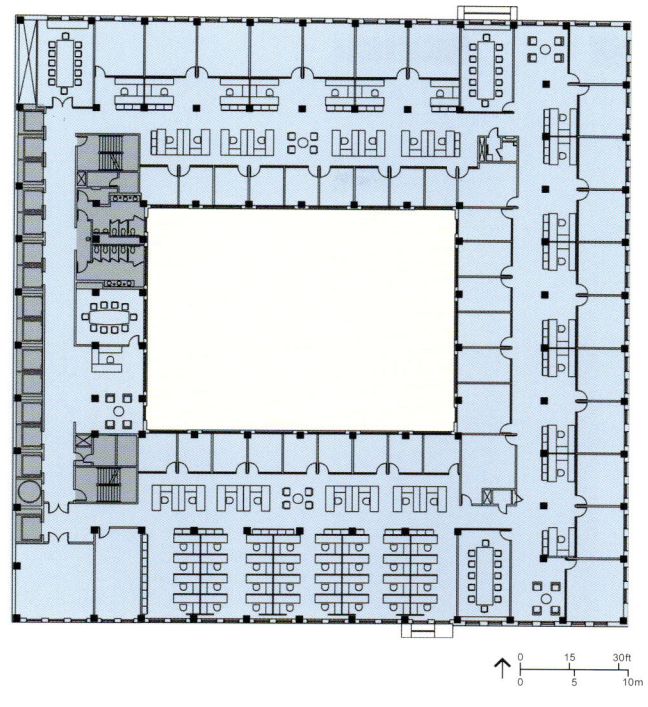

*120 South LaSalle Street*

Chicago, Illinois
Design/Completion 2002/2005
Client: The Dorchester Corp.
520,000 square feet (48,310 square meters)

# 35 East Wacker Drive

### Site
The office building occupies a prime site along the Chicago River in the city's central business district.

### Program
The 38-story landmark had undergone routine maintenance and improvements but no significant long-term enhancements. This renovation included the lobby, main entry, and storefronts. The elevator system and cabs were modernized, and the mechanical, electrical, plumbing, and fire protection systems were upgraded. In addition, corridors and toilet rooms on the office floors were renovated, and tenant design standards were developed.

### Concept
When the Jewelers Building opened in 1926, the terra cotta-clad office tower was the tallest building outside New York. This carefully planned renovation restores its notable classic design elements and repositions the building for a more exclusive market.

In the lobby, a 1970s security desk was moved from its central location to re-establish the original volume of the space. Existing marble floors, walls, borders, and bases were repaired, and elevator doors were refinished in bronze to match the lobby's original finishes. By referring to the building's initial marketing brochure and a small section of intact cornices, the architects recreated gilded column capitals and an ornamental painted, coffered ceiling. Three main entrances were restored, including the floors, steel framing, bronze cladding, revolving and swing doors, lighting, and vestibule ceiling. In addition, a 25-year-old "off-the-shelf" storefront was replaced with an aluminum storefront that closely matches the proportions and the center-entry doors of the building's original design.

### Elements
Bronze and marble

Repositioning

35 East Wacker Drive

# Firm Profile

214 Office
220 Partners
226 Staff
230 Project Chronology
250 Selected Works Project Credits
251 Selected Works Collaborators
252 Acknowledgments
253 Photography Credits
255 Index

Chicago, Illinois
Design/Completion 2002
Client: Goettsch Partners, Inc.
22,500 square feet (2,090 square meters)

# Office

### Site
The firm's offices are located on the top floor of the historic Railway Exchange Building, now known as the Santa Fe Building, which was designed by Daniel Burnham and, upon completion in 1904, housed Burnham's offices.

### Program
The 22,500-square-foot floor plate provides space for 64 workstations, six partner offices, two large conference rooms, a variety of work areas for non-technical personnel, and a reception area. Semi-private meeting areas, breakout areas, a library, model shop, and lunchroom are also provided.

### Concept
The office entry is defined by a full-glass enclosure with doors that slide on a unique stainless steel support system. A white Carrara marble floor flows through the reception area and around the atrium, identifying primary circulation and unifying the space. The office design responds to a number of the building's unique features, including prominent 7-foot-diameter circular windows, a donut-shaped plan, and a large, skylit atrium.

The open-plan studio is fitted with low, linear workstations that allow clear views to the windows and skylight while providing enough privacy to provide a contemplative and productive work environment. Reinforcing the firm's modern aesthetic, all meeting rooms and executive offices respond to the rhythm of the circular windows and are separated from circulation corridors by full-height glass partitions.

### Elements
Carrara marble and carpet flooring, custom millwork workstations, glass partitions, classic modern furniture

*Firm Profile*

Office

Firm Profile

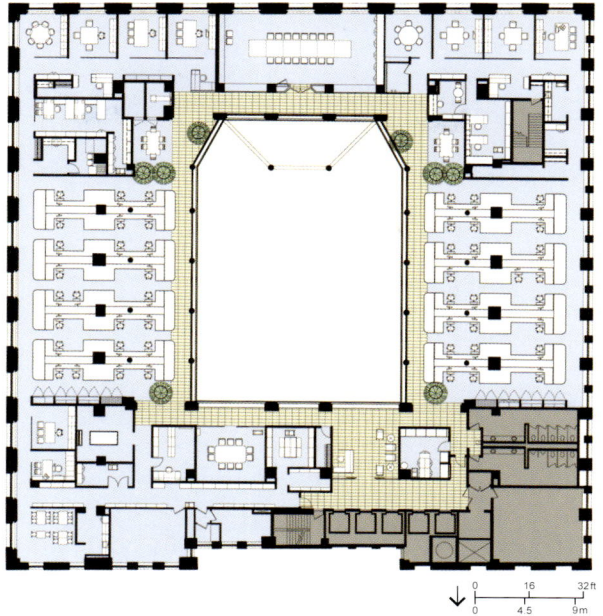

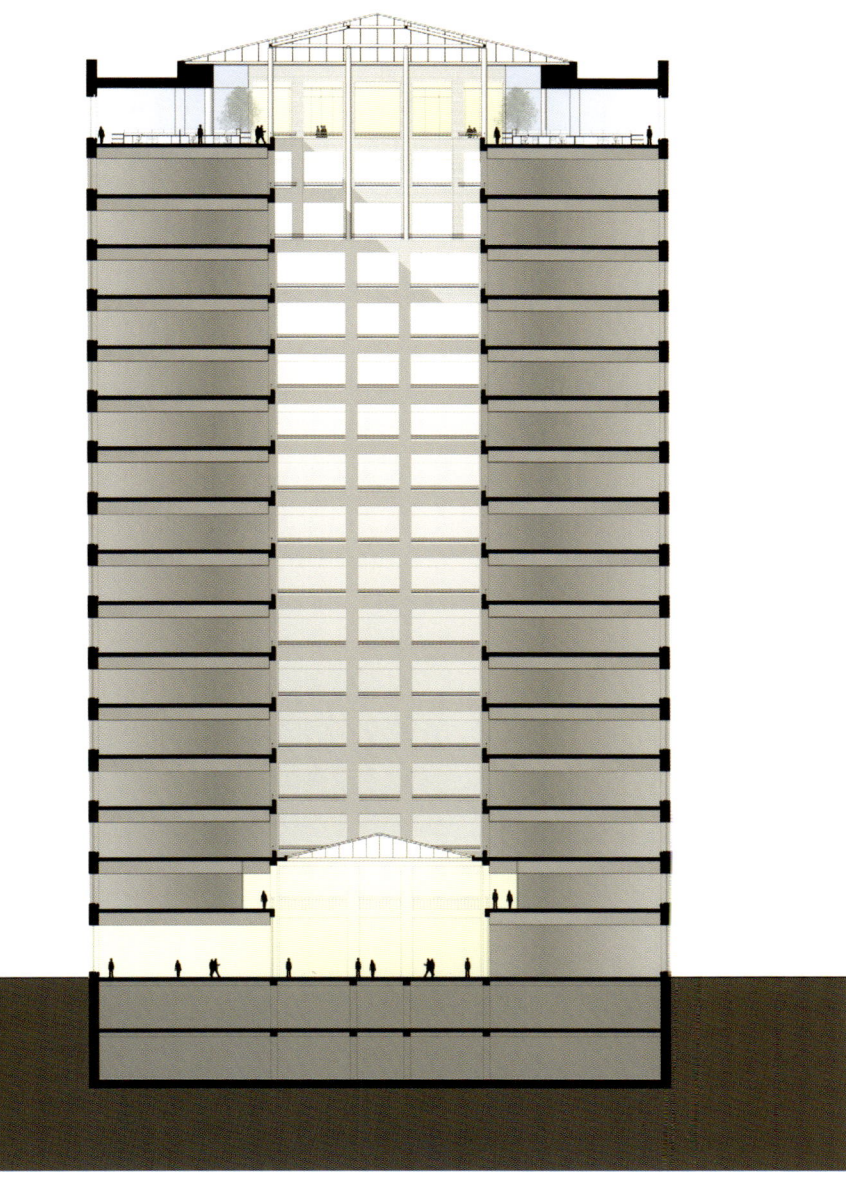

*Firm Profile*

Office

# James Goettsch, FAIA
# Partner

James Goettsch joined the firm that now bears his name in 1992. Since then he has served as design principal, later president of design, and now president of the firm. He oversees the firm's design direction with active projects on four continents.

Mr. Goettsch is a native of Davenport, Iowa, and graduated from Iowa State University in 1967. He jokingly refers to the architecture school at Iowa State as "non-denominational," by which he means that his education exposed him to a variety of styles ranging from classic modern to eclectic. An openness to a diverse range of ideas still marks his design approach.

Goettsch's first significant design responsibilities came after he was hired by Murphy/Jahn in Chicago in 1971. He took a leading role in major projects by that firm, including Xerox Centre and the State of Illinois Center, now known as the James R. Thompson Center. He remained with Murphy/Jahn for 19 years in a variety of positions, including executive vice president and principal in charge of the New York office.

When he joined his present firm, Goettsch took responsibility for the design of commercial and high-rise buildings, blending innovative construction with striking architectural form. The Chicago headquarters for Blue Cross Blue Shield of Illinois (1997) was his first major commission in this capacity. This design signaled a stylistic shift for the firm. The highly praised Blue Cross project led to a series of other large-scale urban projects in Chicago, including UBS Tower (2001) and 111 South Wacker (2005). Goettsch not only takes pride in his ability to create dramatic design features—such as the atrium at Blue Cross and the cable-net wall for UBS—he insists that significant architecture can also be inspired by client demands that include economy and other highly functional considerations.

Goettsch's work abroad underlies the universality of his approach; the cultural variables encountered in different countries find their way into the strong profiles and efficient plans that mark all of his buildings. This is especially true in China where he has led design teams on 12 major commissions, including the master plan and five buildings in Suzhou Industrial Park, one of China's most successful new towns. His work in China reflects the need for a "signature" on new urban landscapes and the increasing sophistication of Chinese clients who need to balance strong design statements with efficient, economical design.

Goettsch's contributions to the profession have been recognized in a number of honors and awards. He was elected a Fellow of the American Institute of Architects in 1988. His designs were selected for the Distinguished Building Award from the Chicago chapter of the AIA six times. He has been a key contributor to projects that have received two national AIA honor awards and two Progressive Architecture design awards.

In his position as director of design and president of Goettsch Partners, he has been central in broadening the firm's focus with strengthened practices in several specializations, including historic restoration, planning, interiors, and technical services. "Modern architecture is successful when a complex program can be reduced to something that is simple and clear," he says.

# Michael Kaufman, AIA, LEED AP
# Partner

"What sets our firm apart is that we apply an economical structure and optimal function to virtually every project," says Michael Kaufman, a member of the firm since 1979. Kaufman heads design teams that handle a diverse range of building types, including museums and hotels as well as renovation, repositioning, and historic preservation projects.

Kaufman has a deep understanding of the values of modern architecture, having studied at IIT, where he graduated in 1977. He studied under Professor John Heinrich who taught students to "think in a modern way, but since he was also a developer, to think about the marketplace and the real world," Kaufman says. Now his career proves how the basic tenets of modernism—rationality and spare structure—apply to different kinds of projects and with highly different results.

Kaufman approaches each project by developing a thorough understanding of a client's needs. This understanding was critical, for example, in the Regenstein Center for African Apes at Chicago's Lincoln Park Zoo, where the science of primatology provided an array of insights that led to an important design. The zoo also had requirements about blending gracefully with the existing urban-park setting. The outcome was a building with brick and limestone finishes that established a rapport with the adjacent historic buildings, yet was modern and distinct. It also created an environment that dissolves barriers between animals and people and between indoor and outdoor space.

His work for the domestic and international hospitality industry recognizes the necessity for distinctive design as one important means that hotels use to differentiate themselves. Yet his efforts to achieve striking profiles and luxurious finishes are tempered by cost constraints, site conditions, and other requirements that must be incorporated fully into any effective design. Results can be as diverse as two of the firm's projects in Mumbai, India: the Grand Hyatt, which is a vast six-story complex, and the Four Seasons, a dramatic high-rise.

Ultimate proof that modernism meets contemporary needs is the work that Kaufman directs in the firm's renovation, repositioning and historic preservation practice. With the objective of creating an appropriate architecture, the adaptive reuse or "repositioning" process achieves objectives similar to new construction: maximizing natural light, occupant utility and comfort, introducing modern infrastructure to existing construction, and even creating up-to-date planning modules in buildings that were not designed for our modern work environments. The end result is state-of-the-art utility in formerly obsolete buildings.

The range of Kaufman's skills is evident in the number of duties that he undertakes for the firm. Besides design management, his role involves oversight of the firm's finance and administration, and under this mantle he also leads loss prevention for the firm and reviews all contracts. Kaufman is also a LEED-accredited architect with strong skills in environmentally sustainable design and leads the firm's internal sustainable education. "The need to save energy and reduce emissions is so well accepted that it's second nature to us," Kaufman says. "We integrate sustainable design in everything we do."

# Steven M. Nilles, AIA, LEED AP
Partner

As technical design principal of Goettsch Partners, Steve Nilles specializes in the integration of advanced engineering concepts with architectural design. This integration is a key part of major high-rise and mixed-use projects that must include both strong aesthetics and optimal efficiency.

Nilles joined the firm in 1998. Since then, he has overseen major design and construction projects from the concept stage through project completion. Nilles takes responsibility for the performance of the product. This end result involves tenant-friendly design features, economical construction, sustainability, and the long-term satisfaction of clients and subsequent building owners.

Nilles attended Notre Dame University, where he earned a five-year Bachelor of Science in Architecture in 1980. He began his career in Cleveland, where he worked for Dalton, Dalton and Newport. In 1982, he arrived in Chicago, which he believed stressed better than any city the relationship between technology and design. In Chicago, he joined Murphy/Jahn and became vice president and director of production, coordinating the construction of many major projects, including Munich Airport Center and the Sony Center in Berlin.

Optimizing economy in a distinctive structure is the essence of modern architecture, according to Nilles. "The trick in technical design is to pay attention to the small details that make a building function without losing sight of the big idea," he says. This approach is not an ivory tower mindset; rather it's learned by "working in the trenches" from the earliest planning stages through the successful completion of a building.

Nilles is an expert in understanding new construction technologies and incorporating them into progressive designs. While working on projects in Germany, he helped pioneer cable wall systems to achieve unprecedented transparency in projects such as the Munich airport. He later used this technology in designs for speculative office buildings in Chicago. He works with composite structural systems and modern elevator systems, all of which figured into Goettsch Partners' UBS Tower, a design noted for aesthetic distinction and inherent economy.

One of Nilles' responsibilities is to integrate a sustainable design approach in projects at an early stage. So-called "green" design considers site selection, construction techniques, materials, and eventual energy consumption. Nilles incorporates sustainable elements into projects, monitors their impact, and educates clients about these features.

The complexity of modern commercial architecture increasingly involves client interaction related to cost concerns, space needs, and many other functional realities. To this end, Nilles' role is to understand client concerns in detail, convey them to his design teams, and usher their development through project completion. In such a role, Nilles was responsible for many aspects of the firm's 111 South Wacker project, including the innovative lobby enclosure. "To us, architecture is an expression of engineering driven by economics," he says, "but these buildings need to be eye-catching as well as economical to be successful."

# James E. Prendergast, AIA, LEED AP
## Partner

Jim Prendergast leads Goettsch Partners' interior architecture practice as an extension of the firm's progressive design philosophy. The interiors practice works in close collaboration with the firm's core architectural design practice as well as on independent, stand-alone tenant commissions.

Prendergast has directed projects for a variety of clients, notably law firms, print and broadcast news organizations, national consulting firms, and corporate headquarters. This diverse experience has enabled him to understand how strategic needs drive office design, and how a profound and intelligent understanding of the dynamics of a business organization can drive the architectural design of new buildings.

Prendergast is a native of Connecticut, raised in Ohio and a graduate of the University of Cincinnati, where he received his Bachelor of Architecture in 1984. He joined the national interior architectural practice of ISD after graduation and assumed a major role in several corporate projects, including executive offices for Stone Container and the law offices of Katten Muchin Rosenman and Jones Day. In 1987 he joined Perkins+Will and helped build an interiors practice that became the third largest in the United States. A.T. Kearney, Coca-Cola, Deloitte Consulting, Time Warner, Turner Entertainment Networks, and the United Nations were major clients in this period, during which Prendergast emerged as a nationally recognized, cutting-edge thinker incorporating sociological and user-centered human organizational methodologies into this designs.

"Historically, office design has been a spatial translation of hierarchical relationships," Prendergast says. "Now, it reflects the realities of efficient work flow and quality-of-life issues and these, in turn, drive design inventions." He believes the design process holds an increasingly high priority in modern companies. In one recent project, the client CEO was directly involved and mandated that no single personal office would be more important than any conference room. In this client's view, conference rooms generate strategies and innovation; private offices are where the tactical outcomes of those strategies and innovations are executed. In the design for a new all-digital, high-definition broadcast center for WBBM-TV/CBS 2 Chicago, Prendergast's team tailored its design to the requirements of the "improvisational culture" of television news.

Goettsch Partners' goal is to optimize the unique functional and aesthetic opportunities that are embedded in every design challenge. Prendergast's interiors, such as those for law firms Freeborn & Peters, Sonnenschein Nath & Rosenthal, and Jenner & Block, have been praised not only for their efficiency but also for their impact on the client's corporate image and the freshness of the design despite the passage of time. These designs typify his objective for Goettsch Partners: to see design contribute materially to building architecture, and to create workplaces that facilitate growth, increase efficiency, and enable innovation.

Prendergast is a frequent speaker before professional forums and university classrooms. His design work is regularly honored with interior architecture awards from AIA Chicago. He received an AIA National Honor Award for Interior Architecture in 2002 and the AIA Chicago Young Architect Award in 1999.

# Lawrence Weldon, AIA
# Partner

Larry Weldon leads Goettsch Partners' Enclosures Group, an in-house specialty group perhaps less publicized than the firm's design studios but one that's equally critical in any project that integrates function, economy, and optimal architectural form. Technical services are increasingly important in contemporary architecture because curtain wall and related building enclosure systems constantly change and can be key in designs that are not just distinctive and beautiful but optimally efficient as well.

Weldon has the longest tenure of anyone with the firm. After graduating from IIT in 1977, he joined Fujikawa Conterato Lohan and Associates, the direct successor to Mies van der Rohe's practice and predecessor to Goettsch Partners. He started on the drafting tables and in the model shop, where he learned the minute details of building techniques and their use in expressive design. Today, Weldon is a world-recognized expert in construction technologies, and his role is a safeguard against inefficiencies and failures in building performance. His group reviews all contract documents, specifications, and drawings.

Weldon's strengths include his ability to evaluate new construction products as they come on the market and to understand the capabilities of local contractors to build them. His knowledge of unitized curtain walls and building systems is unmatched. He advises the firm's design teams about the suppliers and products that figure into their designs. Weldon's group is often hired by clients on a consulting basis to solve specific problems; these short-term assignments related to building enclosure integrity and economic performance often lead to full commissions for the firm on larger architectural projects.

Weldon's group is involved in every project undertaken by the firm. In some cases, the group's role is critical in overcoming potential difficulties. In Mumbai, the firm, with Weldon's assistance, designed a Four Seasons hotel with one of the most advanced curtain wall constructions in India. Weldon was also brought in to analyze, conceive, and coordinate the replacement of the curtain wall on the Grand Hyatt Seoul, a job that resulted from the firm's relationship with Hyatt, and which led to more work for other clients in South Korea.

"Large modern buildings require more efficiency than ever, especially given current economic conditions," Weldon says. "We make the construction stage more efficient and also improve long-term function simply by understanding building materials and systems as well as anyone." These construction techniques are also critical because they are now more evident in the spartan designs of modern commercial buildings.

Weldon's contributions to the firm attest to the importance of technology in modern architecture and of relationships with suppliers and contractors. The technical knowledge that Weldon's group brings to the firm assures clients that their designs are the most advanced in terms of architectural form and the critical efficiencies of function.

# James Zheng, AIA
# Partner

James Zheng, the youngest partner in the firm, is director of Asian operations and maintains hands-on management of the firm's active practice in China. While based in Chicago, Zheng travels to Asia monthly to oversee projects in Shanghai, Beijing, Suzhou, Nanjing, and elsewhere. His ability to provide personal service and skills ranging from design to marketing and management reflects the strengths of Goettsch Partners at large.

Zheng is a native of Shanghai and studied architecture at Tongji University for two years. He then set out for the U.S., based on his ambition to achieve a level of professionalism not then available in China. He enrolled at the University of Illinois at Chicago, where he was introduced to the ideas of classic modernism. He then joined Goettsch Partners in 1995, attracted by the firm's modern design philosophy and its early efforts to develop business in Asia.

Zheng's career has grown simultaneously with the sophistication of the client base in China. When he first arrived, the firm was competing for projects where investors wanted mainly "to be considered 'unique,'" as Zheng explains. This meant that they were enamored with the pyrotechnics of modern construction; what they lacked was an understanding of what constituted an optimal, efficient building. Part of Zheng's job is to educate clients as to how architecture contributes to overall project success.

Zheng's strength is that he can work effectively as a project designer, working closely with design partner James Goettsch, and also as a marketing representative and construction manager. This combination of skills puts him in a position to interact with clients, meet Chinese critics, and produce designs that target the dynamics of the Chinese market. "From the beginning, the Chinese liked our style," Zheng says. "They found it to be simple, elegant, and powerful." More difficult was making clients see less visible ingredients of architecture such as floor plans and construction systems. Zheng's job is to introduce elements of form and function that lead to permanent efficiencies.

Zheng has been intimately involved in a variety of successful projects in China, including the master plan for the Suzhou Industrial Park and the designs of several individual buildings in that development: the Hyatt Regency Suzhou, two government buildings, and Suzhou International Tower. He has managed such projects as Nanjing International Center, Lujiazui Diamond Tower, the Grand Hyatt Guangzhou, and the Xi'an Greenland Mixed-Use Development.

Recognized for his well-rounded skills, Zheng received the AIA Chicago Young Architect Award in 2004 and was named in *Crain's Chicago Business* 40 Under 40 in 2005. Zheng is a consummate business professional who recently received his MBA from Northwestern University's Kellogg School of Management. "Architecture is a business that also involves marketing, management, and finance," he says. "All of these elements are important to the ultimate objective: good buildings and happy clients."

# Staff

### Partners
James Goettsch
Michael F. Kaufman
Steven M. Nilles
James E. Prendergast
Lawrence C. Weldon
James Zheng

### Principals
Joseph Dolinar

### Associate Principals
Randall Chapple
Leonard Koroski
Patrick Loughran
Susan G. Pratt

### Senior Associates
Michael D. Byun
Joseph D. Cliggott
Paul De Santis
James M. Hall
Ming C. Lai
Frank Mraz
Scott Seyer
Travis Soberg

### Associates
J. Jeffery Johnson
Joseph Patrick
J.C. Sanchez
Hiroshi Sango
Joseph Schultz

### Staff
Ross Barney
Amanda Beelman
Patrizia Bischoff
Ashley Blake
Michael J. Bretz
Natalie Brzozowski
Jason D. Cain
O. Nathaniel Cho
Ady Chu
Allan Chung
Susanna J. Craib-Cox
Kathleen Deckard
Bashar Elayyan
Lisa K. Hill
James C. Horton, Jr.
Cheri Jacobs
Yuan Ji
Lisa Krichilsky
Matthew C. Larson
Pao Lertsiri
Yue Lu
Jerry Mattio
Yong Mei
Brian C. Miller
Carol Nawracaj
Anna Ninoyu
Gao Qiu
Alan L. Salchow
Denise Sims
David L. Spangler
Andrew Tarcin
Jeevan Vijayan
John Zacherle
Austin Zike

*Firm Profile*

*Current Staff*

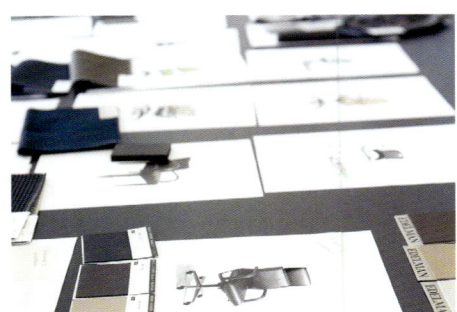

*Firm Profile*

Office Environment

# Project Chronology

| | **Firm History** |
|---|---|
| 1938–1969 | Ludwig Mies van der Rohe |
| 1969–1975 | The Office of Mies van der Rohe |
| 1975–1982 | Fujikawa Conterato Lohan and Associates |
| 1982–1986 | FCL Associates |
| 1986–2002 | Lohan Associates |
| 2002–2005 | Lohan Caprile Goettsch Architects |
| 2005 | Goettsch Partners |

**McDonald's Corporate Campus**
Office
Oak Brook, Illinois
1979/2005

**TRW World Headquarters**
Office
Lyndhurst, Ohio
1981/1985

**Frito-Lay National Headquarters**
Office
Plano, Texas
1982/1984

**Motorola Training Center**
Office
Schaumburg, Illinois
1983/1986

**Oceanarium
John G. Shedd Aquarium**
Institutional
Chicago, Illinois
1983/1991

**Chicago Museum Campus**
Master Planning
Chicago, Illinois
1984

**Cityfront Center**
Master Planning
Chicago, Illinois
1985

**Dean Witter Financial Services and Riverwoods Corporate Place**
Office
Riverwoods, Illinois
1986/1989

**420 East Ohio Street**
Hospitality/Residential
Chicago, Illinois
1987/1991

**Ameritech Center**
Office
Hoffman Estates, Illinois
1987/1991

*Project Chronology*

**Gaviidae Retail Center**
Retail
Minneapolis, Minnesota
1987/1989

**Amerika-Gedenkbibliothek**
Institutional
Berlin, Germany
1988

**Dain Bosworth Tower**
Office
Minneapolis, Minnesota
1988/1991

**Eli Lilly Headquarters Lobby Renovation**
Office
Indianapolis, Indiana
1988/1992

**John T. Richardson Library
DePaul University**
Institutional
Chicago, Illinois
1988/1992

**Devon House**
Hospitality/Residential
Ada, Michigan
1988/1992

**Steelcase/Stow & Davis Showroom**
Interiors
Chicago, Illinois
1988/1989

**Safety-Kleen Corporate Headquarters**
Office
Elgin, Illinois
1989/1992

**John C. Kluczynski Building Renovation**
Institutional
Chicago, Illinois
1990/1994

**Center for Curatorial Studies
Bard College**
Institutional
Annandale-on-Hudson, New York
1990/1992

**Ann and Alfred Goldstein Academic Center
Pace University**
Institutional
Pleasantville, New York
1991/1995

**231 South LaSalle Street**
Repositioning
Chicago, Illinois
1991/1996

200–203

*Project Chronology*

**Gleacher Center**
**University of Chicago**
**Graduate School of Business**
Institutional
Chicago, Illinois
1991/1994

**Ace Hardware Headquarters**
Office
Oak Brook, Illinois
1992/1994

**Checkpoint Charlie Office Complex**
Mixed-Use
Berlin, Germany
1992

**Campus Master Plans**
**Pace University**
Institutional
New York, Pleasantville and White Plains,
New York
1992

**Snap-on Tools Corporate Headquarters**
Office
Pleasant Prairie, Wisconsin
1993/1994

**Sky Pavilion**
**Adler Planetarium & Astronomy Museum**
Institutional
Chicago, Illinois
1993/1999

**182–185**

**Administrative and Training Campus
AmSouth Bancorporation**
Office
Birmingham, Alabama
1993/1995

**American General Center**
Office
Nashville, Tennessee
1994/1997

**Blue Cross Blue Shield of Illinois Headquarters**
Office
Chicago, Illinois
1994/1997
Expansion 2006/2010

**54–67**

**Max Planck Institute**
Institutional
Munich, Germany
1994

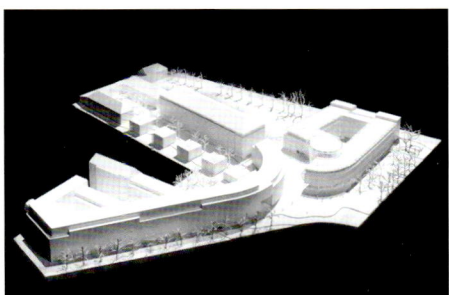

**Oak Brook Comprehensive Plan**
Master Planning
Oak Brook, Illinois
1994

**120 South LaSalle Street**
Repositioning
Chicago, Illinois
1995/1998

**204–207**

*Project Chronology*

**Library and Master Plan**
**Barat College**
Institutional
Lake Forest, Illinois
1995/1996

**Farnsworth House Restoration**
Plano, Illinois
1996/1998

**Grand Hyatt Mumbai**
Hospitality/Residential
Mumbai, India
1996/2004

**128–131**

**Jin Hui Plaza**
Mixed-Use
Shanghai, China
1996

**Central Regional Office**
**Department of Transportation**
Institutional
Kansas City, Missouri
1997/1999

**Cantera Hotel**
Hospitality/Residential
Warrenville, Illinois
1997

*Firm Profile*

**Charles Square Center**
Office
Prague, Czech Republic
1997/2002

**24–33**

**Mary and Leigh Block Museum of Art Expansion
Northwestern University**
Institutional
Evanston, Illinois
1997/2000

**76–83**

**Suzhou International Tower**
Office
Suzhou, China
1997/1999

**94–97**

**School of Law and Law Library
Pace University**
Institutional
White Plains, New York
1997/2000

**Västra City**
Mixed-Use
Stockholm, Sweden
1997

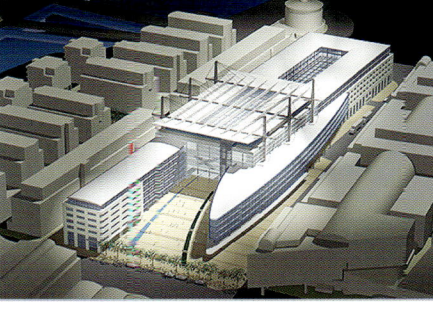

**33 North LaSalle Street**
Repositioning
Chicago, Illinois
1998/2000

**St. Mary of the Annunciation Church**
Institutional
Mundelein, Illinois
1998/2002

**Central Headquarters**
**Chicago Police Department**
Institutional
Chicago, Illinois
1998/1999

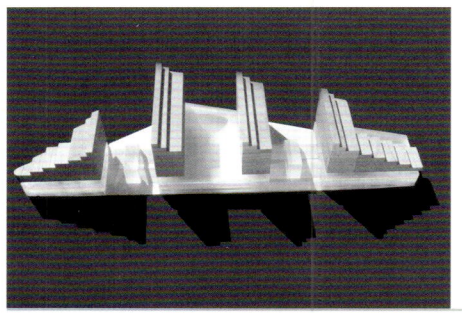

**Europe Gate**
Mixed-Use
Prague, Czech Republic
1998

**Grand Hyatt São Paulo**
Hospitality/Residential
São Paulo, Brazil
1998/2002

68–75

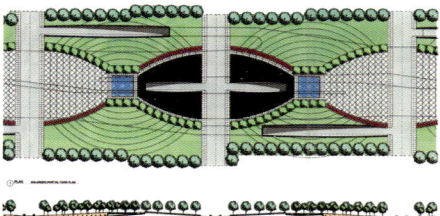

**Kennedy Expressway Park**
Master Planning
Chicago, Illinois
1998

**UBS Tower**
Office
Chicago, Illinois
1998/2001

34–43

**360 North Michigan Avenue**
Repositioning
Chicago, Illinois
1999/2001

**194–197**

**1 North LaSalle Street**
Repositioning
Chicago, Illinois
1999/2002

**198–199**

**Newton Grove Condominiums**
Hospitality/Residential
Singapore
1999

**North Burnham Park and Soldier Field Redevelopment**
Institutional
Chicago, Illinois
1999/2003

**84–91**

**Värtahamnen**
Mixed-Use
Stockholm, Sweden
1999

**Wolf Point**
Master Planning
Chicago, Illinois
2000

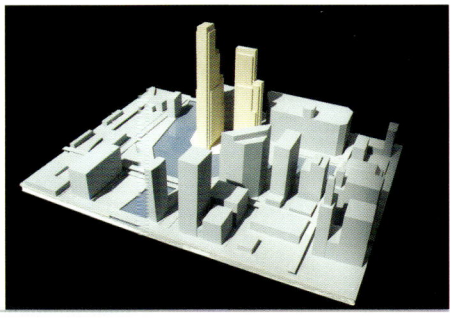

**Regenstein Center for African Apes**
**Lincoln Park Zoo**
Institutional
Chicago, Illinois
2000/2004

**178–181**

**Cityfront Center Plaza**
Hospitality/Residential
Chicago, Illinois
2000

**111 South Wacker**
Office
Chicago, Illinois
2000/2005

**14–23**

**Blue Cross Blue Shield Claim Center**
Office
Amarillo, Texas
2001/2007

**Beijing Silvertie Center**
Mixed-Use
Beijing, China
2001

**166–167**

**Four Seasons Mumbai**
Hospitality/Residential
Mumbai, India
2001/2006

**138–139**

**U-505 Submarine Exhibit
Museum of Science and Industry**
Institutional
Chicago, Illinois
2001/2005

**168–171**

**Grand Hyatt Seoul
Curtain Wall Replacement**
Hospitality/Residential
Seoul, Korea
2001/2003

**Westgate Center**
Office
Prague, Czech Republic
2001

**Sunbelt Tower**
Office
Chicago, Illinois
2001

**112–113**

**35 East Wacker Drive**
Repositioning
Chicago, Illinois
2002/2005

**208–211**

**Goettsch Partners**
Interiors
Chicago, Illinois
2002/2002

**214–219**

**Hyatt Lodge at McDonald's Campus**
Hospitality/Residential
Oak Brook, Illinois
2002/2005

**122–125**

**Bridges for Chicago**
Institutional
Chicago, Illinois
2003

**Shanghai Sanzhi Hotel**
Hospitality/Residential
Shanghai, China
2003

**Government Center Master Plan
Suzhou Industrial Park**
Master Planning
Suzhou, China
2003

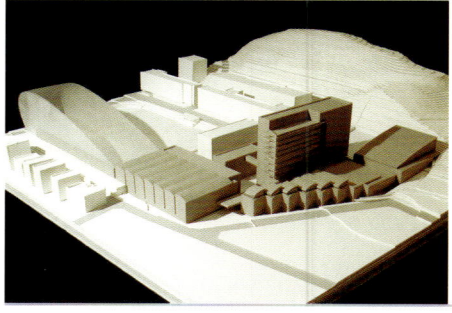

**Athletic and International Exchange Center
Dong Seoul College**
Master Planning
Seoul, Korea
2003

**SIP Administration Center
Suzhou Industrial Park**
Office
Suzhou, China
2003/2005

**98–101**

**Chicago Tower**
Institutional
Chicago, Illinois
2003/2011

**186–189**

**Suzhou Genway Tower**
Suzhou Industrial Park
Office
Suzhou, China
2003/2005

**44–53**

**Nanjing International Center**
Mixed-Use
Nanjing, China
2003/2009

**144–149**

**Theory and Computing Sciences Building**
**Argonne National Laboratory**
Institutional
Argonne, Illinois
2004

**Equinox Fitness Club**
Interiors
Chicago, Illinois
2004/2005

**Enhance Anting Golf Club Complex**
Hospitality/Residential
Shanghai, China
2004/2008

**126–127**

**Grand Hyatt Guangzhou**
Mixed-Use
Guangzhou, China
2004/2007

**156–157**

**CCS Bard Hessel Museum
Bard College**
Institutional
Annandale-on-Hudson, New York
2004/2006

**172–177**

**J.W. Marriott Grand Rapids**
Hospitality/Residential
Grand Rapids, Michigan
2004/2007

**140–143**

**R&F Edinburgh Plaza**
Office
Beijing, China
2004/2008

**Walter Payton Center Building Improvements**
Institutional
Lake Forest, Illinois
2004/2005

**Shanghai Oriental Art Center Hotel**
Hospitality/Residential
Shanghai, China
2004

**Greenland Mixed-Use Development**
Mixed-Use
Xi'an, China
2004/2007

150–151

**Ningbo Marriott**
Hospitality/Residential
Ningbo, China
2004

132–133

**Union Station Towers**
Mixed-Use
Chicago, Illinois
2004

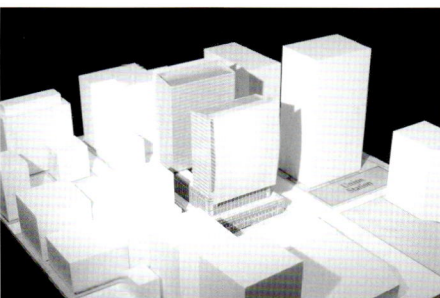

**CBS 2 Broadcast Center**
Interiors
Chicago, Illinois
2004/2008

102–103

**Hyatt Regency Suzhou**
Hospitality/Residential
Suzhou, China
2004/2009

134–137

**155 North Wacker and
222 West Randolph**
Office
Chicago, Illinois
2005/2009

116–121

**The Park Monroe**
Hospitality/Residential
Chicago, Illinois
2005/2009

**Freeborn & Peters**
Interiors
Chicago, Illinois
2005/2007

**114–115**

**Hyatt Regency at Chicony Plaza**
Mixed-Use
Chengdu, China
2005/2007

**154–155**

**Huangzhou Dragon Hotel**
Hospitality/Residential
Huangzhou, China
2005

**Bahagia Mixed-Use Development**
Mixed-Use
Kuala Lumpur, Malaysia
2005

**164–165**

**National City Tower**
Repositioning
Louisville, Kentucky
2005

*Firm Profile*

**Product Research and Data Service Center**
Mixed-Use
Shanghai, China
2005

**152–153**

**Riverwoods Corporate Center**
Office
Riverwoods, Illinois
2005/2006

**Jenner & Block**
Interiors
Chicago, Illinois
2005/2009

**110–111**

**Dongjiadu Residential Tower**
Hospitality/Residential
Shanghai, China
2005

**Ovation Plaza**
Mixed-Use
Milwaukee, Wisconsin
2005/2009

**158–161**

**Suzhou Jinji Lake Yacht Club**
**Suzhou Industrial Park**
Institutional
Suzhou, China
2005/2007

**190–193**

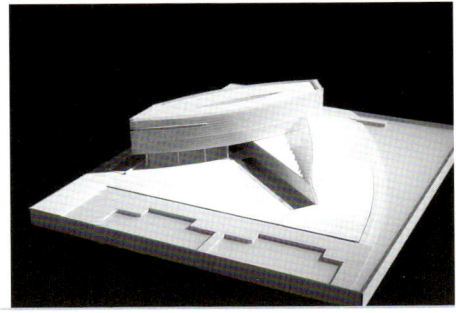

*Project Chronology*

**Westin Chosun Seoul
Renovation Master Plan**
Repositioning
Seoul, Korea
2005

**Xi'an City Gateway**
Mixed-Use
Xi'an, China
2005/2008

**Lujiazui Diamond Tower**
Office
Shanghai, China
2005/2009

**104–109**

**Shanghai Caohejing Development**
Mixed-Use
Shanghai, China
2006

**162–163**

# Typologies

## Office
111 South Wacker
155 North Wacker and 222 West Randolph
Ace Hardware Headquarters
Administrative and Training Campus, AmSouth Bancorporation
American General Center
Ameritech Center
Blue Cross Blue Shield Claim Center
Blue Cross Blue Shield of Illinois Headquarters
Charles Square Center
Dain Bosworth Tower
Dean Witter Financial Services and Riverwoods Corporate Place
Eli Lilly Headquarters Lobby Renovation
Frito-Lay National Headquarters
Lujiazui Diamond Tower
McDonald's Corporate Campus
Motorola Training Center
R&F Edinburgh Plaza
Riverwoods Corporate Center
Safety-Kleen Corporate Headquarters
SIP Administration Center, Suzhou Industrial Park
Snap-on Tools Corporate Headquarters
Sunbelt Tower
Suzhou Genway Tower, Suzhou Industrial Park
Suzhou International Tower
TRW World Headquarters
UBS Tower
Westgate Center

## Interiors
CBS 2 Broadcast Center
Equinox Fitness Club
Freeborn & Peters
Goettsch Partners
Jenner & Block
Steelcase/Stow & Davis Showroom

## Hospitality/Residential
420 East Ohio Street
Cantera Hotel
Cityfront Center Plaza
Devon House
Dongjiadu Residential Tower
Enhance Anting Golf Club Complex
Four Seasons Mumbai
Grand Hyatt Mumbai
Grand Hyatt São Paulo
Grand Hyatt Seoul Curtain Wall Replacement
Huangzhou Dragon Hotel
Hyatt Lodge at McDonald's Campus
Hyatt Regency Suzhou
J.W. Marriot Grand Rapids
Newton Grove Condominiums
Ningbo Marriott
The Park Monroe
Shanghai Oriental Art Center Hotel
Shanghai Sanzhi Hotel

## Mixed-Use
Bahagia Mixed-Use Development
Beijing Silvertie Center
Checkpoint Charlie Office Complex
Europe Gate
Grand Hyatt Guangzhou
Greenland Mixed-Use Development
Hyatt Regency at Chicony Plaza
Jin Hui Plaza
Nanjing International Center
Ovation Plaza
Product Research and Data Service Center
Shanghai Caohejing Development
Union Station Towers
Värtahamnen
Västra City
Xi'an City Gateway

## Institutional
Amerika-Gedenkbibliothek
Ann and Alfred Goldstein Academic Center, Pace University
Bridges for Chicago
Campus Master Plans, Pace University
CCS Bard Hessel Museum, Bard College
Center for Curatorial Studies, Bard College
Central Headquarters, Chicago Police Department
Central Regional Office, Department of Transportation
Chicago Tower
Gleacher Center, University of Chicago GSB
John C. Kluczynski Building Renovation
John T. Richardson Library, DePaul University
Library and Master Plan, Barat College
Mary and Leigh Block Museum of Art, Northwestern University
Max Planck Institute
North Burnham Park and Soldier Field Redevelopment
Oceanarium, John G. Shedd Aquarium
Regenstein Center for African Apes, Lincoln Park Zoo
School of Law and Law Library, Pace University
Sky Pavilion, Adler Planetarium & Astronomy Museum
St. Mary of the Annunciation Church
Suzhou Jinji Lake Yacht Club, Suzhou Industrial Park
Theory and Computing Sciences Building, Argonne Laboratory
U-505 Submarine Exhibit, Museum of Science and Industry
Walter Payton Center Building Improvements

## Repositioning
1 North LaSalle Street
33 North LaSalle Street
35 East Wacker Drive
120 South LaSalle Street
231 South LaSalle Street
360 North Michigan Avenue
National City Tower
Westin Chosun Seoul Renovation Master Plan

## Master Planning
Athletic and International Exchange Center, Dong Seoul College
Chicago Museum Campus
Cityfront Center
Government Center Master Plan, Suzhou Industrial Park
Kennedy Expressway Park
Oak Brook Comprehensive Plan
Wolf Point

# Selected Works Project Credits

### 111 South Wacker
Design Partner: James Goettsch
Partner-in-Charge: Steven Nilles
Project Architects: Joseph Cliggott, Ming Lai
Design Team: Daniel Biver, Vincent Caporale, Aaron Greven, Ryan Moody, Matthew Myers, Martin Salas, Joseph Schultz, Scott Seyer, Charles Wittleder
Enclosures/Technical Services: Lawrence Weldon, Patrick Loughran, Randall Chapple

### Charles Square Center
Design Partner: James Goettsch
Partner-in-Charge: Steven Nilles
Project Designer: Steven Cavanaugh
Design Team: Joseph Cliggott, Aaron Greven, Marius Ronnett, Travis Soberg, David Swanlund, Bryan Watt
Enclosures/Technical Services: Lawrence Weldon, Randall Chapple

### UBS Tower
Design Partner: James Goettsch
Partner-in-Charge: Steven Nilles
Project Architect: Joseph Cliggott
Design Team: Edwin Denson, Aaron Greven, Ming Lai, Michael Patten, Glenn Serdar, Travis Soberg, Man Hing Tam, James Zheng
Enclosures/Technical Services: Lawrence Weldon, Patrick Loughran, Randall Chapple

### Suzhou Genway Tower
Design Partner: James Goettsch
Partner-in-Charge: James Zheng
Project Architect: Ming Lai
Design Team: Allan Chung, Huili Feng, Hiroshi Sango, Travis Soberg, Tim Vacha
Enclosures/Technical Services: Lawrence Weldon, Randall Chapple

### Blue Cross Blue Shield of Illinois Headquarters
Partner-in-Charge: James Goettsch
Project Manager: Edwin Denson (original), Joseph Dolinar (expansion)
Project Architect: Michael Patten
Design Team (original): Fernando Araujo, Vincent Caporale, Patrick Loughran, Tracy Salvia, Tim Vacha
Design Team (expansion): Joseph Patrick, Scott Seyer
Enclosures/Technical Services: Lawrence Weldon, Patrick Loughran, Randall Chapple

### Grand Hyatt São Paolo
Partner-in-Charge: Michael Kaufman
Project Designer: John Arzarian, Jr.
Design Team: Martin Salas, Tim Vacha, Edwin Witkowski, Charles Wittleder
Enclosures/Technical Services: Lawrence Weldon, Randall Chapple

### Mary and Leigh Block Museum of Art Expansion
Partner-in-Charge: Dirk Lohan
Project Manager: Edwin Denson
Project Designer: Tom Demetrion
Design Team: Phuong-kim Kern, Maren Seibold, Edwin Witkowski
Enclosures/Technical Services: Lawrence Weldon, Patrick Loughran, Randall Chapple

### North Burnham Park and Soldier Field Redevelopment
Partner-in-Charge: Joseph Caprile
Partners: Dirk Lohan, Ben Wood, Carlos Zapata
Project Directors: Joseph Dolinar, Tony Montalto, Basil Souder
Project Architects: Bretton Robillard, James Schubert, Travis Soberg
Design Team: John Arzarian Jr., Vincent Caporale, Allan Chung, Glenn Johnson, Ming Lai, Greg Lorusso, Joseph Patrick, Hugo Prill, Joseph Schultz, Maren Seibold, Denise Sims, Tim Vacha, Charles Wittleder
Enclosures/Technical Services: Lawrence Weldon, Randall Chapple

## Selected Works Collaborators

Advanced Structures Incorporated
AHFsa Structural Engineers
Alfred Benesch & Company
BauTech
Beer, Gorski & Graff
Building Services Group
Chhada, Siembieda, Remedios
Cini-Little International
Constantin Walsh-Lowe
Cosentini Associates
Cosentini Lighting
CS Associates
Drew George & Partners
East China Architectural Design & Research Institute
EDAW
Ellerbe Becket
Environmental Systems Design
Escritio Technico Julio Neves
Gleeds
HPS
Jenkins & Huntington
Joe Karr & Associates
Magnusson Klemencic Associates
MERO Structures
Peter Lindsay Schaudt Landscape Architecture
Peter Walker and Partners Landscape Architecture
Rolf Jensen & Associates
Schuler & Shook
Shiner + Associates
SIAL
Soodan & Associates
STS Consultants
SWA Group
Thomas Ricca Associates
Thornton-Tomasetti Engineers
Tinokwan Lighting Consultants
RWDI
WMA Consulting Engineers
Wood + Zapata

# Acknowledgments

The partners would like to first thank our clients, without whom the work depicted within this monograph would not have been possible. They have provided us with rich and varied challenges, and have been our collaborators throughout. Each client has brought to us a unique opportunity, and we have endeavored to exceed their expectations. It has been our honor and privilege to work with them.

Our projects require the involvement of the highest quality consultants and contractors, and we gratefully acknowledge these key members of the building team.

We would also like to recognize all current and past staff for their contributions. The success of these projects is a direct result of a shared spirit and appreciation of architecture.

Finally, Goettsch Partners would like to express thanks to our entire staff, all of whom at one point or another contributed to the production of this monograph. We are particularly grateful to Susanna Craib-Cox for her unwavering enthusiasm and dedication, her design input and for coordinating the overall effort; Joseph Cliggott and Paul De Santis for their contributions in selecting and editing the graphic content and page design; and Matt Larson for coordinating the written content. We would further like to thank Jason Cain, John Zacherle, Alan Salchow and Andrew Tarcin, as well as Ross Barney, Yong Mei, Susan Pratt, Amanda Beelman, and Susan Larson.

# Photography Credits

| | |
|---|---|
| 196 (upper left, lower left) | Art Institute of Chicago |
| 230 (4) | Wayne Cable |
| 91 | Michael Collyer |
| 200, 202 (upper left and middle) | Continental Bank Archives |
| 10 (middle, lower), 84–85, 87, 88 (left), 90, 238 (1,2), 239 (4) | Defined Space, David P. Seide |
| 243 (5) | Eclipse Development |
| 11 (2), 172–174, 233 (4,5), 237 (5) | Esto Photographics, Peter Aaron |
| 88 (centerfold), 89 | Doug Fogelson |
| 7 (upper left), 68–75, 238 (4) | Estúdiogirão, Eduardo Girão |
| 24 | Golub-Europe |
| 6, 11 (lower), 58–59, 61, 63 (upper), 230 (3), 231 (4), 232 (2,5), 235 (1), 236 (1), 238 (6) | Hedrich Blessing Photographers |
| 209–210, 241 (5) | Hedrich Blessing Photographers, Craig Dugan |
| 122 (lower), 123–125, 231 (5,6), 242 (1) | Hedrich Blessing Photographers, Steve Hall |
| 233 (3) | Hedrich Blessing Photographers, Jim Hedrich |
| 67 | Hedrich Blessing Photographers, Scott McDonald |
| 122 (upper), 230 (1,2), 231 (1) | Hedrich Blessing Photographers, Nick Merrick |
| 8, 11 (1,3), 34–43, 171, 194–195, 196 (upper right, lower right), 197–199, 201–202, 203 (upper), 204–206, 207 (lower left), 208, 211 (lower row), 233 (2,6), 238 (6), 234 (1,2,5), 235 (2,6), 237 (6), 239 (1,2), 241 (1) | Hedrich Blessing Photographers, Jon Miller |
| 241 (2) | Hyatt International |
| 232 (6), 233 (1) | Karant + Associates, Barbara Karant |
| 232 (1,3) | CM Korab |
| 236 (2) | Lambros Photography, George Lambros |
| 220–229 | Michelle Litvin |
| 82 (upper, middle right) | Tim Long |
| 232 (4) | Greg Murphey |
| 140 | Rockford/Pepper Construction |
| 231 (3) | Sadin Photo Group/Van Inwegan |
| 236 (5) | Mike Sinclair |
| 7 (2nd row), 25, 29 (upper row), 33 (left), 237 (1) | Filip Slapal |
| 94–95, 97, 237 (3) | Doug Snower Photography, Doug Snower |
| Cover, 7 (lower), 10 (upper), 14–22, 54–55, 57, 62, 63 (lower), 77–82, 167, 179–182, 184, 214–216, 218–219, 234 (6), 235 (3,4), 237 (2,5), 240 (1,3,5), 241 (6) | Steinkamp Photography, James Steinkamp |
| 20 (lower row), 169–170, 171 (lower left) | Steinkamp/Ballogg Photography, Mark Ballogg |
| 183, 185 | Steinkamp/Ballogg Photography, David P. Seide |
| 26–29, 31–33 | Pavel Štecha |
| Back cover, 7 (upper row right, 3rd row right), 44–53, 99, 101, 126–127, 238 (4), 242 (6), 243 (2,6) | Fu Xing |

# Index

| | |
|---|---|
| 198 | 1 North LaSalle Street |
| 208 | 35 East Wacker Drive |
| 14 | 111 South Wacker |
| 204 | 120 South LaSalle Street |
| 116 | 155 North Wacker and 222 West Randolph |
| 200 | 231 South LaSalle Street |
| 194 | 360 North Michigan Avenue |
| 164 | Bahagia Mixed-Use Development |
| 166 | Beijing Silvertie Center |
| 54 | Blue Cross Blue Shield of Illinois Headquarters |
| 102 | CBS 2 Broadcast Center |
| 172 | CCS Bard Hessel Museum |
| 24 | Charles Square Center |
| 186 | Chicago Tower |
| 126 | Enhance Anting Golf Club Complex |
| 138 | Four Seasons Mumbai |
| 114 | Freeborn & Peters |
| 214 | Goettsch Partners Office |
| 156 | Grand Hyatt Guangzhou |
| 128 | Grand Hyatt Mumbai |
| 68 | Grand Hyatt São Paulo |
| 150 | Greenland Mixed-Use Development |
| 122 | Hyatt Lodge at McDonald's Campus |
| 154 | Hyatt Regency at Chicony Plaza |
| 134 | Hyatt Regency Suzhou |
| 110 | Jenner & Block |
| 140 | J.W. Marriott Grand Rapids |
| 104 | Lujiazui Diamond Tower |
| 76 | Mary and Leigh Block Museum of Art Expansion |
| 144 | Nanjing International Center |
| 132 | Ningbo Marriott |
| 84 | North Burnham Park and Soldier Field Redevelopment |
| 158 | Ovation Plaza |
| 152 | Product Research and Data Service Center |
| 178 | Regenstein Center for African Apes |
| 162 | Shanghai Caohejing Development |
| 98 | SIP Administration Center |
| 182 | Sky Pavilion |
| 112 | Sunbelt Tower |
| 44 | Suzhou Genway Tower |
| 94 | Suzhou International Tower |
| 190 | Suzhou Jinji Lake Yacht Club |
| 168 | U-505 Submarine Exhibit |
| 34 | UBS Tower |

Every effort has been made to trace the original source of copyright material contained in this book. The publishers would be pleased to hear from copyright holders to rectify any error or omissions.

The information and illustrations in this publication have been prepared and supplied by Goettsch Partners. While all reasonable efforts have been made to ensure accuracy, the publishers do not, under any circumstances, accept responsibility for errors, omissions and representations expressed or implied.

gp